The Complete Guide to
PET CARE

The Complete Guide to
PET CARE

JOHN NICHOL

CHRISTOPHER HELM

London

© 1988 John Nichol
Line drawings by Chris Shields
Christopher Helm (Publishers) Ltd, Imperial House,
21-25 North Street, Bromley, Kent BR1 1SD

British Library Cataloguing in Publication Data

Nichol, John
    The complete guide to pet care
    1. Pets
    I. Title
    636.08′87   SF413

    ISBN 07470-2406-5

For Margaret

Typeset by Leaper & Gard Ltd, Bristol
Printed and bound in Great Britain by
Billing and Sons Ltd, Worcester

CONTENTS

HOW TO USE THIS BOOK

No book of this size could possibly answer every query about pets; however, you should be able to find the answers to most of the questions you might ever need to ask. At the back you will find a bibliography that will point you in the direction of many useful books, and perhaps even more useful journals. The latter publications will tell you where to find societies, supplies, livestock and much else, and you ought to find the list of addresses absolutely invaluable. The addresses are all of national bodies and, if you contact them, they will pass your query to a local branch if that is what you are after, but do remember that the officers in many of these organisations are private individuals whose addresses may change. If that happens, the appropriate journal will be able to let you know the new address. When you write to one of the listed bodies, do send a stamp with your query.

If you want a little general knowledge about a particular pet, look up the Glossary of Pets where you will find basic information about the more commonly kept animals: they are listed in alphabetical order. If you are thinking of buying one of the listed animals you should then follow up the information contained in the Glossary by dipping in to the chapters on Housing, Feeding, and so on.

Some of the chapters, such as that on Pet Keepers and the Law, are worth browsing through since they are of importance to all pet keepers, and as far as I know there is no comparable list of British and American legislation on animals from any other readily obtainable source.

When you start to plan an aviary, a fish tank or any other sort of animal home, look through the chapter on Housing and you will find a wealth of useful tips, the result of years of keeping animals, which will save you expense and time.

This is not really a book to sit down and read through from beginning to end, but as a reference guide you ought to find it very useful. But please remember that I have only been able to talk in general terms: for the fine details of animal keeping, you need to go to the more specialist books and journals, and to specialist animal keepers.

Lastly, bear in mind that your pets will probably not read this book, so if I suggest that an animal eats sunflower seeds, and you find that yours will not touch the stuff, don't blame me; animals never do what you expect them to!

A NOTE ABOUT NOMENCLATURE

Common names for animals vary enormously. In the chapter on Livefood and in the Glossary of Pets you will find the scientific names of all the species mentioned, so that you can look them up elsewhere for more information.

Elsewhere, when I refer to a group of animals I use a small initial, but when I talk of a particular species I use capital initials, for examples:

gerbils	Mongolian Gerbils
tropical fish	Neon Tetras
finches	Cut Throat Finches
dogs	Cavalier King Charles Spaniels
spiders	Red Kneed Tarantulas

ACKNOWLEDGEMENTS

My first pet was a horse when I was less than two years old. Since then I have never been without animals, and during those many years I have received invaluable information from enormous numbers of people. Much of it has gone into the writing of this book, but if I were to credit everybody, I would be here forever. Therefore I would like to say a simple THANK YOU to all my animal friends.

PREFACE

I think it was John Stevens, one of the original exponents of self-sufficiency, who said that there was an awful lot of unnecessary mystique surrounding the subject of growing plants. A plant, he said, had one end brown and one end green, and if you stuck the brown end in the ground and left the green end in the air and watered the thing regularly, it would probably do perfectly well. I have always thought there was a lot of sense in that seemingly fatuous lesson in horticulture. The reality when it comes to keeping plants or animals is that there are some points which need to be watched with care and meticulously attended to, but equally there is much that is best done with intuition and affection. Yet frequently one comes across pet owners who say that though all the books tell them to feed their animal a particular amount of food each day, their pet does not in fact need anything like that quantity. Surely in that case the thing to do is to feed the animal a meal with which it is happy. The trouble is that animals, being living things, are all very different and as such have differing requirements. This book does not pretend to be all-encompassing; that would be an impossible target for one of its nature. What it does do, is cover all the basic essentials and then point you in the right direction, so that you can read up about the particular animals that have attracted you and meet other people with similar interests.

I feel strongly that an animal should never be bought on impulse, but having seen something you like, you should find out everything you can about it before you go out and buy one. And please, please, never buy an animal as a present for someone else unless (a) you know that they really want it and that no one in the family is going to be less than wholeheartedly supportive about it, (b) the recipient has the knowledge to care for it and (c) that the recipient has the equipment necessary for keeping the animal. You would think all that was obvious, yet each year the RSPCA, the WSPA and other organisations kill many thousands of unwanted pets. Despite the heartfelt appeals each Christmas, the weeks afterwards are the peak period for this mass destruction; and let us not euphemistically call it putting the animals to sleep — they are being killed.

In any case Christmas is not the time to introduce a tiny baby into a house. To start with the poor beast is already unhappy, bewildered and frightened at being separated from its mother and siblings for the first time. It then has to find its way around a strange new home, learn to eat an entirely different food and discover where to sleep, defecate and urinate. All the while the house is full of large, noisy people who keep hauling it around to the accompaniment of bangs, whistles and the bleeping of electronic toys as they trundle across the carpet. It must surely seem the nearest thing to hell on earth. If someone really does want a pet at Christmas, give them the cage or other equipment and explain that after the festivities are over the two of you can go out somewhere and choose the animal in peace.

Pets are a part of our life and provide us with pleasure, and by carefully observing them, and recording and photographing what they do, they can add much to our fund of knowledge. But to be honest much of the work of caring for animals can be tedious and mucky, and if your heart is not in it they can seem to live for an awfully long time. I think it must be rabbits for which I feel most sympathy. How many of them do you know that live in a tiny box full of soggy straw at the end of the garden, condemned to solitary confinement except for 30 seconds a day when someone flings in a handful of carrots and pellets? Where is the fun in that for either the animal or the person to whom it belongs. Rabbits are fascinating, gregarious animals when they are allowed to live as they should.

Though I do not agree with them, some people believe that no animals should be kept in captivity. However, if they are to be kept, then they must be cared for properly. I suspect that cruelty is usually either a lack of knowledge or sensitivity, or a loss of interest. A pet is a responsibility and it is not enough just to know what to feed it on. An intuitive awareness of an animal's requirements is essential to a pet keeper. I have sometimes been asked how I know when a snake is sick or a cat wants to go out to urinate and often I cannot say precisely. The snake looks sick or the cat looks as though it has a full bladder. Probably I am picking up tiny signals that many owners miss, though animal people will know what I mean; but to some folk it seems like magic.

Keeping pets can be very rewarding psychologically and after a while you will be surprised at how much you have learnt. You will realise the extent of your knowledge when you start to argue with what is written in books about keeping your speciality. Do not waste the knowledge. Keeping some animals costs a small fortune – just watch how many cans of dog food an adult Old English Sheepdog can wolf down after a ten mile walk, and it seems to me that if you can recoup some of your outlay that is a good thing. I am not talking about breeding hundreds of rabbits to sell to the meat trade because that is not pet keeping, nor am I suggesting that you will make a profit, but a bit extra here and there always helps and there are more ways of earning that than you might think. By all means sell off any surplus stock that you have bred, but that is not the end of it. Take lots of photographs and, if they are different or interesting, it is surprising what you can do with them. All sorts of magazines are constantly looking for animal pictures, and sometimes greetings card companies and even television programmes use them. But for goodness sake do not take pictures of your dog wearing a deerstalker hat and smoking a pipe. If you are not a photographer you can give talks to various groups of people, or on radio and there are all sorts of other potential sources of a little revenue. You might even write a book!

A basic aspect of pet care that is often overlooked is an understanding of the necessary commitment. Will you be willing to take your dog for a five mile walk every day of the year — and there are plenty of them that need this much exercise — or feed live maggots to a lizard, or shovel snow away from the path to the aviary in midwinter so that you can break the ice in the water dishes and re-fill them? There can be times when keeping animals is no fun at all.

But if you do not mind the maggots, can afford the cost and really want to keep an animal, read what you can, talk to other people about it, and go ahead; who knows where your interest might lead. The important thing is to plan the exercise carefully before you start buying anything.

If you are new to a particular type of animal and not sure where to get some of the foods or accessories that may be necessary, ask someone else who keeps them, or a specialist dealer or look up one of the books or magazines that are listed at the end of this volume.

Surveys have shown that most people who keep pets regard them as members of the family. People generally and children in particular lead richer lives if they have pets. There is ample scientific evidence to show that families with animals live longer, do not suffer from high blood pressure as much as other people, and relate well to those around them. Pets in a household reduce stress and provide an escape from daily problems.

Considerable work has been done on using pets in hospitals and prisons and in all the studies they have been shown to have beneficial effects. I would hate to have to live without animals around me and I cannot help but feel that a household without pets misses out on such a lot of things. The first pet that I can remember was a horse called Ginger, and my mother had a photograph of me when I was tiny, wearing a frilly dress and standing solemnly beneath Ginger's belly for security. Perhaps if I had not had to wear dresses I would not have needed the security, but whatever the reason, my behaviour used to terrify my mother. A few months after the photograph was taken I was sitting safely in my basket saddle on the horse's back when an army motorcycle roared past. Poor old Ginger panicked, threw me and galloped off to jump over a precipice to his death. Since then I have kept a host of animals from cats and dogs to Parameciums and Hydras. Generally I do not find as much interest in domestic animals these days, but instead I find wildlife in all its forms forever and totally absorbing. Many pet keepers will argue with my priorities and that is fine. When it comes to keeping pets, the choice is up to you; but do be sure you really want the commitment, to spend the time and the money, to care for your pet properly.

1
CHOOSING AN ANIMAL

When you buy an animal you could be taking on a changed life style. That animal will depend on you for everything and unless you are willing to provide for it you should consider taking up another interest. Furthermore, some animals live for a considerable time. Tortoises and parrots, for example, could very easily outlive you, so think carefully about what is to happen to your pet when you are no longer able to look after it.

Before you go out to get a pet, learn what you will be expected to do for it. A cuddly little puppy may look great in a pet shop but will you be willing to take it for a long walk next February when the snow is thick and your fingertips are turning blue? It is not sufficient to take it around the block, or to the nearest bit of grass for it to defecate. The other point to remember is that dogs and horses and other large mammals are very expensive to keep. The idea of owning a dog may not appeal to you, and you would rather keep a bird or a python, in which case you will not have to mind chopping up an earthworm or dipping your hand into a pot of maggots, or even killing a couple of rats each week. It is no use feeling revolted — the animals require these things and if you are not willing to supply them then you should not be keeping those particular animals. I am often told by someone that they are an animal lover — a term I dislike, with its undertones of bestiality — but on further enquiry it generally emerges that what they mean is that they like dogs, or cats, or feeding the Blue Tits in the garden. I have discovered over many years that the best animal people are those who are interested in everything. An ant is a fascinating little organism living within a complicated social structure, every bit as rewarding to keep as a Labrador, and a Rose Chafer — just a beetle some might say — is just as beautiful as a goldfinch. Look at them again and you will see that what I say is true. So before

1

you take on your pet be honest with yourself about whether you are willing to care for it properly.

Having done that and read up all about it, go out and get everything you will need before the newcomer arrives. It is no use sticking it in a cardboard box till a cage is finished; in many cases, you might need to let the animal's home establish itself for a few weeks before your pet is introduced. The paint may have to dry and in some aviaries, aquariums and vivariums the plants will need time to settle down and become established or they will die, and it is much harder to replace them when the animals are *in situ*. If you are intending to keep a community of some kind and are not sure how many animals to get, make do with less. You can always add more when you are more experienced, and often an enclosure looks better with fewer animals anyway. A fish tank in particular looks good with lots of plants and a very few fish.

Clearly, when you are looking for a pet you have to try and choose a specimen that is young and healthy. Even experienced animal keepers make mistakes sometimes and if you are new to pet keeping the whole business can be fairly daunting, but there is one thing at least which you should never do and that is to buy an animal which looks dejected and unwell, simply because you feel sorry for it. There is a very good chance that it will die whatever you do for it, and if you keep other animals it could very well pass some condition on to the whole lot of them. I know that there are occasions when such an animal will pull through and, in fact, only yesterday someone told me that they had bought a sunbird with a dropped wing and a fungal infection on the mouth, that turned out to be a magnificent specimen after treatment. Even so, do not be tempted. To leave a sick animal in a shop is rough but if people refused to buy such stock the proprietor would not sell it. Look instead for an animal that looks alert, with bright, open eyes and no signs of diarrhoea around the anus or cloaca; and when you are checking this latter point, look at the floor of the cage to see what the droppings are like. There may be several animals in the cage and if the state of the faeces is suspicious leave all of them alone as the condition might be infectious. Check that the animal is active and behaving normally. Put your hand near it and see what it does. It might either rush off somewhere else or it might come over to examine you, or it might sit there and look around brightly with head cocked to one side to see what you are going to do next. All these patterns of behaviour are probably perfectly all right, but if the animal shows no interest at all or leaps off the perch in fright, think very carefully.

Any animal keeper will tell you that a fair bit of intuition is necessary in choosing a pet, and anyone can go wrong occasionally. So, do try to take an experienced friend with you when you visit a dealer to buy your pet. But. if after you take it home, the pet becomes ill or dies, do not blame your friend. He will have done the best for you and the animal may well have been suffering from a condition that was not apparent at the time of purchase.

If you buy a pet by mail order, examine it closely on arrival and if there is anything wrong phone the dealer to tell him and sort something out there and then. If you wait several days to see if the condition of the animal improves, the person who sold it to you might very well say that it was perfectly all right when it left his premises and anything that has happened since could be due to you.

Almost invariably when one buys an exotic animal via mail order it is sent with a guarantee of live delivery only. So if it arrives dead, it is especially important to telephone immediately − do not write − and follow the phone call with a letter returning the animal the same day. Livestock purchased in this way is almost always sent by rail. It is usually despatched one evening so that it travels overnight and the purchaser is advised when it is being despatched. He must then collect his parcel from his nearest station and he should telephone the parcel office to check if it has arrived. I cannot advise that you purchase animals like this unless there is really no other way, as British Rail has had, over the years, a pretty abysmal record with livestock and anyone who has ever sent animals by rail will be able to tell you horror stories about stock being delayed or going astray. Many dealers, in fact, insist that you collect from them.

If your interest is in imported animals of some kind, one day somebody will tell you that importers can obtain a particular animal from the country of origin for a tiny fraction of the price that you pay for it, and you might be tempted to import animals yourself. Don't do it. You will not believe how difficult it is, how expensive, and nobody tells you that you will almost certainly lose money. Leave it to the professionals and do not begrudge them the price you have to pay for an animal, as in addition to the price they have paid the exporter they have to take into account the cost of airfreight and duty, together with transport to the destination country, mortality and sickness and the cost of keeping and feeding animals during a considerable quarantine period before they are released for sale − in addition to all the normal costs of running a business. Another snag, too, when importing animals is that though you may order a particular species something else might actually arrive, or animals of a different sex, or old animals. The whole business is fraught with difficulties.

Periodically there are stories in the press about dealers making vast amounts of money from handling animals. Don't necessarily believe them, for, whereas I do know some dealers who are extremely wealthy, they also deal in a variety of other commodities, and there is certainly no one in Britain, for instance, who is making more than a modest living from importing and selling animals, and many, regardless of the size of their advertisements, are not doing at all well. Furthermore, if you buy one of the Fancy journals regularly over a few years you will be struck by the high turnover of firms that appear for a year or two, only to vanish again.

We were discussing earlier the general points to look out for when choosing a pet. They were all physical aspects of a healthy animal and did not take into account the character and personality of a pet, which is considerably more difficult to assess. It does not matter if you are looking for a new Zebra Finch for your aviary, but the personality of a dog that is to live as a family pet is absolutely vital. Most writers say that you should watch a litter or a cage full of puppies and choose the one that comes forward and wants to play. As a general rule this makes sense but some animals, just as some humans, grow up to be too pushy. So, while you should certainly spend a fair time watching the puppies, kittens, or whatever, assuming they are all healthy select the one whose personality appeals to you. In the end it is the only way. Take it home and care for it and you will probably both get on fine; and if it is a breed of dog which is traditionally mutilated by having its tail chopped off, take no notice of people who insist on this barbaric practice. Leave the tail where it is and the dog will look far more handsome with it.

For the most part, buying animals is common sense. If you do not know what to look for take someone with you who does. Apart from that elementary precaution simply look for an animal that appears fit and, where appropriate, active, and keep an eye on its behaviour. If it is doing something really odd there must be a reason for it. As an example, I would mention cerebral disorders in birds which can occur in a perfectly healthy specimen that suddenly panics, flies up and bangs its head so hard that the fragile skull is damaged and a haemorrhage results. This is sometimes followed by all sorts of odd behaviour such as a twisting round of the head to an apparently impossible extent, or the falling off a perch and tottering around on the floor.

Very often there are no definite answers with keeping animals. Use what knowledge and experience you have together with a good helping of intuition, and do go to a reputable, well-established source for your animals.

This book is about pets and if you are thinking of keeping horses for dressage competitions or Labradors for showing at top dog shows, you really do need far more information than can be obtained in a single book. But, in the belief that you are reading this book because you are interested in keeping an animal about which you know little or nothing, having talked about general points, let us now look at particular animals and what to be aware of when buying them.

DOGS

The relationship between a dog, its owner and the family in which it lives is astonishingly complex. People keep dogs for all sorts of reasons, such as for companionship, for confidence when living alone, as a substitute for children or for someone to talk to and who will not answer back.

When you choose a dog you will almost unconsciously go for one that suits you, but at the same time you do need to make deliberate decisions and the first of these will relate to the size of dog. If you live in a tenth-storey apartment of a tower block, it is obviously nonsense to keep a Great Dane; on the other hand, if you are fortunate enough to live in a large country house with a couple of acres of land but are crippled with arthritis so that you cannot go for long walks, again there is no point in keeping a large, active dog. The other thing to decide is whether you want a puppy or a young adult and there is much to be said for both. Puppies are great fun but they can be a bit of a handful. Older dogs on the other hand, if you choose the right one, can be lovely. A long time ago I met a friend who was taking her dog to the vet to be killed because her new boyfriend and the dog just could not get on. On impulse I said that I would take the dog. Her name was Cindy and at first she was decidedly uneasy in my presence — she had obviously had a bad experience with a man — but in time she relaxed and proved to be a real sweetie. I am not a dog person at all but I was very fond of Cindy. If you do decide to get an older dog, find out if it is house trained. If it has been living in the kennels of a welfare organisation for some time it might not be.

Whether or not to choose a dog or a bitch is up to you. It is hopeless asking other dog owners for their opinions as some would not have anything but a bitch while others are just as convinced that a dog is far the best. But whichever you choose, unless you are determined to breed from your dog, do have it either castrated or spayed. Every year the animal welfare organisations have to kill many thousands of unwanted puppies and it really is irresponsible to add to this mountain of corpses.

Your final consideration will be whether to buy a pedigree dog or a mongrel and once more your choice is personal preference.

With a pedigree dog you know more or less what you are going to get in respect of the size, the shape and the temperament. On the other hand, many breeds do have inherent defects as a result of years of inbreeding. Mongrels can be great characters and one advantage is that they are infinitely cheaper than pedigree dogs. Welfare organisations are always looking for suitable homes for adult mongrels.

After you have considered all these options and come to a decision, start thinking about where to get your pet. Generally I would suggest that you steer clear of pet shops because their dogs are frequently badly stressed and the risk of infection can be high. If you are buying a pedigree dog, go to a dealer who specialises in the particular breed. But if you would prefer a mongrel you cannot do better than go to an animal welfare organisation. There are two advantages to getting a dog in this way. The first is that you help to cut down the number of dogs being destroyed, and the second is that the dogs will have been examined by a veterinary surgeon and given any necessary treatment, which might not be the case if you buy a puppy from a litter advertised in your local newspaper. That is not to say that you should not buy dogs through an advertisement; they are often super animals and will usually be beautifully looked after. Which is often not the case with dogs in other countries, and if you are abroad and find a poor little scrawny waif that you would love to rescue, leave him be. Rabies occurs all over the continent and is racing across Europe at an alarming rate, and populations of stray dogs are often infected with it. I was once attacked by a rabid dog in Calcutta when I disturbed it raiding the dustbin outside my back door and that was no fun at all.

If you import a dog into Britain you must be willing to pay for six months' quarantine as it is only by imposing this restriction that we can keep the country rabies-free. It is a horrid disease that leads to an appalling death, and its introduction would have an effect on the lives of everyone. The legislation in the USA is covered by the Code of Federal Regulations. (CFR), Part 42/71.

Having decided on the type of dog you want and where to get it, check through the general comments about health earlier in this chapter. In addition, make sure that there are no discharges from the eyes and from the ears which should be clean and not smelly. Finally, pick up the dog. It should feel surprisingly heavy. If you are happy with it, take it home.

CATS

Unless you are thinking of showing your cat it is probably better to buy a crossbreed as a pet; pet pedigree cats are frequently the target of cat thieves. If you do decide that you want a pedigree cat you will be faced with a choice of breeds. Your choice will entirely be a matter of personal preference, but remember that long haired cats have to be constantly groomed or their fur soon becomes absolutely foul. Siamese Cats are great characters — I am sure that they think they are dogs — but they can be pretty vociferous and their voice is not very attractive.

If you choose a crossbred cat there are all sorts available and you can pick a tabby or a tortoiseshell or whatever takes your fancy. But whichever you select, do have it neutered whether you buy a tom or a queen. Each year the animal welfare organisations destroy enormous quantities of unwanted kittens and it is not fair to have the babies killed simply because you neglected to have the parents neutered.

Most cats are obtained as kittens which are great fun but can be very demanding and in need of house training, and nothing is quite so pungent in your home as cat urine unless it is the smell of a dog fox! Because of these initial problems it can be a good idea to get a mature cat, though few people think of it; but if you do, keep it indoors for a while or it might set off to return to its last home.

The only place you should go for a pedigree cat is to a breeder. If you are after a crossbreed you have all sorts of options, for the world is full of people trying to get rid of surplus kittens. At an animal welfare organisation you can be sure that the animal has been inspected by a vet and any diseases seen to before the cat is offered for sale. If there are no such places near you, look at the cards in the windows of local shops, in the classified advertise-ments of your local newspaper, or just put the word around that you are after a cat. You will soon be inundated with offers. I will not suggest that you go to a pet shop as the animals are probably fairly stressed and hygiene is often not what it should be, and young felines are especially susceptible to a variety of infections and other illnesses. Do make sure that kittens have been vacci-nated a good week before you collect them — they should have received vaccines against feline influenza (cat flu) and feline enteri-tis; and look at the eyes, the ears and the anus to see that they are all clean and healthy looking.

HORSES AND PONIES

Owning a horse involves a lot of hard work that cannot be shirked and it is an expensive business, as buying a horse admits one into a whole new world with its own calendar and vocabulary. A begin-ner really must take someone knowledgeable to choose a pony and you should only buy from a reputable source where inspection is welcomed. The British magazine *Horse & Hound* is full of advertisements of stock for sale.

Whatever you do, never buy a horse without having a vet check it over and ask him for a detailed report, because horses are prone to all sorts of conditions that are difficult to detect and veterinary treatment can be horrendously expensive. Another reason for this check is to discover if the animal is mentally sound: a crazy horse can do you an awful lot of damage. Before you buy it, ride the horse around the field for a while and see how it responds. Then take it out in traffic and, if a rider from the stable accompanies you, ask to be able to ride on your own for a while, and when you return to the field remove all the harness and release the horse and then try to catch it again. It is surprising what all these little tips will reveal. If the vendor is reluctant to let you do any of this, bid a polite goodbye and go somewhere else for your horse.

DONKEYS

There are all sorts of donkeys from tiny miniatures (which cost the earth) to the large Spanish Donkeys which are over 12 hands. As with horses the best way to buy a good donkey is to take with you someone who understands what he is doing. What constitutes a good donkey is really common sense but if you are not confident ask the Donkey Breed Society for some advice. Donkeys are great characters but they are not as thick and stupid as they look. What is frequently referred to as a donkey's obstinacy is in fact intelligence, when the animal cannot see the point in a particularly pointless exercise that his owner is trying to inflict upon him.

RABBITS

Rabbits are not just white lumps that sit motionless in a box at the end of the garden; they are remarkable animals that are not appreciated by most of their owners. If you want to find out just how amazing they are, read *The Private Life of the Rabbit* by R. Lockley; it will open your eyes. There are many breeds available and if you are thinking of showing them you will need to decide whether to get Netherland Dwarfs, or New Zealand Whites, or any one of the other choices. However, if you just want an attractive bunny it will not really matter which you select. Pet rabbits are very cheap, and when buying them look for the general points given earlier in this chapter. They are gregarious animals and should be kept in a group, but bucks are aggressive and will certainly fight with each other.

If they are to remain tame, rabbits must be handled frequently, but they have fragile bones so do take care, and never pick up a rabbit by its ears. They can have sharp claws and if they are unused to being handled they scrabble like mad and can inflict nasty scratches. It is as well to check their claws every so often as sometimes they become overgrown; if they are too long ask a vet or someone who knows how to clip them.

GUINEA PIGS OR CAVIES

Guinea Pigs should really be called Cavies. The 'Guinea' part of their name was originally Guiana where these South American rodents were raised as food, and indeed are still eaten in that continent. Since they only live for about three years, only babies should be bought. There is a choice between the English Guinea Pigs, which are short haired and the commonest of the pet Guinea Pigs, the Peruvian, which have very long hair and require constant grooming, and the Abyssinian, which have funny little rosettes here and there where the hair grows in different directions. Guinea Pigs are cheap to buy and if your pet shop has no good stock available look in your local newspaper — someone near you is sure to be breeding them.

HAMSTERS

For some reason many people confuse Hamsters and Guinea Pigs, which are totally unlike. The adult Golden Hamster is about 12–15 cm ($4\frac{3}{4}$–6 in) long, and comes in a variety of shades and patterns of brown, fawn and white. Like politicians, hamsters cannot find a good word to say about others of their kind and from the time they are a few weeks old they will fight savagely. Sexing hamsters is not too difficult as the back end of a female is rounded while that of a male is more elongated. Hamsters are nocturnal so do not expect them to be lively during the day.

CHIPMUNKS

Any Chipmunks that you buy in Britain or the USA will have been captive-bred. They can become very tame and are most endearing little animals. Buy them from a breeder if you can to be sure your stock is unrelated. In a pet shop the entire stock might be siblings. A male in breeding condition can be identified by a swollen scrotal sac. Never make the mistake of trying to pick up a chipmunk by the tail for they have a mechanism which enables them to escape a predator. The skin of the tail breaks and you find yourself holding an inside-out sleeve of tail fur while the chipmunk scuttles off with a bald, rat-like tail.

MICE

Domestic Mice are pretty little animals and are very easy to cater for. A single mouse should not be kept on its own as they are gregarious, but unless you want to breed, keep females only as the smell of the urine of a male is pungent and someone might object to it in the house. Similarly, if you feed them cheese or an excess of green food you will end up with smelly mice. Always buy young stock as they only live for a couple of years.

RATS

Domestic Rats, contrary to popular belief, are not in any way offensive. Wild Rats on the other hand are big, fierce, streetwise survivors and not at all suited to live in captivity. They are most interesting animals, but they are not pets. Some people think of rats as king-size mice, but to me they are totally different. They are certainly intelligent and can become tame and affectionate.

They live for about four years so start with youngsters, and do keep them in a group as they like company, but they occupy more living space than you might think. It is not as easy to come across rats for sale as mice, which every pet shop stocks, but by looking through the addresses at the back of this book you will be able to find a supplier and then you too can join the converted. Rats always get a bad press and they need every friend they can get.

GERBILS

Mongolian Gerbils are such attractive little rodents that they won an award a few years ago as a perfect pet. They seem to have gone somewhat out of favour recently and I feel that this is because they are generally kept in a sterile, boring cage with a hamster wheel, where their potential cannot be appreciated. Being a desert dweller a gerbil drinks little and therefore urinates little, and produces dry faeces with the result that the animal is almost odour free. Various colour variations now exist and I find the black ones especially appealing.

In the harsh condition in which they live, gerbils have to compete fiercely for every scrap of food and consequently they are not tolerant of other gerbils. A mated pair will live happily together but any offspring should be removed when they are weaned. If you prefer not to breed from your gerbils you can keep two females, as long as they were brought up together. The best way of all if you have the facilities is to house them in a really large enclosure and remove the more aggressive animals. Males have a more tapered back end than females and there is a greater distance between the genitals and the anus. Pet shops often sell baby gerbils, but keep an eye on the classified ads in your local paper for breeders with surplus stock — sometimes they are even offered free to good homes.

GOATS

Someone is going to argue with anything I say about goats — they are that sort of animal. Goats are a demanding commitment and they are a lot of work, so unless you are really certain that you want goats, take up something less demanding like white-water canoeing.

Goats are big, powerful and determined, and a fully grown billy is heavier and certainly stronger than you are if he is interested in a fight, and even I, with an almost nonexistent sense of smell, can detect one at a hundred paces without difficulty. Yet goats are marvellous characters and I do not know anybody who, having kept them, does not get hooked. They are born escapologists, cantankerous as hell and intolerant of damp.

Go to a breeder to buy a goat. If you want one just as a pet, buy a castrated billy kid which is a rare animal as most billies are destroyed at birth. If you want milk as well, buy two female goatlings — that is, animals which are over a year old. You will be able to have them serviced the following autumn. One can also buy Pigmy Goats which have been bred as ornamentals but they are rather expensive animals, and not easy to find as there is always a waiting list of customers. You may not be aware that there are different breeds of goat, such as Saanens and Anglo-Nubians, and each has its supporters. But each breed is very different, and it is essential to study the different types before you settle on the one which you feel will suit you best.

BUSHBABIES

Since it has become illegal, or at any rate very difficult to import mammals into Europe and the USA, bushbabies have become somewhat expensive, and as they do not breed at all freely specimens for sale are not common. However, if you are determined to buy a pair keep an eye on the dealers' advertisement in the

11

journals mentioned in the bibliography or contact them and ask them to advise you if they get any in stock. People do keep them and they are being bred and I am sure they will become more popular as other species become harder to obtain.

SQUIRREL MONKEYS AND OTHER PRIMATES

Do not buy a monkey, whatever you do. They are terrible pets. The trouble is that monkeys look so appealing. Unfortunately, they are freely advertised these days and inevitably some of them end up in homes to the distress of both the monkey and the owner. Any monkeys for sale in Britain or the USA have been captive bred and some are surplus stock from laboratories where Squirrel Monkeys and Marmosets are now being bred. I am not too keen on this idea since some strains have been bred to be immune to the effect of various drugs, which makes them the very devil to treat when they become ill and they can pick up all sorts of infections. Adult monkeys are pretty professional biters and I have only limited use of the top joint of my left thumb since a Crab Eating Macaque pushed a tooth between the bones.

BUDGERIGARS

Budgerigars must be familiar birds to everyone. It is said, for example, that there are more of them in Britain than people and they are undoubtedly the most popular pet in Britain. They are gregarious birds that live in huge flocks in the wild, where all budgies are green. Every budgie in captivity these days is captive bred from captive parents, and all sorts of colours are available, but they are still gregarious, and as such should not be kept alone. If you are wanting one as a single domestic pet you must be willing to become the rest of the flock. It is no good leaving the wretched bird in its cage all by itself. It must have avian, or failing that, human company. Buy a young bird, either from a pet shop, a dealer or a breeder. Youngsters are known as 'barheads' from the dark grey lines that cover the forehead.

The same points to look for when choosing a budgie apply to most birds. They should look fit, perky and interested. Check that there is nothing obviously wrong such as scabs or cuts or kinky feathers or lumps, and have a look at the vent and the cage floor to check that they are clean, as an infection of the gut might well manifest itself in green, runny droppings. The droppings of a healthy budgie should be hard and black with a patch of white urea crystals on them. A cock should have a blue cere (the bare skin above the bill) and that of a hen should be brown. The beak

The adult Budgerigar, on the left, lacks the barred forehead of a young bird.

and the claws ought not to be overgrown. It does not matter too much if the feathers are a bit ragged as these will be replaced at the next moult.

CANARIES

Canaries, like budgies, are completely domesticated. You may not be aware that there are many different kinds of canaries such as Borders, Glosters and Rollers. Not all canaries are yellow — for example, they can be white, red, brown or mottled as well. If you want a bird that will sing, choose a cock as a hen simply chirrups. Buy a young bird though it must be said that it is often difficult to sex young birds, whatever some experts claim, so if you ask for a cock and you end up with a hen, do not complain as the choice might have been made in good faith. A canary will be happier with a mate and you can expect the birds to live up to 12 years.

FINCHES AND OTHER SEEDEATERS

The choice of species is enormous. If you are interested in native birds they cannot be offered for sale by law unless they have been aviary bred, and close rung to prove this fact (ABCR). Close ringing means that a ring which cannot be removed is put onto one leg of a bird when it is very young — something which cannot be done after the first few days of life. You will find that you can buy ABCR Goldfinches, Bullfinches and Greenfinches and in the same advertisements you will also come across mules for sale —

13

mules are a cross between a British finch and a canary. Like the other sort of mule they are sterile. They are usually pretty non-descript, sparrow-like birds but they sing very sweetly — the cocks, anyway.

There are many different kinds of foreign seedeaters, some priced modestly and others much more costly. Leave the latter to the experienced birdkeeper as they might have very specific requirements that are difficult to provide. If you can buy captive-bred finches, do so. They will certainly be more expensive than imported birds but they will also be steadier, hardier and in better condition. Imported birds have had a really hard time before they get to you and it can take them a good year before they look as they should. Captive-bred birds are generally snapped up quickly and there are not many of them so you might find that you are stuck with buying imported stock. Choose birds that look fit and perky and make sure that their eyes and feet are undamaged and their vents clean of faeces. Take them home but do not mix them with other birds for some weeks until you are sure that they are not carrying a disease of some sort. Finches (a term which in this context includes waxbills, whydahs, weavers and sparrows, so perhaps really ought to be called foreign seedeaters) are almost invariably sold in pairs and being gregarious they must be kept together, so buy several pairs if you can.

SOFTBILLS

The world of aviculture calls softbills those birds that cannot fit conveniently into other groupings such as seedeaters, birds of prey, waterfowl, pheasants and so on. The result is that the term softbill covers an enormous range of small to medium birds that are quite unrelated in their taxonomy and requirements. Some of them are sociable, but many lead solitary lives apart from a short time during the breeding season, and keeping them together is to court disaster. Robins, for example, and tits are absolutely savage and if you make the mistake of housing several in a cage, I assure you that you will end up with a single Victor Ludorum singing his heart out to tell the world what a great chap he is. Softbills eat fruit, meat (frequently in the form of livefood), commercial softbill food of one sort or another, and nectar, but one particular bird does not necessarily take all these. They vary in cost from moderately to amazingly expensive, so if you are starting with softbills leave the real exotics alone until you have learnt to keep a few Pekin Robins, mynahs and bulbuls.

Look for perky, alert birds with clean vents and undamaged eyes and feet. Until you are experienced there is not a lot of use examining the droppings as these are always much more liquid than those of seedeaters owing to a higher liquid content of the birds' food.

Many fanciers bemoan the fact that foreign birds are so expensive nowadays but I feel it is a good thing, since it decreases the likelihood of impulse buying by casual purchasers. When you buy softbills go direct to a dealer, and do inspect the stock first rather than ordering them via mail order. Many of these birds are delicate and all are costly, and it is unwise to buy them unseen.

DOVES AND PIGEONS

I have no idea what the difference is between doves and pigeons. I usually use the word Dove for granivorous species and Pigeon for frugivorous birds, but you will find both words used indiscriminately so do not be too worried about the names. There are many different kinds of Columbidae (their family name) but few are kept in captivity. A few small species such as the Diamond Dove and the Namaqua Dove, which is a dear little soul, are kept in aviaries. Both eat seed. Several colour variants of the former are now available and Diamond Dove cocks have a wider eye ring than hens. They are only slightly larger than a budgie.

Fruit Pigeons are rarely seen in captivity these days. They were never popular with fanciers, and can be very difficult to feed.

Ornamental doves such as Fantail Doves are easy to keep if you have the room for them: the best way of all to keep them is in an outside loft. They look super strutting about the lawn feeding and displaying, but be warned as they do have disadvantages. First, the area in which they live will be covered with droppings. On top of this they are extremely prolific, which is why they were kept by monasteries and noblemen in the first place — there was always a ready supply of squabs, or chicks, for the table. The third disadvantage is that if a neighbour is growing a tasty crop of something in his garden or field he might find a great flock of birds descending on it each day to help themselves. So if you do want some of these attractive birds make sure your neighbours are friendly and that you have somewhere that will take all your unwanted stock. When you first buy them, keep your birds confined for some weeks or they might return whence they came.

Racing pigeons are a way of life and this is not the place to talk at length on the subject. Read up about them and talk to the Royal Pigeon Racing Association which will point you in the right direction.

Incidentally, if ever you find a pigeon wearing a ring, or if someone brings you one, or you come across a dead one, the chances are that it has lost its way during a race, in which case the RPRA would like to hear about it. Return any rings from dead birds and look on the underside of the wing to see if there is a number stamped thereon. If you look after a ringed live bird you will be compensated for feeding it and returning it to its owner. I was recently brought a racing pigeon with a broken ankle which I nursed back to health, but before I contacted the RPRA it shot past me one day and flew up onto the roof to get its bearings before flying off in a determined fashion in a northeasterly direction. It obviously knew where it was going and wanted to get back there as soon as it could.

QUAIL, FOWL AND PHEASANTS

There are two commonly kept species of quail, the Common Quail and the Chinese Painted Quail, both domesticated. The latter are lovable little birds and the tiniest of the type. Cocks are handsome in greyish blue, red ochre and brown while the hens are a typically gallinaceous mottled brown. They are best kept on the floor of an aviary where they will pick up dropped seed (though they need feeding as well). They take a variety of food including insects and whenever the cock finds a tidbit he will call his hen and give it to her, but do not make the mistake of trying to keep more than a single pair in each flight. They lay plenty of eggs, and provided you can persuade the hen to incubate them, or find a suitable foster parent, they breed well. The newly hatched chicks are tiny furry mites like bumblebees, and they can squeeze through 1.2 cm ($\frac{1}{2}$ in) mesh, so if you are having baby quail make sure that there is something along the bottom of the wire netting to stop them escaping. Hens are more delicate than cocks and consequently there is always a surfeit of cheap cocks on the market.

Common Quail are more robust, rather larger, breed easily and are the source of the delicacy 'quails eggs' — and indeed table quail for which market they are bred commercially — but they too can live on aviary floors.

Fowl and pheasants are closely related and from our point of view they can conveniently be grouped together. The only way to keep them other than at liberty on a large estate, is in a large aviary though to optimise the space it can also be used for parrots and other birds which will live in the upper part of a flight while the pheasants spend nearly all their time on the floor. Most gallinaceous birds are polygamous and it is common to keep a cock and two hens together. If an aviary is to be kept solely for pheasants it is a good idea to make a false ceiling of nylon netting below the wire roof as they can fly upwards with tremendous force and scalp themselves. Pheasants are not noisy but if you keep some varieties of fowl they can make an awful din at dawn, and dawn means the time when the cockerel spots the first lightening of the eastern sky, not when you get up to go to work. Peafowl can be a bit noisy too, and will call just before a shower, though I do not mind their calls which sound wonderfully wild and exotic.

PARROTS

Parrots are expensive and are not cage birds, and so-called parrot cages are dreadful. The law says that a bird must not be kept in a cage which is less than the bird's wingspan, and many caged parrots look as though they are in a sentry box. You need a proper set-up with a birdroom and very strong aviaries to keep parrots. Remember that some parrots can chew through chainlink fencing, and wood stands no chance of survival. Parrots are gregarious so they should be kept at least in pairs and they are noisy birds which means that you need large grounds so that the birds can be kept away from anyone who minds their noise.

Nowadays more and more captive-bred birds are coming onto the market and these are the ones you should buy for not only will they be steadier and hardier but they have not been removed from already depleted wild stocks, that in some cases are disappearing very fast. One can gain much pleasure from keeping and breeding parrots, but whatever you do please refrain from buying one of the poor, so-called tame, brain-washed performing birds that are so popular in North America.

COCKATIELS

Cockatiels are parrots, but unlike most of their family they are easier to maintain without all sorts of special facilities. They are about the size of a smallish blackbird with a long tail, they are not too noisy nor destructive, and being peace-loving folk they can be kept in a mixed community with other birds.

They are entirely domestic and though the original form is grey and yellow there are now other colour varieties available. An additional bonus is that they breed well and there is always a demand for surplus stock. In the grey form the cock has a bright yellow head with red cheek patches while the hen's colouring is considerably duller and her tail is grey, barred with yellow whereas in the cock it is plain grey-black.

17

SNAKES

Whenever people ask me what is the ideal pet, I always suggest a snake: it is an infinitely better choice than a dog. Just think of the advantages — it does not make such a noise that the neighbours complain, neither does it grub up the carpet or deposit hairs on the furniture. It certainly does not want a long walk each day and, depending on its size, it only consumes one modest meal every few days, so if you want to go on vacation for a week you do not need to spend money boarding it; and lastly, it will not drive you mad early in the morning by squawking 'Who's a pretty boy?' nor will it leap onto your lap and snag your clothes. None the less, being a cold-blooded animal, it appreciates warmth and although it will never demand attention many snakes enjoy being handled. All this is not to say that a snake should be taken on lightly — as with all animals it is a responsibility. The only reason that I cannot seriously recommend a snake to most beginners is that as yet few of them are bred in captivity which means that they are taken from the wild.

But for pet keepers who are responsible and really care about animals and who feel they cannot live without a pair of snakes, do not be tempted to buy the Grass Snakes that appear in pet shops each spring. They will almost certainly die unless their buyer is highly experienced in snake keeping. Select instead a fair sized snake that is easy to feed, and examine it closely at the dealer's premises. If it looks dry or a little thin or feels light for its size, leave it alone. It has almost certainly been recently imported and is not being cared for properly. It should not be for sale and is probably suffering greatly from dehydration.

Check the inside of the mouth and if there are any peculiar lumps or patches of fungus, go somewhere else for your snake. But if all is as it should be, have a feel along the body to find any bumps or lesions of any sort. As to the sex of the snake, unless you trust the dealer implicitly, take a knowledgeable friend with you.

You may notice that the snake's eyes are dull and whitish blue. This occurs when it is about to slough and as soon as it has done that the eyes will appear normal. But be warned that when the eyes are like this the snake cannot see very well and consequently it feels vulnerable and at a disadvantage, so do not be too surprised if it strikes at you.

LIZARDS

If a lizard looks active and alert and is not dry and thin, buy it and keep your fingers crossed. If, on the other hand, it does not fit this description, leave it strictly alone.

AMPHIBIANS

What I have said about lizards applies equally to amphibians; it is really difficult to tell you what a sick frog looks like. If an amphibian is a bit cold it can look most unwell until it warms up again, whereupon it reverts to normal. So I suppose the best advice is to look for a frog that looks well, or take along a froggy friend when you go to buy amphibians.

FISH

If you are serious about fish, do not take one home from a fair; instead, complain loudly to the stallholder about the fact that he is giving fish as prizes. It is perfectly legal but if enough people complain about the practice, perhaps it will eventually cease. Fairground fish are stressed and ill fed at the very least, and may well be suffering from all sorts of diseases.

Go instead to a reputable dealer and spend a few minutes watching the fish to see that as a group they look healthy. Fish come in all sorts of shapes and they have many behavioural patterns, but while bearing this in mind, look for a fish that does not hog the bottom of the tank or that swims in an erratic fashion or in an unnatural position. Steer clear of a fish that is bloated or has wounds, torn fins or other obvious damage, or that trails a length of colourless faeces from the vent and, as a general indicator, keep an eye on the fins for a fish that is feeling unwell may swim with them closely against the body.

INVERTEBRATES

The only advice to give about invertebrates of any sort is to watch them for a while to see if they look healthy. There is no point in saying that they should be active as well since many of them spend a great deal of time sitting around doing nothing, but while you watch them look for any serious damage. If the odd leg is missing there is no need to worry as it will regenerate in time though it might very well not look as good as new, but in the meantime the animal will manage perfectly well without it. Do look for any damage to the body itself and if there is any, leave the animal alone.

2
HOUSING

The only certainty about housing any animal is that the cage or run or aquarium will invariably be a compromise. Once you have accepted that, you have to decide whether to buy or to make a home and, generally, provided that one's pocket is deep enough, good, commercially made housing is the best bet. If you can only afford models from the cheap end of the market, do not bother; make the thing yourself and it will be far better in the long run. I do not enjoy carpentry at all and I must certainly be the world's third worst carpenter — I always thought I was the worst until I actually came across two people who make even more terrible furniture and cages than I do. The one great advantage to making your own housing is that you can make it exactly as you want it. Before looking at different types of animal homes, there are a few basic points to bear in mind.

1. Always use the best materials you can find. Rectangular welded mesh (weldmesh) is always preferable to hexagonal wire nettings, and cheap wire netting is useless.
2. Always use weatherproof materials, or weatherproof them yourself, even if you intend to use the finished product indoors. I promise you that one day your cage will be housing something in the garden.
3. Do not leave or use anything in the construction that might be harmful. Deal with sharp ends of wire or points of nails sticking out of the wood. And do not forget that paint and preservatives can be toxic.
4. Take care over the design and make the whole thing of convenient sized panels that can be bolted or screwed together; at some stage you are going to need to alter the thing, and it is a nightmare doing it if the structure is not sectional.
5. If the building is for outdoors, make sure that there is a solid floor even if on the face of it you do not want one, as for example in an aviary. There are two reasons for this: one is to stop occupants getting out — even if you build it for home-loving animals, the day may come when it is used to house a

digger or a chewer. The other reason for a floor is to stop unwanted animals getting in. Rats and mice can cause havoc by killing animals and by contaminating food with urine, that may be infected, and that can be fatal to other animals.

6. Use strong timbers or whatever for the basic structure. It might seem strong while it just sits there but if you have to lift it, or someone leans on it, or if a load of snow packs solid on the top, I might suddenly find myself promoted to the world's fourth worst carpenter.

7. Arrange some way of feeding the inhabitants of this new house so that as little disturbance is caused as possible. You will have to work this out depending on what you are going to keep, but a small door with a shelf inside for food pots might be the answer.

8. Always make a safety porch to aviaries and similar constructions, so that you can enter and close the door behind you before opening the next door. If you do not, you will certainly regret it at some time when your prize specimen shoots out between your legs.

9. Make every animal house as large as space and finances permit. If an occupant needs less space he will not use all of it, but in time you are more than likely going to want the extra space. If you are going to have to enter the animal house, do make sure you can stand upright; nothing is more infuriating, for example, than having to stoop inside an aviary.

10. Make the door as small as is convenient — the bigger it is, the more likely it will be that something will escape. Unless you are keeping really large animals, always hinge the door at the top and let it open outwards so that if you forget to close it, it will drop shut anyway. Think carefully about the position of doors. If you are making a cage and you are right handed, the best place is in the right hand wall as you face the front of the cage.

11. Ensure that the cage floor can be cleaned with minimum disturbance.

12. Paint weldmesh or bars black. It is far easier to see through them and they appear much less prominent.

13. Never assume that an animal cannot get through a gap too small for it, as this happens time and again. I caused considerable panic on one occasion when I was travelling from Bombay to Calcutta by train. Part of my luggage was an old suitcase which contained several snakes, each in its own cotton bag which was securely tied at the neck. Halfway across India one of them, a 2 m (7 ft) python, escaped, and pandemonium resulted. When I finally arrived at my destination I examined the case and the bag carefully but I could not find the smallest

opening anywhere; you have been warned. Nor should you ever assume that a container without a lid is too deep for an animal to jump out of, as Goldfish, frogs, tarantulas and hamsters will readily demonstrate when required.

14. Even if you think you are only going to need one cage, flight in your aviary or compartment in your compound, make two. In time you will thank me for suggesting it.

15. When you are siting an animal home, think for a moment about where you would like it to be if you were going to live in it. Window sills which are boiling hot and freezing cold by turn are not a good idea, neither are draughts nor places where you cannot get at the cage to service it easily. Common sense will dictate the best position.

16. Before you introduce an animal to its new home do make sure that all paint is completely dry, that all nails and bits of wire and tools have been removed, that all plants have established themselves or that pieces of plants that you have used as cage furniture are not poisonous and that food, water and bedding is where it should be. Trying to do any of this at a later stage is frequently doomed to failure.

These points are equally valid if your new pet is to live in the house. There should be no dangerous or poisonous things around, doors or windows should not be left open so that a disorientated kitten can rush out onto the road when no one is looking, and food, drink and bedding should be ready.

Once an animal has been introduced, go away and leave it alone to establish itself. It is tempting for everyone to stand and watch, but it really is best for the animal to find its way around in peace.

AQUARIA

Let's get something out of the way for a start: if you have a goldfish bowl, throw it away now. Goldfish bowls are great as ornaments when filled with glass marbles but for keeping fish they are terrible things and should not be used. What is necessary is an aquarium.

Before buying or making an aquarium, an aspiring aquarist needs to work out what sort of fish are going to be kept since the type of fish, their size and their numbers are going to govern the dimensions of their home. Two considerations need to be taken into account — first, there should be sufficient living space for each animal and secondly the surface area must be large enough for the water to absorb enough oxygen from the atmosphere to enable

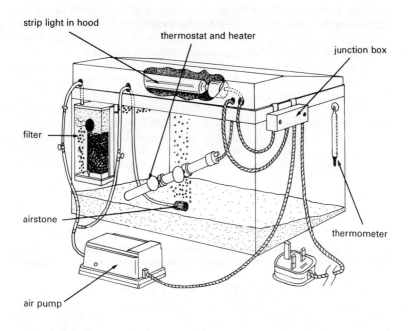

strip light in hood

thermostat and heater

junction box

filter

airstone

thermometer

air pump

The essentials of a good aquarium before you even think about plants and fish.

the fish to 'breathe', and this latter requirement varies according to the type of fish. As a general guide, I always calculate that a tropical freshwater fish ought to have a minimum of 30 sq cm (4½ sq in), a tropical marine fish 120 sq cm (18½ sq in) and a coldwater fresh water fish about 75 sq cm (11½ sq in) per centimetre (0.4 in) of fish. For example: a 90 cm (3 ft) tank will hold 90 cm (3 ft) of tropical freshwater fish, say nine fish × 10 cm (4 in) long or 30 fish × 3 cm (1.2 in) long.

If you intend to keep marine animals, it is imperative that the whole container is made only of glass as seawater will corrode a metal frame. In fact, nowadays, it is almost impossible to buy an aquarium with a frame as this is an outdated form of construction, and all modern tanks are made solely from glass. Trying to make anything waterproof is difficult which is why virtually all fish keepers buy their tanks rather than make them. However, if you would like to make a tank yourself, then you will need five pieces of 6.5 mm (¼ in) float glass for the sides and bottom. Bevel all the sharp edges with emery cloth. The next stage, which is really tedious, is to carefully clean all the areas where adhesive is to be applied with a solvent, such as methylated spirit. Unless every last scrap of fingermark is removed the result could be an empty tank and a great waterfall. Silicon rubber tank adhesive can be bought from aquarist shops and beads of this will need to be applied to the appropriate edges and the whole thing stuck together with sticky tape, and left alone for 24 hours after which further beads of adhesive should be applied to the inside of the seams and run along their lengths with a spatula of some sort to completely seal each seam. Twenty-four hours after that your basic tank is ready. However, if you set it up as it is the water will evaporate, the fish will leap out and, if it is a tropical tank, all your precious heat will escape. It is essential to fit a hood, and to keep this in place a narrow shelf made from strips of glass should be glued in place inside the four walls, 2.5–5 cm (1–2 in) from the top. This not only supports the hood but serves to strengthen the structure appreciably. Hoods of all sizes, completely fitted with lights and feeding hatches and all sorts of refinements, can be bought from a dealer, or can be constructed from glass or aluminium depending on your particular requirements.

Now you can get on with setting up the tank. A tank full of water with a layer of gravel on the bottom weighs far more than you might think, so do not even contemplate moving it unless it is empty. Bear this in mind when you are deciding where the tank is going to live because the supporting piece of furniture will have to be strong. Before you put an aquarium on it, place on top of it a thick slab of expanded polystyrene, the size of the tank, which will even out any surface irregularities, otherwise, you might end up with cracked glass. Have a last think to check that you have an electrical socket nearby and that the tank will not be in direct sunlight, or you are going to be fighting a losing battle with algae, and put the tank in place.

A very important piece of equipment now needs to be considered — a filter, to get rid of all the rubbish that accumulates wherever animals live. There are various types on the market and choice is up to the individual. My own preference is for the under-gravel filter and this needs to be fitted in the bottom of the tank before any gravel is added. Do not be tempted to grab a handful of gravel from your driveway or anywhere else for that matter. It might look fine but could be heavily polluted or could cause a chemical imbalance in the water, either of which is going to give you real problems. Buy proper aquarium gravel which has particles of around 3 mm ($\frac{1}{10}$ in) and spend some time rinsing it in clean running water until the water runs clear. Put the gravel into your tank together with any rocks you might have bought from the same place and arrange it all carefully and artistically, sloping it up towards the back. You will need about a plastic bucketful of gravel for each 0.28 sq m (1 sq ft) of tank base.

You are now ready to add the water, so start filling gently from a tap, but do not let the water whoosh directly onto the gravel or all your careful work will be undone: instead, let it trickle over a rock. Remember not to fill the tank completely or you will have a flood when you start to dabble about while you add plants to the set-up. Tap water is only really fit for human consumption, so do not try to introduce any fish until you have let the water sit for a few days. In the meantime, fit the tank with a water heater and thermostat if you are intending to keep tropicals and put a thermometer handy so that you can keep an eye on the temperature, which ought to be about 24°C (75°F). You can also spend this time installing an aerator which is a device for pumping lots of tiny air bubbles to increase the oxygen in the water, and to cause slight movement which ensures that the water temperature is even.

Whatever fish you have decided to keep will require certain conditions in which to live, so you might need to make the water more acid or more alkaline; a dealer will sell all that is necessary to make your water chemistry just right for your fish. Remember that you will now have several electrical parts on the go — lighting in the hood, an aerator and a filter, both running off a pump, and possibly a heater and thermostat. Make sure these are all doing what they should, and that they are safe.

The next stage in preparing a tank is to introduce some plants, which help the water conditions, provide hiding places for fish, food for herbivorous species and somewhere to lay eggs. Most newcomers to fish keeping are parsimonious with their plants and do not realise that for a 1 m (3 ft) tank you really need about 100 plants. Incidentally, if you are thinking about keeping sea creatures, you can forget all that I have said about plants — marines are an entirely different matter. I can only recommend that you read a specialised book.

When all our greenery has been planted to your satisfaction, do not immediately add the fish to the tank. Wait instead for a few weeks until the plants have established themselves, and show signs of growth. Not only will they survive better but the delay will enable the tank to settle down and look far more attractive than when freshly planted. This intervening period should not be wasted, as the time can be filled by reading up on fish, drooling over the tanks in dealers' premises and window shopping through the advertisements in aquarists magazines; and resisting any aberrant urges to buy divers, treasure chests or Chinese bridges to spoil the appearance of your tank.

25

CAGES FOR BIRDS AND OTHER ANIMALS

For a start, forget all about a chrome plated wire or split bamboo ornamental cage from your local pet shop — they are everything a birdcage should not be — and worst of all are those tall skinny ones. Birds just do not fly vertically, except for quail, and because of this very habit they are no good in cages. Having said that, if you ever do need to keep one temporarily in a cage, make sure that the inside of the top is thickly padded with foam rubber.

Once someone has been keeping animals for a while, cages of all shapes and sizes start to accumulate. In time, not only does the whole collection look untidy, but it is much harder to service, so if you are starting out and intend to keep more than a couple of birds, it is well worth considering making several identical cages at the same time. You can buy, or indeed make, blocks of nine or twelve cages as a single unit, but I consider that the same number of individual cages stacked together is a much more versatile arrangement.

The size of your cage will be determined by what you intend to keep — after all, birds range from ostriches at one end to minuscule waxbills at the other, but a useful all-round size is 91 cm (36 in) long by 30 cm (12 in) deep by 38 cm (15 in) high. Use plywood for the back, top, bottom and two ends. If you use thin plywood for all of them, you may end up having to add a framework. The best idea is to make the two ends of 1.25 cm ($\frac{1}{2}$ cm) ply, the top and bottom of 0.6 cm ($\frac{1}{4}$ in) and the back of 0.3 cm ($\frac{1}{8}$ in). Glue all edges that are going to meet and then nail the thing together, or, if you are more professional than I am, screw it together. Sandpaper any rough bits. For the front of the cage, you can either use weldmesh cut to size — 2.5 cm (1 in) by 1.25 cm ($\frac{1}{2}$ in) is the best for general use — or you can buy specially made cage fronts from dealers and the better pet shops. These are found in three types called 'Budgie', 'Canary' and 'Finch'. The major difference is the gaps between the bars, and unless you know exactly what the cage is going to be used for I suggest you buy 'Finch' fronts which are the narrowest. At this stage it is worth considering whether it is worth being able to partition the cage into two equal halves, and if you decide that it is, fix two pieces of beading on the floor and top of the inside, halfway along the length, and about 0.6 cm ($\frac{1}{4}$ in) apart so that a dividing wall of hardboard or weldmesh can be slid in if the need arises. If you do this you will also need to fix in place two vertical wooden bars in the front, between which to slide the partition.

When you cut the weldmesh for the front of the cage, or buy ready made cage fronts, their vertical measurements ought to be

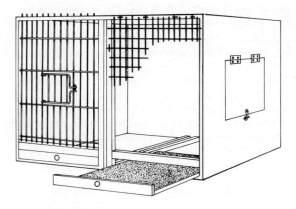

A good box cage. Either weldmesh or commercial cage fronts can be used. The wires of the latter are shown projecting through the top for clarity. In reality they would be cut shorter.

about 7.6 cm (3 in) less than the height of the cage. Place a horizontal bar this distance from the floor, to which you will fix their bottom edges. Remember to cut the weldmesh in two if you have allowed for a partition or you will not be able to slide it in if it is in the way.

The next task to tackle is to make a tray for the cage floor that can slide in easily and simplifies the job of cage cleaning. If you have bought cage fronts you will find that they are fitted with doors. On the other hand if weldmesh is to be used it is far better to make a door in one end of the cage. The cage is now almost complete and needs to be carefully painted inside and out. Any gloss paint or emulsion will do as long as it is lead free, and the inhabitants will show up best if the inside is a light colour and the outside and bars painted dark. I favour white and black but it is entirely a matter of choice.

Finally, when every part is completely dry, drill holes in the frame at the front of the cage to take the long wires on the cage fronts and slot them into place.

For covering the floors of cages I like clean, absorbent paper. Unused newsprint is perfect, and if there is a newspaper or magazine printer nearby you can pick up ends of rolls for a small outlay and they last for ages. If a thick wad of sheets the size of the cage floor are put in once a week when the cage is cleaned, one only needs to remove the top one or two each day to keep the interior tidy. I do not like sand and it gets in eyes and food and any cuts in the birds' feet. Sawdust is equally useless for all of

27

these reasons, and if you use it on the floor of the birdcage, it fills the air like a snowstorm each time the bird flies.

If the cage is for anything that perches or climbs you are going to need perches. Forget about dowel; it is useless. It has no flexibility, and does not allow any exercise for the feet. Instead, find some twigs or branches, bark and all, from some non-poisonous tree — fruit trees are ideal — and wash them well to remove any pollution. When you cut them to size, remember that any forks may need to fit through the door of the cage. Replace them periodically when they have become dry and brittle, and while they are in use clean them every so often. If the cage is for a bird, put the perches as far apart as you can so that it gets as much exercise as possible, but not too close to the roof or the end of the cage, or the scalp or tail may get damaged. And, preferably, do not buy any bells, or plastic clowns, or any other such with which to clutter the cage.

Depending on your animal you might very well need a sleeping box. This is best made of plywood and, provided it has a large enough entrance and is of adequate size there ought to be no problems. Place it at the back of the cage for security: if an animal is arboreal fix it in a top corner; if it is terrestrial put the box on the floor.

All that remains now is to equip the cage with food and water pots. These can be made of anything provided they are easy to

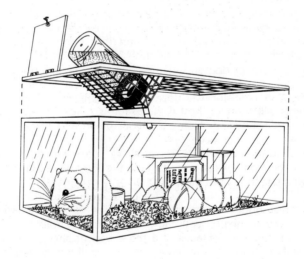

A much better way of keeping rodents than in a commercial cage, is in a properly fitted aquarium.

clean, will not tip up and are animal proof. For most animals a water bottle clipped on the outside of the cage, with the nozzle in a convenient place for the inhabitant, if often best since a dish of water often seems to result in the cage floor ending up awash.

If you are intending to keep rodents, do not be tempted to buy one of those awful metal cages that pet shops sell for mice and hamsters. They are very small and can be absolutely lethal. I have seen a gerbil literally cut its throat on a sharp edge in one of those things. Wood is perfectly all right for rodents — though it is as well not to use very thin wood — provided that there are no edges or corners for them to get their teeth around. In time, all rodent cages end up a bit chewed, but a proper hole is very unusual. Alternatively, small rodents can be kept in aquariums; with a suitable weldmesh lid they are ideal. But do make sure that a door is provided so that the whole top is not lifted off at each feed, and that the lid cannot be easily lifted off by the animal which lives in the tank. For rodents, I find that shredded newsprint is best for the floor and for bedding, and several papier mâché egg boxes and small cardboard tubes make great adventure playgrounds.

You will also have to supply a sleeping chamber and some suitable pots for food and water. You can try an exercise wheel: some animals love them and others just do not want to know. Whatever else you do, though, resist the impulse to buy a hamster ball — a transparent plastic globe in which you incarcerate the poor beast which then rolls it around the floor as he walks about inside. They are nasty things which ought to be banned.

When you are thinking about where to put your cage, always bear in mind that to most household pets you are the size of the Empire State Building, and thus can be very frightening. Therefore, try and put your cage so that it is as near face height as possible. This way there are much less likely to be panic stricken dashes for cover each time you are around. Another point to remember is that it is not a good idea to keep rodents in your bedroom. They spend all night thundering around in their exercise wheel or rustling about while they burrow. It can be very wearing.

AVIARIES AND SIMILAR ENCLOSURES

Whether you intend to keep birds or dogs in an outside enclosure you basically need the same sort of thing, so it makes sense to treat all such animal homes in one place.

To start with, plan the whole thing so that it is as large as possible but only a few cm (in) higher than you are, and in a sheltered, secluded place. This type of structure consists of two parts — an outside flight or run, and a shed of some sort.

Make sure that aquaria are sited near a
power point, that there are no trailing
electrical leads, and that apparatus is
unplugged when not in use.

Make sure all house plants
are non-poisonous

Fit fire guards
to prevent your
pets from
getting burnt
or escaping up
the chimney.

Thought must be given to the safety and housing of animals in the home.

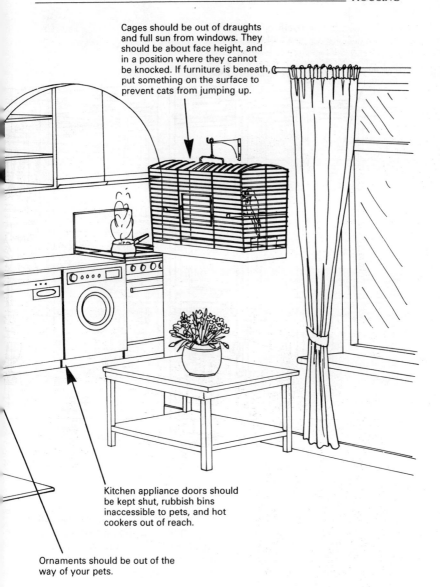

Cages should be out of draughts and full sun from windows. They should be about face height, and in a position where they cannot be knocked. If furniture is beneath, put something on the surface to prevent cats from jumping up.

Kitchen appliance doors should be kept shut, rubbish bins inaccessible to pets, and hot cookers out of reach.

Ornaments should be out of the way of your pets.

31

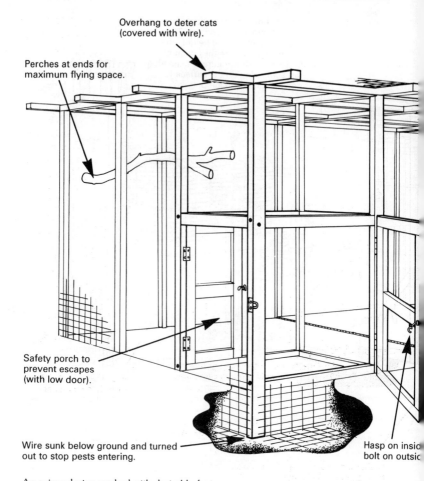

Overhang to deter cats
(covered with wire).

Perches at ends for
maximum flying space.

Safety porch to
prevent escapes
(with low door).

Wire sunk below ground and turned
out to stop pests entering.

Hasp on inside
bolt on outside

An aviary design packed with desirable features.

Try to plan for more than one flight or run. You will find it
invaluable over the years even if you cannot visualise a use for it at
this stage. If the aviary is to have a natural floor, remove the soil
to a depth of 15 cm (6 in) and, after you have built the frame of
the aviary and start to attach the wire, completely cover the floor
with 1.25 cm (½ in) mesh. It will stop your pets from escaping;
just as importantly, it will exclude vermin. Some books suggest that
you dig a 30 cm (12 in) deep trench around the aviary and continue the netting of the walls to this depth and outwards for 15 cm
(6 in), but this is hard work, almost as expensive and not nearly as

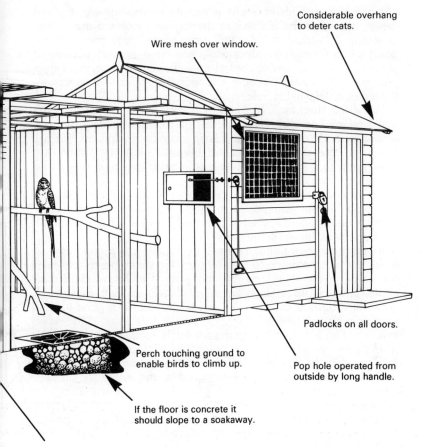

Considerable overhang to deter cats.

Wire mesh over window.

Perch touching ground to enable birds to climb up.

Padlocks on all doors.

Pop hole operated from outside by long handle.

If the floor is concrete it should slope to a soakaway.

Flight made from separate sections for maximum versatility.

effective. After you have wired the floor you can put back all the topsoil.

It is imperative that all timber used for aviaries is made as weatherproof and insectproof as possible. If you are using a commercially made shed the timber will already be treated, and building your own flights onto bought sheds is certainly the easiest way of making an aviary. Somewhere along the side of the shed you will have to make a doorway so that animals can enter or leave the flight, and this door should be constructed so that it can be opened from outside the aviary as well as from inside the shed.

33

When you are thinking about a remote control device, try and design it so that the animals in the flight cannot see the person operating it because the day will come when some animal is not going to go through the door while anyone is around. I have not yet come across a remote control door that is anything better than primitive but perhaps the best is a door that slides in runners with the aid of a detachable pole.

Inside the shed itself is a good place to make the safety porch that I referred to earlier, and in this part of the building one can also store and cut up food and keep cleaning equipment. Do not forget to wire over any windows because otherwise, when you open them to let in a cool breeze, your prize specimen may make a break for freedom.

If your pets need beds or sleeping boxes, make sure they are dry and draughtproof and put them in the furthest corner from the door. A bed inside the shed is best made with short legs as floors can be remarkably draughty places.

If you are keeping birds or small mammals, it is a good idea to make the only entrance to the flight via the safety porch and then the inside of the shed, and the doors ought to be no more than about 120 cm (48 in) high as this will help prevent escapes. A good thick bush at the opposite end to the door is a good idea as your animals will tend to dive into it when you enter at the other end. Planting is important because it fulfils so many purposes. All plants must naturally be non-poisonous and pretty robust, and provide cover at all levels. Birds and small mammals use leaves in nest building and any plants introduced to the aviary should take this into account, as some birds such as weavers use long thin grasses for their nest and others use conventional leaves or moss as a lining. It is a good idea to incorporate plants with flowers and fruit as the former attract edible insects while the latter can themselves be eaten. One thing to be aware of is the final size to which a plant will grow, for the top of a tree or a stout branch can exert such pressure on wire mesh that eventually a hole appears and you wonder why your stock keeps disappearing. It is not a bad idea to trim all your plants so that they do not touch the wire. If ever you are hunting for a hole, it is much easier to find if there is this gap.

The best floor covering is peat. If you try and grow some sort of lawn you will be forever fighting to keep it looking attractive. Gravel can work well too, especially if it is hosed down occasion-ally but it cannot be much fun for quail to trudge about on all day long. Nor can birds have a dust bath in gravel. It may seem obvious, but do not put food or water dishes beneath anything on which a bird may perch, and if there is to be a large birdbath (and there ought to be) do find one with a rough surface and a slope at one end or a bird might be drowned; or if the water level drops, so that it cannot be reached from a tall side, all your charges are going to get thirsty. The easiest thing of all is to make a shallow pond with cement.

If your flight is to have a concrete floor, life will be a lot easier if you incorporate a drain with a soakaway beneath. Arrange your floor at a slight gradient, so that when you hose it down or it rains all the water disappears quickly.

If your aviary is actually going to house birds, neighbourhood cats can become a real pest; indeed, breeding can be completely spoiled because the birds are too nervous about a great fat cat sitting on top of their home. The best deterrent is to extend the wire netting of the roof so that it sticks out beyond the walls of the aviary for about 20 cm (8 in). If this has no framework at the outer edge it is very floppy and a cat that has climbed the wire will find it almost impossible to negotiate this insubstantial overhang. It must, however, extend around the shed because otherwise any self respecting cat will soon learn to climb the building to get on top of the flight. Unfortunately, if your next door neighbour builds a shed on his side of the fence, close to your aviary, a cat will jump across. It applies the other way around, too; don't site your aviary near your neighbour's shed.

Finally, when the whole thing has been built and planted, and the plants allowed to become established, do get yourself a substantial lock for the door. Pet thefts are increasing and pets are valuable. I know it will only keep out honest burglars, but it will help.

OUTDOOR ENCLOSURES FOR LARGE ANIMALS

If you are going to keep horses, ponies and donkeys, or for that matter any other large mammal, you need to be sure that you have enough space. They all take up a fair amount of room which means a fence long enough to surround a paddock, and that costs a lot of money. Horses and donkeys will not try to wreck it, but the best grass is just out of reach beyond the fence which means that it gets leaned on very heavily.

Goats on the other hand will do their utmost to get out of anything. They can climb, they can ignore electric shocks, they can squeeze through the tiniest gaps — they are brilliant escapologists, so, if you are intending to keep them, you must think long and hard about their fence. If you have any doubts at all, do not keep goats. They are great characters but they are demanding beasts.

Once you have established where your paddock is going to go, you will need to provide a draughtproof shed for your animals and, unless you are experienced at making such things, I suggest you buy one. Site it so that the door does not face the prevailing wind, fit it with a concrete floor that can be easily cleaned, and if the building is large enough to incorporate a separate room in which to keep brooms and wheelbarrows and metal bins full of food, life will be a lot easier. The food bins must be rodent proof and you will also need a water tap on the premises.

You will need a regular supply of straw for bedding and a pitchfork and shovel for getting rid of it. A really heavy water container is essential, and a food trough and hayrick from which the animals can feed should be fixed firmly to one wall.

Whether you intend to keep horses, donkeys or goats, they will need to be groomed, so you will need a good brush. You will also need something to remove tightly packed muck from hooves and, in the case of goats, something to trim their hooves with before they become overgrown. Horses need this service as well but it is far better to ask your vet or farrier to do it. Do not be tempted to neglect doing this periodically, or your animal is going to end up with all sorts of foot and leg problems.

TERRARIUMS (VIVARIUMS)

If you are intending to go in for reptiles, amphibians or some invertebrates, like bird eating spiders, or even some small mammals, such as shrews, you are going to need a terrarium.

Basically, a terrarium is a fish tank with a lid. Old aquariums are ideal since for most species they need not be waterproof, though some amphibians, such as Axolotls and Clawed Toads, have to be kept entirely in water. Unless the animals who live in your terrarium are to be found wild in your own latitude, you will need to keep them warm, and by far the easiest way of doing this is to use lamps in the hood connected to a thermostat. However, there is evidence that this is harmful, so the best solution is to heat the tank with ceramic heating bulbs or soil-warming cables, and have a separate bulb whose sole function is to provide light during the day. Whichever system you use, do make sure that it is surrounded by a weldmesh cage so that animals cannot touch it, otherwise they will get burnt. Do not forget a thermometer; the temperature in a tank can rise astonishingly fast if something goes wrong.

Basically this is all that is needed, although you will also have to decide what type of environment to reproduce. If this set-up is for tree frogs, it will need to be humid and contain heaps of growing plants over a peat or loam floor, with 25 per cent activated charcoal. An underlying layer of pebbles will help drainage. On the other hand, if the vivarium is for desert dwelling lizards then all you will have to provide will be a few rocks and a perlite or gravel substrate to keep the animals happy. The only other furniture you will require will be food and water pots, and for humid vivariums a spraying device such as is used for house plants. It is really difficult to have absolute rules when housing animals because even individuals of a single species can have widely differing requirements. I know one person who keeps his pet orb web spider in a hula hoop suspended vertically from the ceiling. The spider has made a web within this framework and is very content to live like that.

Whatever type of animal you are keeping, try and provide conditions as near those that are natural for it and you will not go far wrong.

HOUSING BUTTERFLIES AND MOTHS

Breeding and keeping butterflies and moths is a fascinating hobby, but the adults are very delicate so that special housing is necessary. If you keep them in a conventional cage they will soon have tattered wings, and a tank is useless as the humidity means that the wings adhere to the glass and the butterfly dies fairly swiftly. Butterfly cages are made of fine, soft nylon netting on a wooden frame, which work well for the insects as they can hold onto the mesh wherever they land. Perhaps the easiest way of keeping native species of butterflies and moths is to keep them in a sleeve, which is basically a large cylinder of nylon mesh, kept cylindrical along its length with a few wire hoops. The whole thing is slid over a branch of the tree which is the foodplant of the particular species, and one open end is tied around the wood. The insects are introduced into the cylinder and the other end is similarly attached further along the same branch, so that foodplant and butterflies are all together in this cage, which is simplicity itself to make.

An excellent way of keeping caterpillars is to use an empty plastic fizzy drink bottle. These usually have an opaque bottom and if the transparent bit is cut away from this it can be slipped back on to make a mini greenhouse if a sleeve of the transparent plastic is glued inside the opaque cup. All, then, that is necessary is to stand a pot containing a growing foodplant for the intended species inside, the eggs or caterpillars are carefully placed on the leaves with a paintbrush and the top is slid into place. A small piece of net held in position over the mouth of the bottle completes the job; but do not be tempted to replace the lid, as the

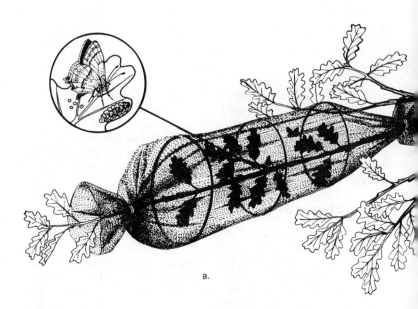

Housing for butterflies and moths. a: sleeving a tree branch. b: covering a living pot plant. c: using a soft drinks bottle.

humidity will build up to such an extent that the little caterpillars will end up glued to the plastic by the film of water, and there they will die.

FORMICARIUM

If you are interested in invertebrates, few are more fascinating to keep than ants, and it is very simple to construct a formicarium. You will need a piece of glass — the size is not critical, but about 30 cm (1 ft) square is ideal. Make a wooden frame to fit around this and tack it very lightly to a plywood baseboard with the same outside dimensions. Drill a hole in the middle of one of the sides and plug into it a cork from an old bottle. Place the sheet of glass inside the frame so that it is resting on the baseboard and press some long plasticine, or modelling clay snakes to the glass so that they will eventually form a network of tunnels and chambers when

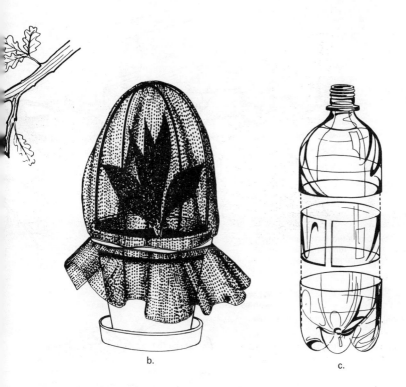

b.

c.

the plasticine is removed. Make sure that a big chamber is adjacent to the plughole so that you can insert ants and food into it. Now mix up some plaster of paris to the consistency of cream and pour it into the frame until it is filled just to the top and leave it to set. When it is, carefully pull out the tacks holding the frame to the baseboard and lift the whole thing free. Apply glue liberally to the top edge of the frame, put the baseboard on to it and turn the whole lot over. Ease out the glass and remove all the plasticine from it and from the plaster. Clean the glass carefully, replace it and tape it to the wood using broad adhesive tape. All you need to do now is to introduce your ants, and periodically some food, through the plughole, but do keep the formicarium covered except when you want to watch what is happening as ants do not like light in their nests.

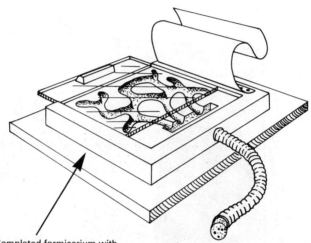

5. Completed formicarium with cork in tube and felt cover to exclude light.

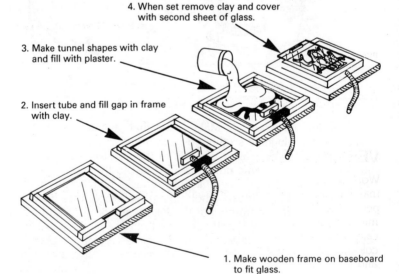

4. When set remove clay and cover with second sheet of glass.

3. Make tunnel shapes with clay and fill with plaster.

2. Insert tube and fill gap in frame with clay.

1. Make wooden frame on baseboard to fit glass.

How to make a formicarium for keeping ants.

40

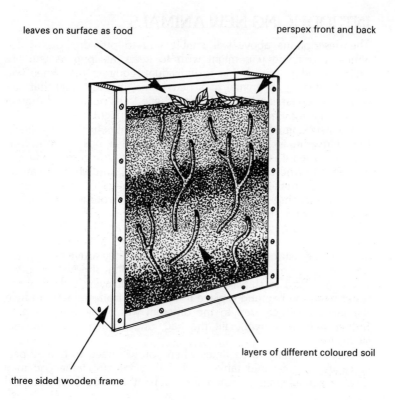

leaves on surface as food

perspex front and back

layers of different coloured soil

three sided wooden frame

A simply made vermicarium for keeping worms.

VERMICARIUM

Wormeries are even easier to make than formicariums. Simply make a three-sided, U-shaped frame of wood and screw a sheet of perspex to it. Turn it over and fix perspex to this side as well. You might need to add a base to keep it stable because it stands vertically with the open side uppermost. Pour layers of different coloured 'soil' into the open top — you can, for example, use sand and peat alternatively so that there is a series of broad stripes but stop about 5 cm (2 in) from the top. Water gently, add some dead leaves as food and introduce your earthworms. Cover with a light-proof cloth.

41

INTRODUCING NEW ANIMALS

The descriptions above will enable you to provide housing for almost everything you might wish to keep, as long as you are willing to adapt any design to individual requirements. When you are introducing an animal to a new home, it is essential that you should be understanding and sympathetic to its needs, and though each one is different a few general guidelines might help.

If a new animal is to join several others already in place, keep the animal in isolation for a while in case it has an infectious disease. When it is ready to be introduced into the community, put it in a cage where it can see everybody else, and where it can be seen, but do make sure it can hide if it needs to. Always introduce it in the morning so that it can find its way around and discover where the food and water is before it gets dark. Do not tip it out of its box with much banging; open the door and let it find its own way when it is ready, and leave it in place to settle down. If you are bringing fish home, let the bag in which they arrive float in the water of the tank for a couple of hours so that the two temperatures have time to stabilise. At that time pour away a third of the water from the bag and replace it with water from the tank to help the newcomer get used to the different water chemistry. After a further half hour gently tilt the bag, under water, until the fish swims free.

There are going to be times when you will need to handle pets in cages, aviaries and tanks, and if they are not tame you may need a suitable net to catch them, and these are best obtained from dealers. It is quite a good idea to have a trap cage built into aviaries, perhaps where the inhabitants are fed (but be careful with this idea in case an animal is unwilling to enter where it has been caught before, or it might starve) so that they can be caught easily.

CONTAINERS FOR TRANSPORTING ANIMALS

If animals are to be sent by public transport, the containers in which they are sent must comply with all sorts of requirements (see the chapter on legislation). This section on the other hand deals with the occasion on which you are moving an animal from one cage to another, or taking it to a vet, or bringing it home from a dealer's premises. If your animal is the size of a cat, or larger, by far the best way of transporting it is to buy a commercial container for it. These are usually either of wicker, or fibreglass. I much prefer the latter as I am always frightened that toes are going to get caught in the gaps of a wicker basket and be pulled off. To be fair, I must say that I have not known that happen, but the design

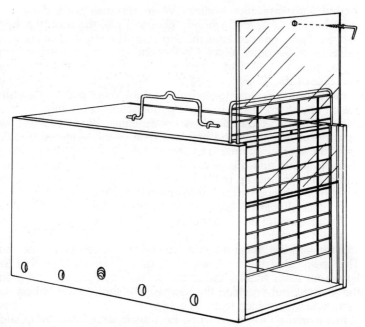

A simple and extraordinarily useful carrying box for animals.

still bothers me. I am not too keen about moving a cat in a cardboard pet carrier. They are fine if the cat is content to be in it, but if it sets its mind on getting out you will have problems. And never, ever transport any animal loose in a car, however tame it might be. Keep it instead behind a grid at the back of the vehicle. I remember a friend taking some tortoises from London to Bedfordshire on one occasion. You would not think that a tortoise on the loose in a car could cause problems would you? Neither did he, but one of them got stuck behind the clutch pedal without being noticed until it was time for the next gear change, and then there was a panic, and very nearly a nasty accident.

It is simple to make carrying cases for birds and small mammals, and it is a good idea to make three or four as they are always useful. The smallest handy size is about 25 × 12 × 12 cm (10 × 5 × 5 in).

You will need two sides of 12 mm (½ in) plywood and a top and bottom of 6 mm (¼ in) plywood. The top should be 15 mm (⅝ in) shorter than the other three pieces. Two vertical grooves need to be cut in the sides at one end so that slides can be dropped in, and a few air-holes drilled through the sides about

43

2 cm ($\frac{3}{8}$ in) from the bottom. When this has been done and everything sandpapered smooth, glue and nail the roof, the sides and the floor together after making sure that one end of the roof is flush with the other pieces. On that end fix a panel of 4mm ($\frac{1}{8}$in) ply as an end wall. Cut a similar piece, but a bit taller to drop into one of the grooves at the other end and then cut a piece of weldmesh of the same size to drop into the other groove. Carefully file off any sharp bits. It is also a good idea to cut a third panel of this size from perspex but it is not essential. When you want to examine an animal in the box you slide in the weldmesh, but to keep the animal warmer and fairly dark so that it does not go dashing about, add the plywood panel as well. So that these two end panels do not slip out, make a hole in the plywood and screw a cuphook through it and into the roof of the cage. Two small screw eyes should be fixed to the top to take a bent wire handle and your carrying box is about ready. If it is used for a bird, push a twig of suitable diameter through the centre air hole as a perch and the bird will travel much more quietly if it can hold onto this. The reason that the air holes are near the bottom is so that the light from them enables the animal to see any food you put in for the journey, but provided the journey is a short one it is best not to include water which tends to get spilt.

Many animals will need to be kept warm while they are in such a travelling box. All sorts of ideas have been tried but to be honest none is very successful, although there are two that work better than the others. First, insulate the box (expanded polystyrene panels are ideal for this), and then either put an angler's hand warmer beneath a false floor in the box, or one of those plastic sachets that you crumple to cause an exothermic chemical reaction which makes it hot for a few hours. Failing that, you can resort to a hot water bottle which everyone has used at some time to keep animals warm.

Snakes and lizards are generally carried in cloth bags, and these should be a good 2.5 times as long as they are wide so that a knot can be tied in the neck. Seams should be on the outside so that fraying edges do not entangle feet. The bags can then be laid in a cardboard box. To make an even better bag for lizards, fold some very strong wire into a box-like frame that can be inserted inside the bag first.

Amphibians are best moved around in plastic boxes, such as margarine tubs with a piece of nylon mesh over the top. The container has to be waterproof since amphibians must be kept damp and to this end it is a good idea to put a piece of damp moss in with them, or failing that a lump of foam rubber, which must not be able to flop about or it may squash your toad.

For carrying invertebrates, I favour a good stout cardboard box. A short length of cardboard tube such as is used for posters is ideal with a plastic push on lid at each end, but whatever is used I do like to enclose some crumpled up newspaper to give the animals something to hang onto. Some animals are not too good in company, so it is a good idea to pack these individually.

While fish are invariably sold in plastic bags, a small flexible polythene container is better and can be easily kept in an insulated box.

HOSPITAL CAGE

If you keep birds, a hospital cage is an absolutely vital piece of equipment. It is also handy for small mammals but you will be amazed the effect it has on avian patients.

Basically, a hospital cage is a box cage with a glass front that you can slide in and out as well as a conventional wire cage front that can also be slid into a second groove at the same time. It is fitted with food pots and perches and a thermometer fixed to the back wall so that it can easily be read. The door is in the side and there is a ventilation panel near the top of the opposite side, but beneath all this is a separate compartment containing two or more electric light bulbs to provide heat, and a thermostat which can be controlled from outside the cage. The floor between the two compartments is best made of a sheet of metal to allow the heat through, though this should be covered with a piece of felt or something similar so that it is not uncomfortable to stand on. You need to be able to raise the temperature in the cage to about 32°C (90°F) and, if you can find them, carbon filament lamps produce more heat than modern ones but they are difficult to come across nowadays for that very reason.

For details on how to make and use hospital cages see the chapter on injuries, diseases and First Aid.

LIGHTING

If you are keeping birds, do make sure that they are on their perches at night before you turn off the lights as it is very difficult to fly up to a perch in the dark and the bird might do himself a fair amount of damage while crashing about in a cage. This is easy enough if you keep a single budgie, but if you have several birds in a birdroom it is worth investing in a dimmer with a time switch so that your birds have time to get back to their roosting perches before dark.

3
FEEDING

Some years ago, I was in a pet shop when a large and boisterous Old English Sheepdog entered like a runaway train, closely followed by a panting woman in her twenties. The dog stuck his nose in a bin of dog biscuits and wolfed down nearly $3\frac{1}{2}$ kg ($7\frac{1}{2}$ lb) of them. The proprietor, ignoring the rest of the queue, turned to the dog's owner and enquired through gritted teeth, 'May I help you?' The girl explained that her dog was a problem — it was so full of energy. In an attempt to correct matters she had stopped feeding the thing on meat which she had replaced with biscuits, but the new diet had not helped matters and she was at her wits' end. What could she do, she asked plaintively.

I do not remember what advice was given to the poor woman by the man in the pet shop. The reason I mention the story is because I was surprised how little understanding the dog's owner had about nutrition. Biscuits are far higher in carbohydrates, which provide energy, than meat and I would have thought that in these times when everyone is talking about healthy eating and diets, most people surely have a basic knowledge of nutrition. Perhaps the trouble is that there is too much confusion due to the wealth of information with which we are daily bombarded, so let us try and simplify things a bit.

All animals take in food which their bodies convert to energy which might be energy to walk about, or energy to keep warm, or energy to bark, or simply energy to keep the body processes going so that the animal stays alive. Energy is measured in calories. You may have heard about kilocalories or kilojoules, but they are only other ways of measuring calories. An animal needs to take in a certain amount of food so that it can do the things it needs to do, so one dog biscuit or carrot or anything else for that matter can be converted into a certain amount of energy. If the animal does not get enough food it is unable to behave normally, which is why when you see television programmes about starving people they are all sitting around apathetically — they are simply not getting enough calories to enable them to rush around and play football, they only have enough to keep the basic body needs going, like the heart pumping and the lungs sucking in air, and so on. On the other hand, if an animal receives too much food, it stores what it does not need now in the form of fat so that if food supplies are scarce, at a later date it can use the calories stored in the fat. That is why chocolate eclairs make you fat — they are rich in calories that you do not need, and you put on weight. The only way to lose it is to cut down on your food. The amount of food an animal needs is related to the amount of energy it uses, so a budgie sitting by itself in a tiny cage will not require as much as one flying around in a 12 m (40 ft) aviary.

Animals also need food to build muscles and bones, and other parts of their anatomy, such as teeth and claws. There are various groups of food and a healthy diet should consist of a good mixture from these groups, together with tiny quantities of vitamins and trace elements. Many foods overlap between groups so, for example, although a particular item may be thought of as protein, it can contain bits of hydrocarbon or trace elements or something else essential. Roughly, the groups are as follows:

— Protein is found in meat and fish, eggs and milk and some vegetables such as lentils and peas.
— Carbohydrates are in bread and biscuits, potatoes and other vegetables and fruit.
— Hydrocarbons are fats and oils.
— Vitamins and trace elements are both required in tiny quantities, and most can be found in other foods though they can be supplied as supplements.
— Water can be obtained from a wide variety of foodstuffs.

The above information is quite enough for most pet keepers, but if you are interested, read something like the *Manual of Nutrition* from the Ministry of Agriculture, Fisheries & Food which you can get from book shops which sell Her Majesty's Stationery Office (HMSO) publications.

Too many people make a meal of diet, if you see what I mean. Give your pet a good mixture and he will do well.

Someone who keeps animals must, in time, develop a sensitivity to the dietary requirements of his pets, because their needs vary all the time. A dog may eat more in the winter than the summer and a bird might change from eating mainly seed to being almost entirely carnivorous during the months when it is breeding, while many animals in the wild have seasonal fluctuations in their diet depending on what is available. In Trinidad, when the Poui tree starts to bloom so that the whole thing becomes transformed into a bright yellow blaze, hummingbirds appear from nowhere to feed

47

on the nectar — dozens busily whirr from one flower to the next. The week after the blooms have fallen, it is back to the Hibiscus and the Canna Lilies.

Everybody who keeps a cat will know very well that there are some foods it will not touch and I am a great believer in taking such fads seriously, unless there is a good reason to alter the diet, but also I think one should experiment with diets; an animal might be bored with the same canned food. After all, if the animal does not want it he will leave it alone and if it is not doing any good the animal will start to go off-colour and the item should be withdrawn. These general principles are valid for most animals but some species are so specialised in their feeding habits that they are intolerant of change and only someone who is very experienced in caring for them should try and experiment with their diet.

However, there is one aspect of feeding, and indeed husbandry generally, that applies equally to all animals and that is good hygiene, which is something that many people neglect. The world is full of microbes, or germs if you prefer — and they are virtually everywhere. All they need is a bit of food, a degree of warmth and some moisture and they can find these simple requirements almost anywhere. Your skin is covered in them, they live on your kitchen table and you would not believe how many are on a square centimetre or square inch of your dog's food dish each morning. Most germs will do you no harm; indeed, we could not manage without many of them. But there are several nasty ones, and if we are not scrupulously careful a few of these can reproduce at a breathtaking rate and before long infections and diseases are cropping up all over the place. At best this might mean an expensive and unnecessary veterinary bill, at worst it can result in the loss of loved and valuable animals.

You should be pragmatic and not paranoid about this, because no one is ever going to get rid of all the villains completely, and it really is very easy to take basic precautions. I was in a café a few months ago. The tables were covered with cigarette ash, sandwich wrappings and other rubbish, when along came a man who had been employed to clear the tables. He removed all the rubbish, and extracted the most disgusting dishcloth from a plastic bowl of water so thick that it resembled soup. The guy sloshed it carelessly over the tabletop and departed to do the next one. The table looked shiny and uncluttered, but it was now far dirtier than it had been before being treated. It was revolting.

Lack of hygiene only becomes a problem if you let it. There is nothing worse than trying to scrub months of accumulated grime from an animal cage, but if you make a point of keeping cages clean there is no problem. For cleaning cages and utensils I favour a mild bleach solution: it kills off everything and can be rinsed away after use. At the same time I know someone who uses buckets full of Savlon all over the place which is fine but it does stink so. However thoroughly you rinse a feeding dish you cannot get rid of the smell, and, when you think how sensitive many animals' noses are compared to ours you realise how horrid it must be to stick your nose in a dish of food that smells of the stuff. The same can be said of all the phenolic compounds; and a point to beware of, if you keep cats, is that many household disinfectants are dangerous to these animals. Read a specialist book on cats or ask your vet if you are worried.

Common-sense hygiene boils down to a few simple rules: wash your hands before you feed or handle an animal, clean and disinfect feeding equipment, and when you have finished, wash your hands again. Do not wash your pet's dishes in your own washing up bowl with the same cloths or brushes that you use for yours. Do wash the dishes in hot soapy water first to remove gross dirt but, if you use bleach, make sure the water is cold — hot water inactivates bleach.

A few other general hygiene tips worth remembering are not to let your dog lick your face (it might transmit the parasite *Toxicara Canis*), making sure children and pregnant women do not touch cat droppings — keep an eye on toddlers and sandpits — and quarantine your animal if it has ringworm. All these suggestions are because other animals can transmit diseases to humans — did you know for example that terrapins and the like can infect you with *Salmonella*?

Before we go into details about feeding individual species, always remember that all animals should have a supply of fresh, clean water at all times, though some might not drink much. If you keep large mammals that live out of doors, do not break the ice on water troughs in the winter unless you change all the water for fresh water at a reasonable temperature. Simply breaking the ice enables the animal to gulp down quantities of icy water which can lead to painful colic. If the animal has to lick the ice for his drink the liquid has time to warm up before it reaches the stomach. Milk is no substitute for water; if your pet likes milk, supply it by all means, but always let it have water as well.

Whatever your animals may be, never try to economise on their food. Always supply good, fresh food which you have obtained from a reputable source. And when you find a good one, stick to it rather than rush down to the local supermarket for a packet of birdseed to tide you over the weekend.

DOGS

Most people get their first dog as a puppy. It should be properly weaned by the time you take it home, and the simplest way of feeding a new puppy is to give it four feeds a day, the first and the last consisting of baby cereal mashed up in warm milk. The other two feeds, at lunchtime and teatime, ought to be a mixture of canned puppy food mixed with rusk. If for some reason you cannot get canned puppy food, you can use canned dog food provided you sprinkle bonemeal onto it. Do not, as older books suggest, feed the little mite on meat alone as it is low in calcium. At about twelve weeks you should find that the puppy no longer requires four meals and at this time one of the cereal and milk meals can be dropped. At six months you can omit the other, and three months after that you must decide whether you would prefer your dog to have one meal a day, or two.

Do not get into the habit of letting the dog eat between official mealtimes or of feeding it tidbits, such as sweets or biscuits. Nor should you feed scraps of food from the table when you are eating and never, ever let it lick up leftovers from the plates. There is nothing wrong with feeding any lean bits of left-over meat to the dog in his dish at his next meal. If the puppy has left his meal, remove it after half an hour. Keep to a regular feeding routine and always leave the food dish in the same place. It does not matter what sort of dish you use except that if your dog has long, dangly ears the dish should be a narrow one so that his face can fit into it while his ears hang outside, because if he gets food all over them dermatitis can result. You have several choices when you come to feeding an adult dog but simply feeding it on meat is just not an adequate diet.

The great advantage to commercial dog foods is that they contain all that your dog needs. The commonest diet for a single pet dog is undoubtedly canned food, but many dog owners have not realised that some of these are complete diets containing cereal while others are just meat; so check the can, and supplement the meat with dog biscuit, either mixed in or served separately. Alternatives to canned food are either semi-moist or dry foods, but if you use these do make sure that there is an ample supply of water.

It is not necessary to give a dog a bone, but if you do, only buy beef bones and keep an eye on the dog while he is enjoying them. Chops and bones from poultry are positively dangerous, due to the danger of splintering.

If you wish to make your own dog food, boil some rice with meat that contains a bit of fat, and which you have minced. Ready made mince is useless as it has far too high a fat content. Measure the uncooked rice and add about half that amount of meat. When the meal has cooled, add a scrap of corn oil, bonemeal, iodised salt and a rather larger quantity of raw liver and mix the lot together.

One of the well-known television chefs was saying the other day that a fan had come up to him at some reception to compliment him. She particularly liked one cake recipe of his and had been making it regularly for five years; her only complaint was that it contained too much lemon. The chef, relating this story, wondered why the woman had never thought of using less lemon. No recipe is meant to be followed slavishly and this applies equally to dog food, so if your dog is lactating or obese or old, adjust the recipe to suit the circumstance.

Someone keeping a dog for the first time is frequently concerned about how much to feed and is confused at the ambiguous answers. But the answer does depend on so many factors, such as the size of the dog, how much exercise it gets — even on how warm the day is. There are tables for working out all this but play it by ear and you are not likely to go wrong. If the dog starts to put on weight, cut down slightly on the carbohydrates. If the dog is frantic for food at mealtimes, give it a bit more, but if you are still not happy here are some typical figures for a very small dog such as a Chihuahua and an enormous great thing like an Old English Sheepdog.

	Dried Food	Semi-moist Food	Canned food (complete diet)
Adult small dog	67 g (2½ oz)	76 g (2⅔ oz)	230 g (8 oz)
Adult very large dog	608 g (21½ oz)	690 g (24½ oz)	2070 g (73 ozs = 4½ lb)

Pregnant bitches will require about one and a half times these amounts. When they have had their puppies and are nursing them, this should be increased to three or four times the above figures, while the puppies themselves, when they are weaned, require twice as much.

CATS

Let us get one thing sorted out right at the start — cats do not live on fish. Of all the species of cat in the world, one, Geoffroy's Fishing Cat, is the only one which subsists entirely on fish though I have watched Jaguars in South America catch fish sometimes and

I daresay most carnivores will eat an occasional fish if conditions are right. But domestic cats, like wild felines, eat meat. Even then if you watch a cat in the wild, when it has killed its antelope or whatever, it will almost always eat the half digested vegetable contents in the stomach.

When you first receive a kitten it ought to be fully weaned but it will still require four meals a day, of which alternate ones should consist of a little baby cereal mixed with some milk. Remove what has not been eaten in half an hour. The other two meals ought to be finely chopped cat food from a can. As the kitten grows and requires fewer meals, first one of the milk feeds can be dropped and then the other. When the cat is on two meals a day, you can feed him on canned cat food to which you should periodically add a little bit of cooked offal, or cheese or cooked vegetables, or even a scrap of crumbled toast. If at any time your cat is suffering from swallowed hair balls, a bit of cooked, boneless, oily fish will help him to expel them. Some cats continue to enjoy a bit of milk but even if they do, water should be available at all times, and water is especially important if you are feeding dry or moist foods. There have been incidences of kidney disease caused by insufficient water being given with these foods.

The occasional hard boiled egg will be good for your cat, provided that it is occasional, but never feed raw egg white. And do not worry if you see your cat eating grass or wild plants, provided you do not use toxic chemicals in your garden: it is perfectly natural.

HORSES AND PONIES

A horse's needs depend very much on how it is kept, what work it does and the kind of horse it is, and horses are such a big commitment that it is essential to talk to a number of people in the horse world about diets before you take on an animal. Grass is a pretty good food throughout the spring and summer, when it is young and fresh, though later in the year it becomes tough and less nutritious. But it is no use leaving your animal simply to feed on grass. He should have an ample and constant supply of hay at all times, suspended in a net at a convenient height for his muzzle. The net needs to be thought about carefully because when it is empty it will hang down and the horse could catch a foot if it is near the floor of the stable, breaking a leg as a result. Nor should the net be suspended from a nail banged into the wall or you may find an injured horse one morning.

In addition to the hay, the animal will need four regular daily feeds of grain, which usually means crushed oats, mixed with bran

Hay nets should be hung so that they do not trail on the floor when empty, and care should be taken not to hang them from nails which can damage eyes.

or chopped hay, or nowadays these can be replaced by horse or pony nuts. If the animal does not have access to grazing, he will appreciate some freshly cut grass or clover during the spring and summer; in the winter, this can be replaced with a kilo (2 lb) of chopped apple or carrot. A salt lick is essential and a constant supply of clean water must be available. If his bucket is empty, let your horse have a drink before he feeds.

RABBITS

Contrary to what many people still think, a rabbit will not live on lettuce alone, and the best basis for a rabbit's diet is to let it have unlimited supplies of good hay. In addition, each morning give it a handful of concentrates which you can buy from a pet shop as Rabbit Mixture. Vary this with an occasional meal of rabbit pellets, and in the evening feed a good double handful of fresh vegetables and fruit. Most varieties will be eaten, including wild plants such as dandelion, plantain and hedge parsley, but do wash all fruit and vegetables to remove petrol residues, herbicides and so on.

Naturally, the rabbit will need a constant supply of drinking water and this is best provided via a fountain clipped to the outside of the cage. A mineral lick is essential.

GUINEA PIGS

Feed as for rabbits, replacing the concentrates with a commercial Guinea Pig Mixture. Guinea pigs are great chewers and should have a piece of branch from a non-poisonous tree to munch — a fruit tree is ideal.

HAMSTERS

Hamster Mixture from your pet shop is a good basic diet for these animals and can be supplemented with a little green food, which can either be vegetable or fruit. An occasional piece of wholemeal bread or hard boiled egg is a good thing but these should not be a major part of the diet and, when greenfood wilts and goes stale, remove it from the cage. Some hamsters will take the occasional mealworm which is fine, but I do not agree with books that suggest feeding a scrap of meat or canned dog food on occasion, as the animal might well hide it in his food store and if it goes bad it will not be good for him, and also it will smell horrible. Dog biscuits on the other hand are good hamster food. Hamsters only need to be fed once a day, but fresh water should be available at all times.

CHIPMUNKS

Chipmunks should be fed as hamsters though they should also have three or four mealworms a day — not more — or else another form of livefood such as crickets or maggots.

MICE

The one thing you should not feed to your mice is cheese. Mouse pellets or a mixture as described for gerbils will suit your mouse, and you can add very small quantities of fruit and vegetables. Some people find mice smelly — this is because the males produce a chemical compound containing acetamide which they use to mark their territory. Females do not do this but like all mice they urinate freely, so provided you only keep females and clean the cage regularly and do not feed too much greenfood, you ought not to have smelly mice.

RATS

Hamster Mixture is great for feeding rats, or you can buy special pellets for them, though I am not in favour of these since rats are intelligent and must get very bored if they only have pellets. Otherwise feed as for hamsters. Rats drink a surprising amount of water, so do keep an eye on it.

GERBILS

Buy some Hamster Mixture from your pet shop and mix it with an equal quantity of Foreign Finch Mixture and this forms a super Gerbil Mixture. Supplement it with a little daily greenfood and, if the gerbils will take them, a couple of mealworms a day; finally, provide a piece of fruit-tree wood to chew. Gerbils drink less than many animals, nevertheless a fountain of water must be available at all times. Feed once a day.

HEDGEHOGS

Although these animals are not normally kept as pets, it always seems that at any one time, someone is temporarily looking after a hedgehog. In the wild about one quarter of a hedgehog's food is beetles, one quarter is caterpillars, another quarter is earthworms and the remainder is made up from eggs, millipedes, slugs and snails, assorted insects and a few odds and ends. Most people who find that there are hedgehogs in their garden put out a saucer of wholemeal bread and milk, and a hedgehog will happily eat this as a supplement to his diet, but if the hedgehog is kept in captivity for a while, perhaps because it is injured, a look at the natural diet will show that he should be fed on a mixture of invertebrates to stay healthy.

GOATS

Goats will eat the most amazing variety of vegetation though it would be wrong to suppose that they can be fed on anything at all. A constant supply of good quality hay is essential and this must be supplemented with daily feeds of goat pellets or a mixture of concentrates as supplied for goats. It helps when you are milking if you can let the nanny feed at the same time — she is far less likely to become impatient if she is feeding.

Such a diet should be regarded merely as a basis, for you should also give copious supplies of hedge trimmings, root vegetables and suitable wild plants, ensuring that these are not collected from areas that have been sprayed with toxic chemicals or contaminated by petrol fumes.

Great care must be taken to eliminate poisonous plants from any mixtures that you feed to your goat. Another point to watch is the feeding of large quantities of material that may ferment in the gut; this can happen if a goat is in an orchard when fruit falls.

BUSHBABIES

In the wild bushbabies eat fruit, nectar and insects and some species are specially adapted to eat gum and resin. In captivity, they need a good variety of chopped fruit and vegetables together with plenty of insects such as crickets, locusts, mealworms, stick insects and waxmoths. They should also have a constant supply of primate cubes and a variety of baby foods. Canned foods are fine, as are rusks soaked in milk or milk and glucose, though not all bushbabies will take milk. Multivitamin supplements must be added to the food on alternate days, and they must be given a few drops of cod liver oil on a chunk of wholemeal bread, or on fruit, once a week. A multivitamin compound such as Vionate or SA 37 may be obtained from your vet. Clean water must always be available.

PRIMATES

Squirrel Monkeys, marmosets and the like are super animals but they make terrible pets and are definitely only for the experienced animal keeper. On top of that, in Britain they are classed as Dangerous Wild Animals according to the 1981 Act which means that anyone who keeps them will have to pay an annual licence fee of about £25 per animal. They should be fed similarly to bushbabies. In the United States, primates cannot be kept as pets.

BUDGERIGARS

In the wild, the Budgerigar eats grass seed and shoots, as well as the buds of trees. There is some evidence that they also take small insects and some fruit. In captivity, the simplest way to feed budgies is to buy a good commercial Budgie Mix — it is best not to change the brand, but if you want to make up your own, a mixture of four parts of plain canary seed to one part white millet and one part yellow millet is fine. In addition, as with all seedeating birds, budgies must have mineral grit. Since birds do not have teeth a budgie swallows whole seeds which go into the crop where they are broken down by muscular action on the seed and the grit together. The sharp edges on each piece of grit chop up the seeds into easily digestible particles. A bird will not eat much grit but it must have access to the stuff at all times. If you keep a single budgie, a small packet will last over a year. A commercial vitamin mixture should be given on a regular basis.

You should put a piece of cuttlefish bone in the cage to provide the budgie with calcium, and he will appreciate as many millet sprays as you care to give him. If you soak a spray in water for a few hours, then rinse it well and put it in an open topped jamjar for a day and then rinse it again and put it back in the jar and keep doing this, you will find in two or three days that all the seeds on the spray start to sprout. When they do, give it a final thorough rinse and hang it in the cage. If you do this once a week you will be providing your bird with all sorts of vitamins that he otherwise would not have. To add some variety to the diet, especially if you want to breed budgies, you can also try tidbits of greenfood, such as pieces of fruit or vegetables that have been well washed, but not all budgies will take them. In any case, such items should only be supplied very sparingly, especially if you have only one budgie in a cage. Seeding grasses, thistles and other wild plants are good foods if they are not covered in contaminants. Budgies do not drink much but they should have water at all times.

Incidentally, in the spring when the last frosts are past, if you sow a row of spray millet seeds they will grow, but you will only get a reasonable quantity of decent sized sprays if the summer is a long hot one. You can save a fortune on the things if it is. You cannot grow ordinary budgie seed as it has been dried at a temperature which has killed it.

CANARIES

Buying good Canary Mixture from your pet shop is the easiest way of feeding your bird, but if you want to make it up yourself mix three parts plain canary seed with one part red rape. To this you add a very little yellow millet and a teaspoon of so-called Tonic Mixture which consists of a variety of seeds such as niger, gold of pleasure, linseed, maw and hemp. Canaries, like budgies, are seedeaters and need mineral grit, and they also appreciate some well-washed greenfood and fruit. They should be given cuttlefish bone and clean water at all times.

ZEBRA FINCHES

Some breeders say that a diet of panicum millet and plain canary seed is a suitable staple diet for Zebra Finches, but the way I like to feed them is to fill one pot with plain canary seed and another with a mixture of half panicum millet and half mixed millets. They

57

will need mineral grit at all times, and a good supply of chickweed, seeding grasses and other non-poisonous wild plants should be provided when they are available. Cuttlefish such as is used for budgies is essential and sprouted seed is invaluable throughout the breeding season. If a fresh supply of stale wholemeal bread soaked in milk is presented to the birds at this time they will happily take it, but it goes off pretty fast in warm weather so it must be replaced frequently in well washed pots. An occasional few drops of cod liver oil mixed in with the seed is beneficial but this is best given through the winter as it too can deteriorate quickly in summer.

FOREIGN FINCHES

Every single fancier has his own recipe for keeping foreign finches and in time you will develop yours, but if you start by following my suggestions you will not go far wrong. Bear in mind, though, that each species of bird has slightly differing requirements, so although my recommendations will suit a mixed community in a large cage or an aviary, if you are intending to keep a single pair of Red Eared Waxbills or Cut Throat Finches or Black Headed Nuns you might very well find that part of the food is not being eaten, in which case simply alter the proportions of the ingredients. Provided that your local pet shop sells first class seed, by all means get it. The seeds should be plump and shiny, and should not have little holes in which show that weevils have got there before you. There should also not be a lot of dust in the bag of seed. This is an expensive way of buying seed, but if you keep a single pair of birds that will not matter since they eat so little. If you want to maintain a collection of birds, it is much more sensible to buy your seed from a well-known big supplier, and by buying in bulk you can easily pay less than a third of the retail price.

When most pet keepers start to keep these birds, they buy a ready-blended Foreign Finch Mixture, which is fine, but I prefer to make up my own selection of seeds, and if you would like to do the same, the proportions of seeds are 60 per cent yellow millet, 30 per cent white millet and 10 per cent plain canary seed. Although this is a basic diet, on which some unfortunate birds are fed for years, there are several other elements that must not be omitted if you are to keep the birds properly. To the basic mixture I like to add a mixture of so-called tonic seeds. You can buy Tonic Mixture from the good seed dealers and if you only want a small quantity this is the best way to get it, or alternatively you can make it up yourself from species like cress seed, white lettuce, gold of pleasure, teazle, red rape, linseed, niger, maw, hemp and safflower. You only need a handful of this mixture to about 6.3 kg (14 lb) of basic foreign finch food. Throughout the spring and summer your birds should have a daily dose of sprouted seed mixture, which contains essential nutrients. You will need to buy a special mixture for soaking. To prepare them for your birds, soak the seeds overnight and pour off the water, rinse them well and leave them, still damp, in a jamjar. The next day rinse and drain them again. After three or four days they will be well sprouted at which time they ought to be given a final good rinse through a sieve, allowed to drain and offered to your stock in a separate pot. Millet sprays, alfalfa seeds and mung beans can all be treated in this way.

Millet sprays should be constantly available and, of course, mineral grit and cuttlefish bone. The reason for the grit is that birds do not have teeth, so the seed and the grit are mixed together in a muscular organ known as the gizzard, and the sharp bits of grit break down the seed into a digestible paste. On top of all these assorted seeds, birds will have to have a daily supply of greenfood which has been washed well. Whole lettuce heads will soon be torn to pieces and half oranges and tomatoes, groundsel, chickweed and other wild plants will all be eaten avidly. Your garden is a rich source of food, as long as it has not been sprayed with chemicals. If you have thought far enough ahead to grow broadbeans or Canada balsam, you ought to have a good healthy crop of aphids for your birds which can do with all the livefood they can get, especially during the breeding season.

During the winter, a tiny weekly dose of cod liver oil sprinkled over the seed is a good thing and if you sprinkle a pinch of powdered yeast mixture over the seed at the same time it will help. Throughout the spring and summer I like to feed some stale sponge cake soaked in a honey/water or honey/milk solution, and occasionally a drop or two of multivitamin compound can be added to this concoction. Finally, I consider it important to let the birds have a pot of commercial softbill food at all times, and you will soon discover that they love it. In an aviary all these things can be supplied in separate pots but in a cage you can put the seed in one, the sponge cake in another and everything else in a third. The birds need a constant supply of fresh, clean water, — both in a fountain, and in a wide shallow container for bathing.

There are many other things you can do to keep your birds in perfect condition and to make your hobby more rewarding. Experiment with as wide a variety of foods as you can — there are all sorts of things you can feed. Some people add powdered seaweed to the menu and although I have not tried it, fanciers who have, swear by it. If there is a long hot summer you can grow spray millet with no difficulty, but it will not ripen in Britain if the season is not a good one.

The diets described above will keep most foreign finches in excellent condition but there are some species that are specific in their requirements, such as the Pintailed Nonpareil which will need paddy rice, which is not at all the same as rice from a supermarket. It is still in its husk and can be bought from the better seed dealers. Many of these finches will take surprisingly large quantities of insects, especially during the breeding season, and this should be borne in mind. It is quite a good idea to keep a Fruit Fly culture going in an aviary throughout the summer, though rain must be prevented from entering or you will lose the lot.

SOFTBILLS

'Softbills' is a vague term that is, however, well understood by people who keep birds. Basically a softbill is any bird that is not a seedeater, a parrot, a bird of prey, waterfowl or some sort of gallinaceous bird. You may feel there are not many left after all those exclusions, but you would be surprised at the number of species that are classified as softbills, and because they are so diverse one can only lay down broad guidelines for feeding them. Some have such specific requirements that they would not survive long on the general softbill diet that I will describe. For this reason, it is essential to go to a book that specialises in the particular birds that you want to keep.

To start with, you need a commercial softbill mixture which can be bought from good pet shops. There are different varieties suitable for different birds, but often the finer grade is known as Nightingale Mixture for small birds like zosterops, tits, yuhinas and wee sized birds, while the coarser food is called Universal and is more suitable for larger birds such as mynahs, starlings and bulbuls. I cannot suggest that you make your own though if you look in books about keeping softbills you will find recipes, but if this is what you want to do, only refer to modern books. The older ones, while superb in many ways, are pretty grim when it comes to nutritional matters. It was hardly the writers' fault, it is simply that in the last few years our understanding of nutrition has advanced enormously.

When you buy a packet of softfood and open it you will discover that it looks rather like compost, rich and brown and slightly moist and crumbly. It smells absolutely divine, as though it would be really nice to eat. Look at it closely, however, and you will see that it contains bits of insects and all sorts. Still, it is what the birds want though it is no use expecting a softbill to survive only on this commercial mixture. Each day you will need to chop up quantities of fresh, ripe sweet fruit that you have first washed thoroughly. Any fruit in season will do, but oranges, grapes and tomatoes all cut in half are good standbys, but do go easy on banana. To this one must add considerable amounts of livefood. All your birds will love mealworms but do not feed too many of them, but by all means give the birds as many other insects as they will take. This diet does mean that a softbill's faeces are pretty wet and if you keep the bird in a cage you will need to clean it thoroughly and frequently. Softbills all seem to have prodigious appetites, so these birds can work out expensive to keep. The answer is to keep them in a large aviary planted with fruit and berry bushes where they can eat fruit and catch insects to help out with the food bill, though you will still have to feed them properly.

Sprouted seed will be taken by some softbills and details of how to do this are given in the Foreign Finch section above. Stale sponge cake soaked in a thin honey and water mixture will be taken greedily by all softbills, and they will need a constant supply of fresh water.

PIGEONS (ORNAMENTAL)

Assuming that your fantails or other ornamental pigeons are to be kept at liberty, the best thing on which to feed them is a commercial Pigeon Mixture of seeds which contain cereals, maize, chickpeas and the like, or you can buy pigeon pellets. Special pigeon grit and fresh clean water must be provided at all times. If you grow vegetables, forget about eating them yourself — your pigeons will finish them long before harvest time!

QUAIL AND DOVES

Fruit Doves should be fed as softbills (see above). The tiny Chinese Painted Quail and the rather larger Japanese Quail should be fed as Foreign Finches (see above) with the addition of a little wheat.

All the larger species should have a mixture made up of 75 per cent equally mixed plain canary seed, yellow millet and white millet, plus 10 per cent hemp and 15 per cent wheat or wheat and crushed oats. Greenfood should be provided and quail are all insectivorous to an extent so maggots, mealworms or other livefood are indispensable. Mineral grit of a suitable particle size is necessary to digest the food and fresh clean water must be available at all times. As a matter of interest, pigeons are the only birds that are able to put their beaks into water and suck it up. All other birds have to scoop up a beakful at a time, tip their heads back and swallow it.

WATERFOWL

You can buy commercially prepared diets for waterfowl, or you can make up a good duck feed with 60 per cent wheat, 20 per cent bran and 20 per cent flaked maize plus a little fish meal. Waterfowl cannot eat dry food so it must be supplied twice a day in water — either in the pond if it is big enough not to be polluted, or a trough of water. If available, you can add bits of dry bread or cake to the mixture. Your birds will supplement their diet by foraging for insects, snails and other livefood, and grazing on the grass in their enclosure. Naturally, they require a lot of water as it plays a large part in their lives. It is no use trying to keep a duck in a pen with an old sink in it and hoping that it will thrive.

PHEASANTS, FOWL AND PEAFOWL

Although many people consider these birds to be granivorous, in fact they will eat almost anything that they come across. The best way to feed them is on either a commercial Pheasant Seed Mixture or on pellets which contain all that the birds need together with prophylactics to prevent the onset of common diseases, but whatever you feed the birds they will spend the greater part of the day looking for things to eat. You can feed root crops and green-food of all sorts and a handful of maggots will be attacked voraciously. During the three months before the start of the breed-ing season, some extra rolled oats, hemp and maize is beneficial. The birds must, of course, have oyster grit of a suitable particle size, and clean, fresh water should be available at all times.

PARROTS

I recently heard of a pet shop proprietor who told an interested customer that all parrots were simplicity itself to feed, subsisting as they do on sunflower seed and water. Believe me, nothing could be further from the truth and if a pet shop proprietor tells you that, go somewhere else for your parrot. Nor should it be thought that all parrots are fed in identical fashion, for there are many different types of parrot from the cockatoos and macaws which almost everybody would recognise, through to the conures and lories and long-tailed parakeets, on to the nectar-feeding lorikeets and the strange little hanging parrots which are no bigger than a sparrow. Parrot diets are every bit as different as the birds themselves, but all parrots are great demolition experts, they can destroy chain link fencing, and it really is important to supply branches of fruit trees or willow for them to chew, not only to distract them from chewing their aviary — or even your finger — but because they consume some of the bark that they strip from the wood and there is evidence that they might actually need it.

Because parrots vary so much from tiny to enormous, and because of their different requirements, it is impossible to recommend a definitive parrot diet. However, depending on your bird, its diet should comprise as wide a selection from this list as possible:

Sunflower seed	Wild plants
Peanuts	Hemp seed
Nuts of all sorts	Plain canary seed
Rolled oats	Assorted millet seed
Sweet corn,	Fruit
dried, fresh and cooked	Green vegetables (raw)
Cooked rice	Root vegetables (raw)
Bluebottle pupae	Potatoes (cooked)
Mealworms	Fresh ant pupae
Spray millet	

Wholemeal digestive biscuit mixed with hard boiled egg to a moist, crumbly consistency
Stale bread or cake soaked in a honey/water solution or a honey/milk solution
Stale bread soaked in fruit juice

Some parrots require special treatment, but they are beyond the scope of this book. All these birds should have a regular supply of mineral grit of a suitable particle size and, of course, fresh clean water.

COCKATIELS

I like to feed Cockatiels on a good Budgerigar Seed Mixture to which is added about 10 per cent striped sunflower seed and a few crushed oats and a meagre scattering of peanuts. This should be supplemented with millet sprays, sprouted seeds (see Foreign Finches, above) and well washed fruit and vegetables. Some birds will take Bluebottle pupae. When Cockatiels are rearing chicks, they should be provided with crushed wholemeal digestive biscuits mixed with hard boiled egg to a moist crumbly texture over which should be sprinkled fresh ants eggs. Do not bother buying dried ants eggs from an aquarium supplier — they are a complete waste of money. The birds, being seedeaters, will need a constant supply of mineral grit and fresh, clean water at all times.

SNAKES

In the wild, most snakes eat whole animals; their anatomy does not permit them to take bites from their prey. They kill the animal they are going to eat either by injecting venom, by constriction, by a good hard bite that causes so much damage that the animal dies, or in some cases they will eat it while it is still alive in which cases the digestive juices in the snake's stomach will kill it. Nothing is more surrounded by myths than the feeding habits of snakes. Snakes do not hypnotise their prey before attacking, nor does a constrictor break every bone in an animal's body — it is unusual for any bone to be broken. What actually happens is that the snake strikes very fast, grabs the animal with its teeth, and quicker than you can see, it flings a coil or two around the victim, which, now, is probably completely immobilised. It is certainly helpless and the snake can, if it needs to, put a couple more coils around at leisure. Each time the prey animal exhales, the snake takes up any slack so that the animal cannot breathe, and finally suffocates.

When the snake is convinced it is dead, it will relax its hold and, starting at the head, it will completely ingest the prey which might be larger than the snake's head. A snake is able to deliberately dislocate its lower jaw so that the sides of the mouth can be stretched to take large prey. Furthermore, the lower jaw is in two halves so to swallow its prey a snake will open its mouth round the head of the dead animal and reach forward with one half of its lower jaw in which all the teeth face backwards. It will pull the animal towards its throat and when the jaw is back in position it will reach forward with the other half, then the first half again, and so on until the whole prey is swallowed. When the dead animal has travelled far enough down to feel comfortable, the snake will settle into position to digest its meal, which may take days. When it is settled it will usually yawn a couple of times to get its jaws back into position. If the snake is disturbed, irritated or frightened before the prey is well digested, it will vomit up, as it is somewhat vulnerable with a great lump of undigested animal inside; so when your snake has fed, leave it in peace.

It is illegal to feed a captive snake with live food, so when your snake looks hungry you must give it a freshly killed animal. Sometimes a lot of coaxing is required before a snake will take a dead animal, or even a lump of meat, but if you hold the thing with long forceps — not your hand — in front of the snake's face and move it as though it is alive, you will usually be successful in persuading your snake to feed.

Most captive snakes feed on rodents or chicks though aquatic snakes need fish. Small baby snakes may take worms. You might not think so but snakes can be really fussy about food, not merely as regards the species of the prey but even the colour. There are snakes that feed on other snakes, there are some that eat lizards, and there are even some that eat eggs.

If you find that your snake is reluctant to feed, turn up the temperature a couple of degrees. If it still refuses to eat, remove the prey after about half an hour or it will start to go rotten. Some snakes can go for some time without feeding — if they are really large they can fast for months, or even a year — though small snakes may need feeding twice a week. Do not put your hand in the snake's tank if you have been handling food animals, until you have had a wash, or you might be mistaken for a rat. Just occasionally you might have to force feed a snake but this operation should be avoided if at all possible since it is very stressful for the snake, and in any case, never attempt it until you have been shown how to do it by an experienced herpetologist or you might do your snake serious damage. In any case, when your snake is coming up for a slough it will not be interested in feeding. Fresh, clean water must be available at all times, and just after sloughing (pronounced 'sluffing') a snake is generally thirsty, and might be ready to eat as well.

LIZARDS

Most lizards are entirely carnivorous. Really large ones will take mice or day old chicks, and may eat a small lizard, but most of them will need insects such as crickets and other forms of livefood. Before feeding, sprinkle the prey with a multivitamin powder — you can shake the two together in a polythene bag. Some lizards will take a little fruit, and Common Iguanas are almost completely vegetarian. As with snakes, lizards cannot bite chunks from their food, so iguanas must be fed a variety of fruit and vegetables that have been cut into suitably sized chunks, but in addition they need livefood, such as mealworms, calcium carbonate and vitamin D3 which should be given in the proportions 2 parts calcium carbonate and 1 part D3, sprinkled on the food together with a multivitamin powder such as vionate or SA 37 from your vet. Not more than one capsule of D3 should be fed each week, and on one day a week the iguana should not be fed at all though fresh, clean water must be available at all times. Mineral grit in a separate dish aids digestion, and a little canned dog or cat food can be added to the menu, but not more than three times weekly.

TORTOISES

If you feed your tortoises in the same fashion as iguanas (see Lizards, above) they will thrive. Do not feed banana which can ferment in the gut, nor the grit that is suggested for the iguanas. When a tortoise first wakes from hibernation, have a dish full of water ready for him to drink as he will be very thirsty — never mind what they might say on children's TV programmes about offering cucumber and the like, water will be the tortoise's first requirement. Do not feed a tortoise solely or almost entirely on lettuce, and as autumn approaches make sure that your pet eats a lot so that he has plenty of reserves to see him over the winter hibernation.

TERRAPINS

Terrapins are carnivorous, and need livefood. Some people suggest feeding pieces of fish and meat, but this could lead to tank pollution. When the animals are tiny, feed them on Tubifex in the water. As they get older they will take a variety of prey from mealworms to fish, mice and so on.

AMPHIBIANS

All amphibians are carnivorous after the early days of tadpolehood when they scrape algae from surfaces underwater. If your amphibians are at an aquatic stage they will need aquatic livefood. They are not usually fussy about its nature as long as it is a convenient size, since like most of the reptiles they cannot bite pieces out of it, and this continues to apply after the animals have left the water to take up a terrestrial way of life. Some amphibians are quite large enough to eat whole mice which must be supplied freshly killed though if they have not been eaten within a short time, the mice should be removed from the tank or they will putrefy.

FISH

There are three things to be aware of when feeding fish: the quantity of food to give, at what level fish feed, and what they eat. As to quantity, the best way of getting the amount right is to feed as much as your fish will eat in five minutes, and until you are sure how much that is going to be, start with a little and see how long that takes to eat, then add some more, and so on. When you have discovered that it takes three lots of a quarter of a teaspoon you know next time that you can feed three quarters of a teaspoonful in one go. If you feed too little your fish are not suddenly going to float upside down to the surface — they will just be a little hungry. If you feed too much, once again they will not die, but the uneaten food will sink to the bottom and may start to pollute the tank. Excess pollution will kill the fish, but if you discover that you have inadvertently put too much food in the tank you will have time to clean out the whole system. Try feeding your fish in the morning and in the evening. If you are going on holiday, feed them well for a couple of weeks in advance and they will not come to any harm being left on their own for a few days. If you need to leave a neighbour in charge of your fish, divide up the food into daily packets and leave instructions that only one packet a day must be fed. If you have a pond in the garden, and it has been set up properly so that a good community of plants and animals exists, then you ought to have no need to add food.

Some species of fish feed at the surface, some at different levels in the volume of water, and some at the bottom, so you will need to choose a food that satisfies the fishes' requirements. As to what they eat, some fish are herbivorous, some are carnivorous and some are pretty well omnivorous. Some people resent their herbivorous species eating plants in the aquarium, but if you use lots of plants rather than the three or four that you see in most aquaria, and regard the expense of lost plants as part of your food bill, you will not feel so bad about it and your fish will feel happier.

There are all sorts of basic fish foods available that will fulfil most of your pets' requirements and, provided that you choose a food appropriate to the feeding level of your fish, you can select what you like. Some pellets sink straight to the bottom, some sink slowly and some foods, like the multicoloured flakes, sit on the top for a while until they become waterlogged and then they slowly sink. What is crucial to fish is the size of the food particles. This basic diet can be supplemented by all sorts of scraps of food, cut up into suitably tiny lumps, such as cheese, fresh vegetables, fish and meat; but remember what I said about pollution.

Commercial foods and household scraps are all very well but your fish will be delighted if you feed them suitably sized aquatic livefood (see the chapter on Livefood), but if you sweep for it in a pond, check that no predatory beasts like dragonfly larvae are hidden amongst the Daphnia. Livefood is great for fish, not only in nutritional terms, but because it gives the fish something to do since they have to hunt for it. A good portion of livefood tipped into the tank before you go on holiday will keep the fish going for a couple of days.

Very tiny, newly hatched fish are best started off on infusoria (see the chapter on Livefood) and small Brine Shrimp, and as they grow they will learn to take some of the other items. But watch the parents, as many of them will eat small fish with the same gusto with which they will eat *Daphnia*.

SPIDERS

All spiders are carnivorous for the whole of their lives. When they are hatchlings they should first be given instar crickets or something of similar size, and as they grow a variety of livefood can be supplied, of a size appropriate to the spider. An adult will not necessarily feed every day and the amount of prey it takes will vary. Really large spiders will take baby mice or even those that are half grown and these should be supplied freshly killed when you think your spider is hungry; but if they have not been eaten within a short time they should be removed from the tank or they will begin to decompose. All spiders should have a constant supply of fresh clean drinking water. A spider considers anything that moves and is smaller than itself is suitable for eating, and this includes other spiders, even its own offspring, so do not consider keeping more than one spider in a tank.

STICK INSECTS

All stick insects are vegetarian and live entirely on leaves. The common Indian Stick Insect will take privet or bramble but they are reluctant to change, so if you start them off on one of these food plants, keep to it. I prefer to feed them on privet, as bramble is not so easy to find during the winter, and what leaves are available are usually very tatty and tough. Whichever you use, do make sure that it has been thoroughly washed first to remove any pollution, and never collect leaves from an area where herbicides or pesticides may have been used — this often includes hedgerows around farmland as the crops may have been subject to aerial spraying. And never use an insecticide in the room where you keep your stick insects, or any other insects for that matter. There are several species of stick insect, and one or two need leaves such as rhoddodendron or ivy, so do check up with the supplier of your stick insects.

The well washed sprigs of foodplant should be stood upright in a jamjar, or something similar, full of water in the middle of the insects' tank. The water helps to keep the foodplant alive, but make sure that the neck of the jar is packed solid so that no insect can walk down a stem and drown — tiny babies are especially vulnerable. There is no need to replace the food until it is nearly eaten, unless it starts to wilt. Put a jar of new food alongside the old one and wait till all the insects have climbed from one to the other before removing the old one, as stick insects are fragile animals that should not be handled. Before the old plant is thrown out, though, check it carefully for any still hiding on it. These animals are experts at camouflage — after all, they look just like sticks.

BEETLES

There are thousands of species of beetle in the world, and they eat all sorts of things; some are carnivorous, some feed on rotting wood, some on vegetation and others on cereals so the only general advice one can give is to ask the supplier what your beetles eat. If he is a dealer, treat his advice with caution: he may be knowledgeable but equally he may be guessing — he could very well be importing the animals and selling them without having to feed them. If a beetle is a big one and bites hard and moves fast there is a good chance that it is a carnivore.

LOCUSTS

See under Livefood.

BUTTERFLIES AND MOTHS

Many adult butterflies and moths feed on nectar in the wild, and this can be duplicated in captivity either by providing nectar rich flowers, or by making a solution of sugar and water and impregnating a small piece of sponge rubber in a dish with this mixture. Or you could try placing some overripe sweet fruit in the cage. Some butterflies will suck perspiration from your skin.

Caterpillars, which are the larvae of butterflies and moths, all live on the leaves of a specific foodplant, so for example, Red Admiral caterpillars eat the leaves of nettles. Before you obtain any of these animals, first ascertain what foodplant you need. Whatever it is can be supplied in one of three ways: as for stick insects (see above), by putting a potted plant in the cage, or by 'sleeving' a leafy branch of a suitable tree. This involves making a long cylinder of nylon mesh which is kept open along its length by several wire hoops. It is slid over a tree branch and one loose end tied around the wood. The caterpillars are introduced and the other end is similarly tied so that the insects are held captive inside this sleeve where they can eat the leaves contained within it.

GIANT LAND SNAILS

These fascinating snails, which usually belong to one of the genera *Achatina* or *Oblongus*, are easy to feed on a wide variety of freshly washed clean fruit. They seem to like pieces of soft pear that have started to grow fungus.

GIANT MILLIPEDES

Feed as for Giant Land Snails (see above). They also like a bit of stale bread soaked in sweetened milk, but remove it before it goes sour.

4
LIVEFOOD

You can feed a huge range of pet animals on canned food or birdseed or whatever, but there are many species that need to eat other animals, either solely or as part of a mixed diet. For the sake of convenience, I am including in this chapter a few species of animals that are fed to others freshly killed rather than actually alive, such as day-old chicks.

If the animals you keep are going to need livefood you will either have to buy it or breed it. There are plenty of firms which exist solely to supply animal keepers with livefood and there are many advantages to buying it from one of them, even if you have the facilities for producing it yourself. Though not always more expensive than breeding your own, it can be so, but it does solve an awful lot of aggravation. I find that people who breed their own livefood are usually interested in the animals for their own sake. Breeding locusts or stick insects for example is totally absorbing, and Fruit Flies are exquisite little animals that are absolutely fascinating and they have such a short lifespan that they are used in the study of genetics as one can follow a strain through several generations in a few months. Sorting the virgin females from the males shortly after they have emerged from their pupal cases and mating them with another strain and waiting for the results is something that people spend a lifetime doing. Try it — you could get hooked.

If you want to buy small quantities of livefood the best place to start looking is your local pet shop or aquarist, or for maggots, an angling shop. If you cannot find what you want or you need large quantities, have a hunt through one of the journals listed at the back of this book or consult the suppliers' advertisements. Many of the forms of livefood that animal keepers require are insects and other small invertebrates, and you can catch all sorts of insects to add variety to your pets' diet throughout the warmer months of the year. The best way of doing this is to sweep or beat for them but you must ensure that you do not do it in an area where pesticides and other toxic chemicals are likely to be found. Sweeping is done with a wide mouthed, deep net on a short handle which you

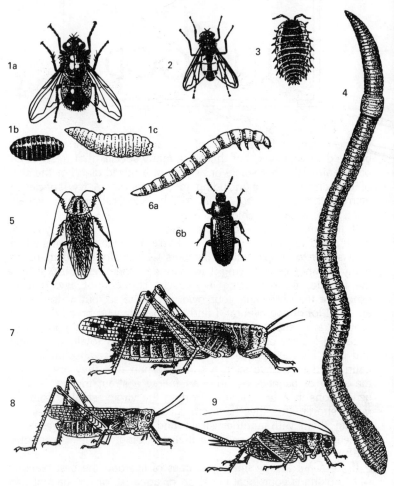

A wealth of useful livefood: 1. Bluebottle, a. adult, b. pupa, c. larva (maggot).
2. Housefly. 3. Woodlouse. 4. Earthworm. 5. Cockroach. 6. Mealworm, a. larva,
b. adult. 7. Locust. 8. Grasshopper. 9. Cricket. 10. Stick Insect. 11. Caterpillar.
12. Glassworms. 13. Mosquito larvae. 14. Cyclops. 15. *Daphnia* (Water Fleas).
16. Tubifex. 17. Freshwater shrimp.

sweep from side to side before you as you walk through the long
grass or nettles. You must keep the net moving all the time or
your catch might fly out again. When you stop sweeping flip the
top of the net over to close the bag. You will find it full of a
mixture of grass seeds and other bits of vegetation together with a

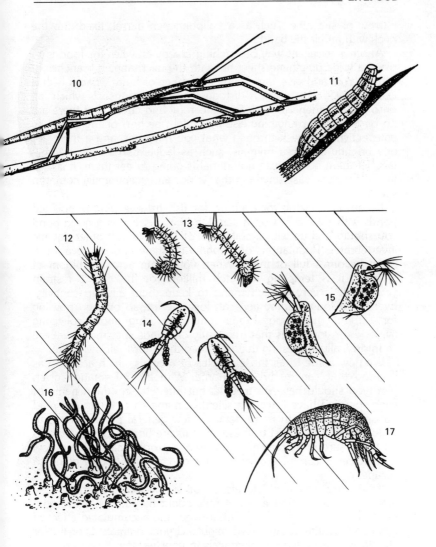

host of insects and spiders. The best way of feeding them to your stock is to tip them into a container which can be closed leaving a very small hole so that only one insect at a time can escape. If you tip the lot into the cage or aviary half of them will fly away. A good container to put your catch in is a polythese bag with a narrow plastic tube, such as a ballpoint pen barrel, fixed into the neck with an elastic band.

Another excellent way of catching creepy crawlies for food is to place a large polythene sheet beneath the overhanging branches of a hedgerow and give the shrubs a number of hefty whacks with a walking stick. This process dislodges all sorts of insects which fall onto the polythene. But please be careful and check that there are no birds' nests or anything else that might be hurt or frightened by your activities. Check through what you have got, and if there are any brightly coloured animals, such as ladybirds or furry caterpillars, let them go because no animal is going to eat them. It is also important to release anything that is not an exceptionally common species.

If you are looking for livefood for fish try sweeping unpolluted ponds with a large net on a very long handle. If it is a good pond you should end up with a collection of *Daphnia* and other aquatic invertebrates. Populations of *Daphnia* fluctuate and on occasion a pond becomes full of them. When you come across a bloom of *Daphnia* it is tempting to catch millions of the things; restrain yourself, it is very difficult trying to keep them alive in captivity. Even on a long journey you can lose the lot, so only go trawling for *Daphnia* near your home. The nice thing about collecting livefood for yourself is that frequently one finds specimens that are so intrinsically interesting that you keep them for their own sake.

We now come to all those species of animals which are used as livefood that can be bred at home. With the information given here you should have no trouble, but after the common name of each species I have listed the scientific name so that you can read up on the animals in more detail. A few general points are worth making first. First, most of these animals are born escapologists, so do make sure that containers are escape proof. I can tell you now that however careful you are, some of your livefood is going to escape.

If you are breeding crickets or other invertebrates, never use insecticides in the house — not only might they kill your livefood, but if the insects take in sub-lethal doses the accumulated effect of eating a quantity of such feed might kill your animals as well. Nor should you use any toxic chemicals in your garden, if you are ever to collect livefood from it, or if you have an aviary, since an infected insect can fly from a sprayed part of the garden to the aviary and be eaten. An animal keeper's garden will be a mini nature reserve and plants that encourage quantities of insects, such as aphid-covered broad bean plants are invaluable to a bird keeper, and a good crop of mosquito larvae in a pond are a godsend to an aquarist. But when you are collecting aquatic livefood for your fish, do take care not to introduce any predators, such as dragonfly larvae, hydras or Water Boatmen, into your tank.

Another point to watch is that several of these animals need warmth, which is best supplied by electric lamps, but things like crickets will munch their way through the insulating covers of electric leads. An additional hazard is that moisture is an important part of culturing some forms of livefood, so you really must be careful, and never forget that Bluebottles, House Flies and so on can be a risk to health, not just to us but to the animals that are meant to eat them. On more than one occasion an animal keeper has found that his animals have been nibbled by crickets or had eggs laid on them by flies. Nature is tough and you cannot blame the cricket or the fly, but you have a responsibility to your charges to prevent this sort of thing happening.

One further tip worth noting is that the food value of many of these creatures is increased by dusting them with a powdered yeast compound, before you feed them to your animals.

BRINE SHRIMPS *Artemia salina* (for fish)

Brine Shrimps are an invaluable source of livefood for coldwater and tropical fish but they are remarkably expensive to buy so it is well worth getting some eggs and hatching them. Strictly speaking one cannot breed them in captivity − it is difficult to persuade them to mate − but you can keep a culture of *Artemia* on the go so that you have a constant supply of different sized shrimps for your fish.

Brine Shrimps live along the edges of salt lakes in the United States, where the eggs are collected in colossal quantities before being dried for export. To hatch them out put them into a tank of water containing three or four per cent common salt (sodium chloride). Keep the temperature at 14°C (75°F) and the eggs will hatch in about a day, and if you keep the water well aerated your losses will be less than if the whole thing is stagnant. To feed the *Artemia*, scrape some green algae from the inside of an aquarium and put that in the Brine Shrimp tank, or you can use very small quantities of yeast suspension. When you want to collect the shrimps, either catch them with a net or strain them through one and rinse them several times to remove the salt. Put them into a small quantity of freshwater and tip this into your fish tanks.

Brine Shrimps are fascinating, highly decorative little animals that have been advertised in a whole variety of journals as pets, in which case they are sold as 'Sea Monkeys'; but their minute size makes them somewhat unrewarding as 'pets'.

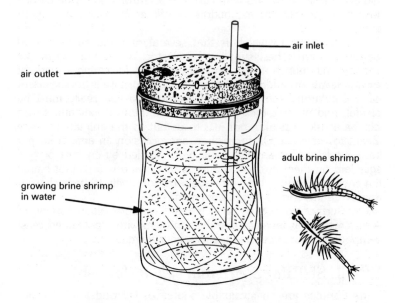

air inlet

air outlet

adult brine shrimp

growing brine shrimp
in water

A basic container is adequate for maintaining brine shrimp providing a constant supply of air is bubbled through the water.

CHICKS *Gallus gallus* (for birds, mammals and reptiles)

Assuming that you are not going to breed your own chicks, the best way to obtain dead, day-old chicks is to look for advertisements in a journal which caters for bird or reptile keepers. The reason there are so many of them for sale is that hatcheries which are raising laying hens do not want cocks, so they kill them shortly after hatching. They have sackloads for disposal, and often these are bought by firms to supply pet keepers. They are usually sold frozen, but if there is a hatchery near you give it a call and ask if they can supply you. These culled chicks are very cheap.

COCKROACHES *Blatta* spp. and *Periplaneta* spp. (for any carnivorous animals)

Cockroaches are interesting, primitive insects. One of the commonly bred species is the Chinese Cockroach, which is a gigantic beast. They are not at all difficult to breed as long as they live in an atmosphere so humid that it is nearly saturated, and as long as the temperature does not drop below 20°C (68°F). The best container in which to breed cockroaches is either an old aquarium or a glass sweet jar, depending on the quantities you require. You will need to make a high rise tower block and the easiest way to do this is to insert a length of stout wire into the centre of a square 1.25 cm (½ in) thick wood, whose dimensions are slightly smaller than those of the container, so for example if your container measures 25 cm (10 in) along each side, cut the wood 2.5 cm (1 in) shorter. The idea is that cockroaches should be able to move freely between the edge of the wood and the glass wall of the tank.

The floor of the tank should be covered with 1 cm (⅖ in) of sawdust and the square of wood stood on this. Cut the wire on the same level as the top of the tank and then cut several pieces of 4 mm (⅛ in) plywood to the same size as your original piece of wood and drill a hole in the centre of all of them to take the wire. Drop into the wire a bead with square top and bottom, or several washers or a short length of garden cane as a spacer and slide a piece of plywood down to sit on it.

You should now have a square of plywood sitting on a spacer of some sort which should be about 1 cm (⅖ in) high. Add another spacer and another piece of plywood and continue like this until the top piece of ply is about 2.5 cm (1 in) below the top of the tank when the bottom piece of wood is resting on the layer of sawdust. It is quite a good idea to add a dab of glue to each spacer and piece of plywood to keep the structure solid, and finally bend the top of the wire to form a loop. This is your cockroaches' tower block. Stand it on the sawdust and put some bits of food here and there between the floors. Almost any vegetable matter will do, like porridge, biscuits, flour or cabbage leaves — cockroaches will eat anything, even meat, but if you use that you might end up with a nasty smell. Spray the inside of the tank to provide the necessary humidity, introduce a handful of cockroaches and put on a lid that lets in just a little air. Cockroaches like to be in the dark so an excellent place for them is an airing cupboard. Before long you ought to have huge numbers of insects; provided you keep it damp and warm, and continue to add food as necessary, your cockroach culture should last for ages.

The best way to harvest them is to carry the whole thing into the bathroom and stand it in the bath. You should keep a spare plug for this operation which is not attached to a chain. The whole point about this exercise is that cockroaches move very fast and

77

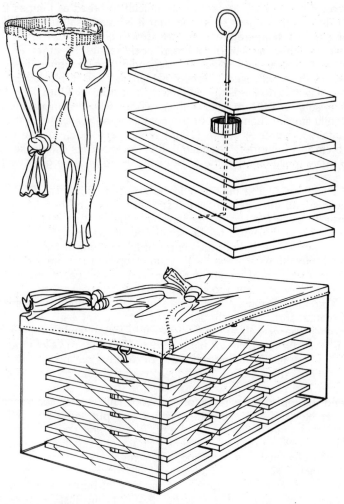

A tank for breeding cockroaches, using part of an old pair of nylon tights as a security sleeve to prevent escapes.

escape easily, so you have to increase the odds in your favour when you want to harvest them. Take the lid off the culture, lift the tower block by the loop at the top and lay it on its side next to the tank. Tap it sharply two or three times on the bottom of the bath to dislodge the insects and return it to its place. Replace the lid and, making sure there are no cockroaches on the outside of the tank, lift it onto the floor. You may find it helps to have a crumpled sheet of newspaper on the bottom of the bath so that the insects can hide. It is now fairly simple to pick them up one at a time and put them into a small container to take to your animal room as they cannot climb the sides of the bath as efficiently as they could a rougher surface; but do not fool yourself that they cannot climb at all; given time some of them definitely will and however careful you are the odd escape is inevitable.

CRICKETS *Gryllus gryllus* (for almost any carnivorous animal)

Crickets really are the livefood *par excellence* and their only drawback is that they will eat anthing. They are a sort of insect goat, only more so, for crickets will eat each other and any animal they might come across. For this reason it is imperative that you do not put more crickets into an animal's cage than it requires for its immediate needs. Similarly, you ought not to introduce them into a cage where the animal is likely to be immobile for a long time. Having said that, it is unusual to have any problems with the diner being eaten by the dinner, but it is as well that you should know.

Crickets come in all sorts of sizes from tiny, newly hatched babies to adults, which makes them a very useful form of food. They get everywhere throughout the house, but despite that you will need crickets if you keep any sort of carnivorous animal, and fortunately they are very simple to breed.

Start your culture with an old aquarium and an airing cupboard, or some other suitable heat source, for the temperature must be about 21–26°C (70–80°F). The only difficulty is providing an escape proof lid and I find that the best thing of all is a pair of women's discarded tights provided that any holes are at the feet end. Cut off one leg at the top of the thigh and the other at about the knee and throw away the two pieces with the feet attached. You are now left with the top part, one long leg and one short leg. Tie a knot in the short leg. The waistband of the tights is now slipped over the top edge of the tank to make an inelegant but effective nylon mesh lid. The other leg is used as a sleeve through which to insert your hand into the tank, and when it is not being used it should be twisted shut or loosely tied. But when I said that crickets eat almost anything I was not joking, so keep an eye on the tights and renew them if you see a hole appearing.

However, before you put the tights over the tank you will need to set up the interior, and for this you should get hold of a

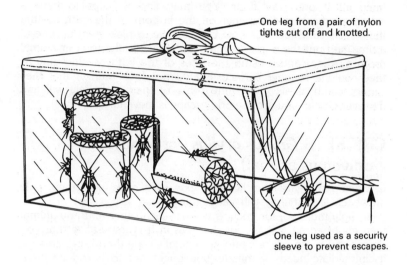

One leg from a pair of nylon tights cut off and knotted.

One leg used as a security sleeve to prevent escapes.

An arrangement for breeding crickets, using old nylon tights for the top, but beware because crickets eat anything so keep an eye open for holes.

quantity of corrugated card, of which the best is the kind that has a flat sheet to which is glued the wavy bit without another flat sheet on the top. Cut it into strips about 15 cm (6 in) wide and roll them up tightly until you have a cylinder about 4 cm (1½ in) in diameter and glue a strip of brown sticky tape around the outside to keep it in shape. The number of these you need will depend on the size of your container, but when stood vertically these cylinders should occupy about half the total floorspace. It is an idea to put an elastic band around bundles of three of these cardboard rolls, so they do not fall over constantly. Put several layers of newspaper cut to size on the floor of the tank and stand all your cylinders on end. It makes no difference whether they are all together or separate. Put some food in the form of bread or cereals, together with a little apple to provide moisture, into the tank and two or three glass jars full of sterilized damp sand in which the females will lay their eggs. Introduce 20 or 30 crickets and leave them in peace somewhere warm and dark.

Crickets can be obtained by sending off to a specialist supplier or sometimes they can be found in pet shops, where 30 or 40 are sold pre-packed in a plastic tub. This is an extremely expensive way of buying them but it will provide you with enough stock to set up your culture. The reason for all the rolls of cardboard will become apparent as soon as you put the insects into the tank as they will vanish in a flash into the corrugations, and apart from when they are feeding they will live in the rolls for most of the time. This makes it fairly simple to harvest them. Take a small container, such as a jamjar into the tank, and then take each roll in turn, put one end into the jar and tap it sharply several times to dislodge the insects. Since you should only collect enough for a single feed at a time, it does not take long to collect this quantity. However, when the time arrives to have a good clean out of the tank, you have to be very careful or you end up with crickets everywhere. The best thing to do is to put the whole tank into the bath, after you have put in a plug which is not fixed to a chain. Put a clean tank into the bath as well and as soon as you remove the cardboard tubes full of crickets from the old tank you can put them straight into the other, which leaves only comparatively small numbers to transfer individually before they escape.

When you feed crickets to your pets you will discover that provided you feed them at the same time each day, the animals will be waiting to snap them up the moment you tip them into the cage.

EARTHWORMS *Lumbricus* spp. (for birds, amphibians and some young snakes)

A large wooden box full of garden soil, which has been sterilised in the oven at 200°C (400°F) for 30 minutes with a layer of dead leaves on the top is a good place to breed earthworms. The soil should always be slightly moist and a piece of sacking, cut to the size of the container, laid on top of the dead leaves will help to cut down water loss; but do not let the thing get too wet. When you have set up their home, go and catch your earthworms and put them in a bucket of cut grass overnight. In the morning discard any dead or injured worms and put the rest in your vermicarium. Worms do not appreciate being overcrowded so you should not introduce more than about 40 of them per .03 cu m (1 cu ft) or so. They like to be cool and a temperature of 16°C (60°F) will kill them. It is quite a good idea to breed earthworms if you have animals that will eat them since wild specimens are virtually unobtainable during the winter, and in captivity you can sterilise the soil in which they live, which could be important, because there have been stories of wild worms causing the death of the animals to which they were fed due to nasty things that they had picked up along the way.

FRUIT FLIES *Drosophila melanogaster* (for birds, small amphibians and baby lizards)

There are all sorts of different varieties of Fruit Flies, and if you are going to feed them to a terrestrial animal it is best to start off with a culture of wingless *Drosophila*, which you can obtain from a supplier of biological materials. Schools and colleges sometimes have stocks of Fruit Flies so it might be worth approaching those in your area. On the other hand if you want them for birds the whole business of breeding these delightful animals is simplicity itself. You can buy all sorts of special culturing mediums, but the way I get a culture going is to put some over-ripe bananas into a small bucket, together with a couple of over-ripe oranges, cut in half. Don't use just one banana in a small pot, for it will dry out rather than ferment. The culture should be set up when the weather is warm: there is no point trying to do it in the winter, though once you have the culture going you can keep it all year round.

Leave the bucket in a warm spot in the garden where the rain cannot get in — inside a shed with the window open is ideal, and you will find after a few days that the bananas are covered in tiny white *Drosophila* larvae which look like small maggots. You will sometimes see these better if you look underneath the top few bananas where it is nice and moist and warm. You may also see a few tiny flies on the surface of the culture, and the whole thing will have a lively, rich, fermenting fruity smell. What has happened is that wild Fruit Flies have been attracted by the smell and laid their eggs which have then hatched into larvae. At this stage take the bucket into your animal room. You can put small quantities of the gooey banana into narrow necked containers such as test tubes, and put one of these in each cage, if you have cages, otherwise simply leave it standing in the bucket on the floor. Very shortly the Fruit Flies will hatch out and your animals will have a great time catching them. You can encourage the flies to certain spots by baiting them with bits of overripe fruit. Now, providing that you keep your animal room at between 18°C–26°C (64°F–79°F) throughout the year, and providing that you periodically add a couple more bananas to your bucket, the Fruit Flies will continue to breed with no problems. Occasionally a culture becomes infected with tiny white mites but they cause no problems and can be left in peace. When you enter the animal room, if you tap the bucket sharply a few times a whole swarm of tiny flies will emerge to be snapped up greedily by all your animals. If you have enough it might be worth your while to keep several buckets on the go in sequence so that every so often you can clean out the old ones when they dry out and are no longer productive.

Fruit Flies really are very easy things to rear, and when you have the opportunity examine one closely under a hand lens. The red eyed forms are particularly attractive.

HOUSE FLIES *Musca domestica* and BLUEBOTTLES *Calliphora vomitoria* (for birds, lizards, amphibians, small mammals and carnivorous invertebrates)

Bluebottle larvae, which most people know as maggots but anglers call 'gentles', can be bought during the fishing season from angling shops, and a culture can be started from these. The alternative is to use a big cage, perhaps one that has become damaged, or you can use a large, chrome plated budgie cage. Make a container from a piece of wire mesh so that it is nearly as large as the cage, and hang it from some wire hooks inside the cage. The apparatus is hung inside a cage, so that every bird in the vicinity will not pick the maggots from your culture before you can get at them. The floor of the cage should be taken up with a large plastic tray about 2.5 cm (1 in) deep. Some cages are already fitted with one of these. The wire mesh box should neither touch the bars of the cage nor dangle below the top edge of the tray which you should fill with bran. Some people substitute sawdust for bran, and it works every bit as well, but I do not like it in case any small splinters adhere to a maggot and are swallowed. The next thing to do is to fill the wire mesh basket with scraps of meat, or preferably fish heads, guts and so on. Make sure that the basket is full because if there is only a small quantity it will dry out rather than putrefy and you will not get any maggots. Hang the cage as far from people as you can — breeding maggots is a smelly business.

What happens is that Bluebottles and House Flies are attracted by the meat and lay their eggs on it. In a few days these become maggots and feed on the meat and eventually drop onto the bran where they wriggle about. The bran cleans all the putrefying meat juices from them so they are ready to use and are no longer offensive. Do not try to feed the maggots to your animals until they have been cleaned in the bran. When you judge that the bran is a seething mass of maggots, tip the lot into a suitable container, refill and replace the tray, and if necessary the meat, and you are ready to go a second time. Both the maggots and the adults are taken as food, and some animals such as Chipmunks will also eat the intermediate stage, the pupa. It is a good idea to keep two or three

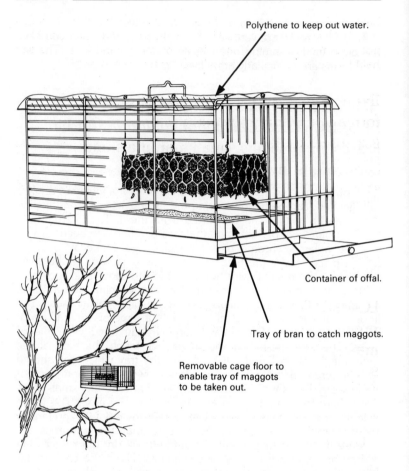

Polythene to keep out water.

Container of offal.

Tray of bran to catch maggots.

Removable cage floor to enable tray of maggots to be taken out.

A maggot breeding device to be set well away from the house!

cultures at different stages so that you have a steady supply of maggots. The breeding process could be continued through the winter in theory, but it would have to be situated in your heated animal room where it would be so smelly that I cannot imagine anyone wanting to do it.

Maggots can be made to last longer before they pupate by keeping them in a refrigerator, but whatever you keep them in it should not be airtight as the whole lot start to 'sweat', the moisture builds up, they stink and soon you lose the lot. The best thing is to cover the top of the container with a piece of women's nylon tights held in place with an elastic band and then, if the flies do hatch out, they cannot escape and fill the refrigerator. And, of course, do not keep them in a refrigerator in your kitchen; that is a disgusting habit. Keep them in a special animal room refrigerator.

INFUSORIA A mixture of minute aquatic life forms (for young fish and newts)

Boil a handful of hay in a pan of water and after it has cooled pour the water through a sieve and throw away the hay. This is all you need to do though you will have better results if you add an equal quantity of pond water. After a few days you ought to find the water teeming with life, which is so interesting that it is worth examining under a microscope. One of the fascinating things about infusoria is that many of the organisms inhabit quite separate parts of the container, so for example *Paramecium* can be found at the surface and *Amoeba* lives on the bottom. Two or three drops of the water contain a whole enthralling world of little animals.

LOCUSTS *Locusta migratoria* and *Schistocerca gregaria* (for birds, lizards, amphibians, small mammals and invertebrates)

Before I go any further, let me say that there have been reports that locusts can be poisonous to animals that eat them. I have fed locusts to many animals with no trouble and I do not know anyone else who has experienced any problems; but I make the point anyway.

Locusts are fascinating animals that are easy to breed. To start with, you will require a wooden box cage with a glass front. Minimum dimensions should be about 60 cm (24 in) high × 45 cm (18 in) wide × 30 cm (12 in) deep. There should be a light inside connected to a thermostat to maintain the temperature at about 32–34°C (90–93°F) during the day, dropping to about 28°C (82°F) at night, so there must be a thermometer in the cage to enable you to check this. It is important that the light bulb is not in a position where it can scorch the wood or you might end up with a fire, and I prefer to put a wire mesh cage around it so that the locusts cannot hurt themselves. You need a false floor about 13 cm (5 in) above the bottom of the cage and you will have to make a few holes in this large enough to take a plastic tube − I like to use the top part of the type of budgerigar drinking fountain that fits on the bars of the cage. Drop the tubes, open end uppermost into the holes so that the top edge is flush with the false floor and fill them with rather moist sterilised sand. When they are full to the top, cover the whole floor with the same sand. You can sterilise the sand in the oven after you have rinsed it well several times. Some twigs with lots of branches should be set upright in the cage for the insects to climb. A shallow dish of bran and a small glass jar packed tightly with grass is all that is needed in the way of food. The grass stalks should be in water to keep them alive and the reason they are packed tightly is so that a locust cannot drown in the water. Only trial and error will tell you how much grass to use — too little and cannibalism will result; too much and the cage will get sweaty and smelly. The cage must in any case have a gauze ventilation panel.

One special point about the construction of the cage door. If you make a conventional door, some locusts will escape, so the door must be hinged at the top so that it swings inwards, and around the outside of the door frame fix securely one end of a long leg from a pair of women's nylon tights. Cut off the foot so that you are left with a nylon mesh sleeve. Each time you insert your arm into this tube it fits snugly around your arm so that when you open the cage door no insect can possibly escape, but do make sure the tube is empty before you close the door and extract your arm.

The locusts will live through most of the year on the bran and the grass. I spray the grass with water before I put it in the cage. During the winter, when it may be difficult to find some nice appetising grass, it can be replaced with sprouting wheat seeds on some damp cotton wool.

A cage of the suggested minimum size will house about 60 or 70 adult locusts or up to a thousand newly hatched babies, which are called hoppers, but to start your colony you need only obtain one or two dozen adults. After they have mated the females lay their eggs in the deep tubes of sand. You can either leave the tubes where they are or remove them and stand them upright in a corner of the cage and replace them with new tubes in which case you will get more eggs. Humidity in the tubes is critical. If they are allowed to get too dry the eggs will become dehydrated and die, and if too wet a fungus will kill them. If you want to be sure of results and do the thing properly you should fill the tubes with 100 parts sand to 15 parts distilled water and weigh them. Each day they should again be weighed and more distilled water added to make up any weight loss. Follow the same sort of procedure after eggs have been laid.

The little locusts hatch after four or five weeks and thereafter they shed their skins every so often, each time emerging a little larger. Each stage is called an instar, so newly hatched insects are known as first instars, and then second instars and so on. Do not be at all surprised when you start to lose the babies. Losses are high, sometimes as much as 80 per cent die before reaching maturity. Clean any bodies and other rubbish from the cage daily.

At each stage the locusts are a valuable source of food for your animals, and obviously the larger the animal the larger the locust it will take. When you first start to keep locusts remember their reputation — you will be astonished at the amount they eat, but do not worry if a few escape; it is far too cold for the insects to survive for long in the open in Britain, so you are not going to wake one morning to find that the countryside has been defoliated overnight.

MEALWORMS *Tenebrio molitor* (for birds, amphibians, lizards, some invertebrates and small mammals)

Mealworms are one of the commonest and most useful of livefoods. They are not worms at all, but rather the larvae of a beetle which is closely related to the so-called Mexican Jewel Beetles. In Mexico, the beetles are caught to have small pieces of coloured glass, sequins and so on glued to their backs together with a short length of fine chain. The beetle on the end of this chain is pinned to the collar of a girl's dress as a fashion accessory. The origin of the habit is interesting as Mexican folklore tells of a handsome prince who was turned into a beetle by a witch. The princess who loved him was worried that he would be trodden on, so she tied a short piece of chain to him and pinned that to her collar so that she could be sure her boyfriend was safe until she could find a way to break the spell. They are easy to culture but the life cycle is a long one, so if you want livefood quickly, breed maggots.

I find the best container to be an old aquarium, but anything of a suitable size will do, and as I write there is a 4-litre (7-pint) plastic ice cream tub on the floor beside me which houses my stock of mealworms. Half fill the container with dry porridge oats and lay a couple of pieces of dry bread on the top together with a bit of vegetable or fruit such as half an apple and cover the surface with two or three sheets of newspaper cut to the size of the tank. This is about all really, except to keep it warm — mine lives near the radiator during the winter. Every so often you will need to add some more food — mealworms will eat almost anything veget-able, and on various occasions I have thrown in bits of hamster mixture, apple cores and pieces of boiled potato. After about six months, you can start harvesting your crop. I find the best way is to tip a quantity of the contents onto several large sheets of newspaper and spread it thinly with your fingers. If there are any adults I put them straight back to continue breeding, but you can feed them to your animals. After that you will find that the mealworms start to move around and they are easy to pick out and put into a pot. It is best to collect a couple of weeks supply at a time, to save disturbing the colony too often. Tip all the porridge and rubbish · back into the culture. Never throw it away, nor indeed any dried up food, because the stuff is full of tiny eggs. If you suffer from hay fever wear a mask for this operation. I find the dust makes me sneeze after I have been sorting mealworms. The only thing to watch is that the culture never becomes damp or you can soon lose the lot. Some people like to cover their mealworm colonies but I have found that humidity can soon start to build up, and I have had no problems without lids, though it is true that on one occasion a single beetle escaped and turned up in the bathroom.

One point to note with mealworms is that they have fairly tough skins so that very small baby lizards have considerable trouble digesting them. On one occasion, I lost several tiny Jones' Zonures for this very reason.

MICE *Mus musculus* (for snakes, large lizards, birds and some amphibians, invertebrates and small mammals)

For cultural instructions, see page 226 in the Glossary of Pets.

It is illegal to feed a live mouse to an animal, but do get someone who knows how to show you how to kill a mouse humanely. Usually the person from whom you bought it will do this. Mice are an excellent food for all sorts of animals and can be fed either when newly born when they are referred to as pinkies, or when they have grown larger.

RATS *Rattus norvegicus* (for snakes and large birds)

For cultural instructions, see under Rodent in the Glossary of Pets.

It is illegal to feed a live rat to an animal but do get someone who knows to show you how to kill a rat humanely. Usually the person from whom you bought it will do this.

STICK INSECTS *Carausius morosus* (for birds, amphibians, lizards and invertebrates)

The lifespan of a stick insect is a lot longer than all the previously described insects — it can be well over a year, but they are prolific and extremely easy to care for. Keep them in an old fish tank with fine netting over the top, and cover the floor in clean newsprint. You need a glass jar full of water, into which you place as many leafy twigs of privet as will fit, so that there are no gaps to let an insect get to the water and drown.

Start off with half a dozen insects and place them on the privet leaves. Some books say you can but honestly it is wiser not to handle stick insects for they are very fragile: pick up babies with a soft paintbrush. Stick insects should be kept at room temperature but do watch that they do not become damp or you could lose them. They will defecate small, shrivelled droppings; they will also lay great loads of eggs, one at a time. They are the same colour as the droppings so you have to look carefully, but they are hard and round with a little lid at one end. I find the best thing is to change the privet whenever most of the leaves have been eaten, being careful that the insects climb onto the new leaves first or you might inadvertently throw them out. When you have done that, pick up all the eggs and put them into an open match-box tray in the corner of the cage and then get rid of the droppings. Incidentally, you will not come across any male stick insects — not of this species, anyway — they are all female. After some months the eggs will hatch out and newly hatched babies are very thirsty so you will need a shallow dish with a scrap of water; an upturned lid of some sort usually works. After this first drink they do not take water again until just before they die. Newly hatched babies look like a 1 cm (0.4 in) long piece of thread with legs. They shed their skins periodically, getting bigger each time until they are adult, and when they are about nine months old they start to lay eggs themselves. You can feed them to animals at any age depending on the size of the animal.

WHITEWORMS *Enchytrea* spp. (for fish, small newts and salamanders)

Start off a Whiteworm culture as described for earthworms, then poke something like a pencil into the soil to make a number of small tunnels into which you should push some bread that you have soaked in milk. Whiteworms can be bought at aquarists' shops and even some pet shops, and a few should be placed on each piece of bread. Rake the humus over the top and put a lid on the container to retain the humidity. As with the earthworm culture, keep your Whiteworms cool. When the bread disappears, add some more, and after about a week you ought to be able to start harvesting. If any of the bread goes mouldy or sour, take it out or you will have problems.

5
INJURIES,
DISEASES
AND FIRST AID

Injuries and diseases are as much a part of your pet's life as they are of yours and when somebody takes on a pet they ought to realise that veterinary costs could become very expensive indeed. Most animals are put together in much the same way as you or I; that is to say that they have limbs for walking, eyes for seeing, lungs and hearts and livers and kidneys, so it should come as no surprise to anyone that they can suffer from much the same diseases and injuries as ourselves. But, just as we can contract conditions specific to our species, so can many animals, and if all that was not complicated enough most animals cannot communicate too well about their symptoms. When you need to call in a veterinary surgeon to diagnose, and to treat, a suffering animal, do not begrudge his charges. If you feel that you will not be able to pay veterinary fees during the life of your animal, do not take it on in the first place, however much you are attracted to it.

If you are interested in keeping exotic animals check before you become a client whether or not your local veterinary surgeon has any knowledge of or interest in your particular animals. If he does not, contact the Royal College of Veterinary Surgeons, who have lists of members with interests in treating the more exotic species.

Apart from veterinary surgeons, no one in the United Kingdom is permitted to treat an animal and charge for doing so, but you will find that the RSPCA Inspectors and the clinics of that organisation or the PDSA are most useful to know and can be really helpful. Welfare organisations, and there are hosts of them, some existing specifically for a certain type of animal, will all help you in return for a donation.

If you are going to start keeping animals, it is a good idea to get yourself a book or two on first aid for your special interest. Some fanciers are remarkably well served in this respect, and it is surprising how often it is the older guides that have survived and still work best, so for instance I feel that the best book on diseases of birds is *Diseases of Canaries* by Robert Stroud, the birdman of Alcatraz; though it was written specifically about canaries, it is equally applicable to most birds.

BASIC FIRST AID KIT

Once you have got the information to hand should you need it, start to put together a first aid kit. You might feel this is unnecessary as quite a lot of the items you may require are probably already in your home but when an emergency occurs you will wish that it was all together in one handy box. What you choose to keep in your first aid box kit will vary depending on the sort of animals you keep, and experience will tell you what else to add, but some items are pretty basic and ought to be available anyway.

The list may seem unnecessarily complicated, and for whatever reason you may decide to replace any of the items on it, but unless you are willing to take this sort of trouble over an animal, you should not really be keeping a pet.

1 pair of small scissors	— Small cutting jobs
1 pair of medium scissors	— Clipping fur, cutting lint, etc.
1 pair square-ended forceps	— Holding small items
1 pair artery forceps	— Invaluable as they stay closed without having to hold them
1 small bone snips	— Handy for trimming nails and beaks
1 stubby bulb thermometer	— Taking temperatures
1 pack of cotton buds	— Cleaning ears and invaluable for cleaning wounds
1 Styptic pencil	— Stopping small hameorrhages
1 narrow bandage	— Dressing some injuries
1 wide bandage	— Dressing some injuries and for restraining an animal if necessary
1 roll of adhesive tape	— Holding dressings in place
1 pack gauze	— Dressing wounds
1 large pack of cotton wool	— Vital for cleaning fur, feathers and wounds
1 pack of polythene bags	— Protecting dressings from getting wet
1 bottle of solvent	— Alcohol, carbon tetrachloride or something similar to clean paint, tar, oil and other noxious substances from your pet — but, because of solvent abuse, do be careful with it

1 large container of disinfectant	— You cannot have too much of this and it should be used liberally and frequently to cleanse wounds, first aid instruments, cages, feeding bowls (but rinse well and repeatedly afterwards) and anything else. But do please read the note at the end of this list before buying any disinfectant
1 tube of antiseptic cream	— Treating wounds
1 small plastic bowl	— For water. You can never find one in a hurry when you want one
1 packet of roundworm/ tapeworm tablets	— Treat according to instructions. Internal parasites are commoner than you may think
1 largish magnifying lens on a stand	— If you keep Great Danes do not bother. If you keep small animals, such as birds or frogs, this is handy to see what you are doing
1 container of wound dressing powder	— Treating open wounds

A warning about disinfectants, if you keep cats. Many common disinfectants are dangerous to cats, so choose carefully. The best one of all to use is Dodecine. Other such as Cetrimide are probably safe if diluted strictly according to instructions, but the phenolic compounds and the iodine compounds must not be used; so check the ingredients on the bottle before you buy it.

INJURIES

An animal that has suffered an injury that requires treatment is likely to be pretty distressed. If the injury is a small one, treat it yourself. If it is severe, or if you are not sure what to do, take the patient to the vet as soon as you can after taking emergency precautions. You might find that due to the pain and fear an injured animal is difficult to catch. Do not rush about; you will only panic the animal further and could exacerbate the injury. Stop for a moment and think. The animal should be caught as quickly and efficiently as possible to minimise the trauma, and often the easiest way to do this is to persuade it to enter a confined space where it can be more readily caught. Mind you do not get bitten and remember, if the animal is a cat, that not only has it got sharp teeth, it has sharp claws as well. Often, the best thing to do is to wrap the animal in something like a towel to immobilise it and

93

hold it still, and talk to it calmly until it can be treated. What you say might not help the animal too much but it will help you to stay calm and think clearly, and that is important to your pet. If the patient is a dog and it is snapping at you make a muzzle from a length of bandage, provided that the dog is not a short nosed breed or has injuries that affect respiration.

Once you become known in your community as being good with animals, pet owners are going to come to you in emergencies. If they tell you that you have no need to worry as Fido never bites, or Tabby has never hurt anyone, do not believe them however convincing they may sound. Until I learnt this lesson the hard way I was bitten and scratched more times than I care to remember.

Mammals, from hamsters to horses, sometimes end up with a wound of some kind. When this happens, call a vet if it is serious or you are not sure what to do about it. However, if it is only a small injury, clean the wound well with a tepid disinfectant solution, while keeping all parts of your own anatomy away from the biting, scratching, kicking and butting bits of your patient, and then treat the wound with either an antiseptic ointment or wound dressing powder. If the animal is one of those rare creatures that do not worry about bandages and other dressings, put one on to keep flies and other baddies away from the injury until it begins to heal. Keep the animal warm and quiet and, when you have done that, check its cage or paddock or stable or wherever it lives for the source of the injury and remove it.

Many animals will not tolerate bandages or other dressings and, if these are needed, they should be left to the vet as he will know the best way to make sure that they are as pet proof as possible, though it must be said that some animals will accept them far better than others. This advice — going to the vet — cannot be bettered for mammals, but as you become more experienced it is possible to do a good job yourself on small birds. The commonest injuries to small birds are broken limbs. If the limb is a wing and the skin is not torn and there is little or no bleeding beneath the skin, or swelling, the best thing to do is to match the ends of the bones as well as you can and tape the wing to the body so that it cannot be moved. Then keep the bird warm and quiet for a couple of weeks before you remove the dressing. If you are very lucky the wing might have healed, but very often there has been more bleeding and swelling and the whole thing is worse. This is so frequently the case that with an injury such as I have described it is often easier to do nothing except to isolate the patient, and again keep him warm and quiet. In this case the wing will often heal but rarely is the bird able to fly again. If there is an open wound at the site of the fracture, the chances of mending the whole business successfully are minimal and the best thing might be to take the bird to your vet and ask him to amputate the wing. A broken leg presents much the same sort of difficulties if the injury is above the tibio-tarsal joint, but if it is below that, repairing it is a lot easier. You need to apply a splint and the two easiest ways of doing this are either to wrap some bandage around the leg and then smear a good thick layer of melted candle wax all over it: the wax will set to form a splint. Or, alternatively, again wrap bandage around the

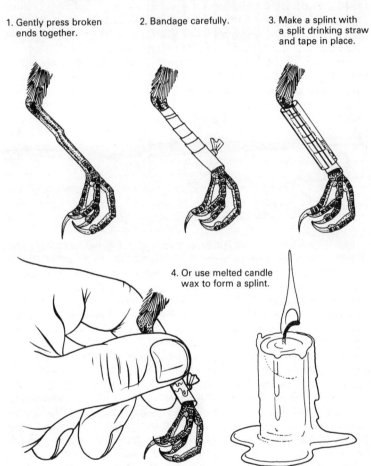

1. Gently press broken ends together.

2. Bandage carefully.

3. Make a splint with a split drinking straw and tape in place.

4. Or use melted candle wax to form a splint.

Mending the broken leg of a bird using either a length of plastic drinking straw as a splint, or a coating of candle wax.

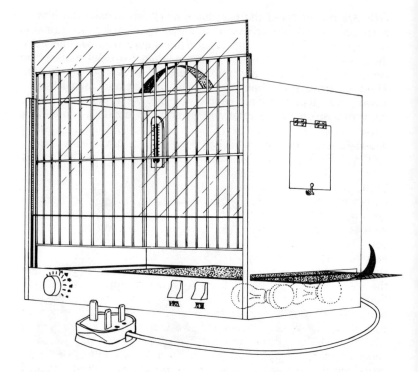

An ideal hospital cage showing a removable perforated zinc floor covered with a piece of felt.

limb and then slide over it a length of plastic drinking straw that has been split along one side. Sellotape this closed. After two or three weeks, carefully remove the splint and all should be well.

A general tip that works wonders for birds is to raise the temperature in a hospital cage to 32°C (90°F) and put the bird into it. Very often this alone will bring about a recovery. When the bird is better, reduce the temperature a little each day until it is back to normal, and then return your bird to its cage or aviary. But, whatever you do, do not take it straight from 32°C (90°F) and put it into room temperature. One can buy hospital cages but they are fairly expensive. Nevertheless if you can afford one it will be the most useful piece of equipment you buy. If you cannot afford to buy one, it is perfectly possible to make this vital component of successful first aid.

The size will depend on what birds you keep, but for the usual small seedeaters, such as the Zebra Finch, a cage about 40 cm

(16 in) high × 30 cm (12 in) ×30 cm (12 in) is about right. It is best made of thick plywood. There should be a false floor or perforated zinc about 10 cm (4 in) from the bottom, and beneath this are situated two or more ordinary electric light bulbs, or, if you can find them, carbon filament lamps, that act as the heat source. These need to be connected to a thermostat to raise the temperature in the chamber above. Make sure the heat from the lamps does not cause the wood to scorch. This compartment should have a solid front suitably equipped with switches and controls; you need to be able to raise the temperature in the cage to about 32°C (90°F). The compartment for the birds should be fitted with channels at the front so that you can slide in a weldmesh cage front, and outside that a sheet of glass. The glass keeps the heat in, but the mesh is also necessary as birds will often keep flying at glass and hurt themselves. This compartment should have an adjustable ventilation panel and a door in the right hand wall, if you are right handed, hinged at the top. A thermometer that is easy to read should be situated in the centre of the back wall, and suitable provision made for food and drink pots, remembering that the water must not spill as there is electrical apparatus beneath. Perches must be fitted, and finally a piece of thick felt or something similar must be laid to cover the floor or the bird may burn its feet on the metal. Burn the felt after each patient and replace it with a new piece. Fit a handle to the centre of the roof, as hospital cages are surprisingly heavy, and being bulky are difficult to carry especially if you need to open doors on the way. You can add refinements to a hospital cage, such as insulation to cut down on the energy consumption, but whatever is wrong with your pet, and whatever kind of pet it is, the essential is to give the animal warmth, and peace and quiet.

You might find, or someone might bring you, a racing pigeon that has landed, exhausted and perhaps lost. Often, all that is necessary is to provide rest and food for a day or two until it is fit enough to resume its journey. You will know that the pigeon belongs to someone if it has a metal ring on one leg. If the bird was actually on a race when you found it there will be an elastic ring on the other leg. This ring is put on at the start of the race and removed again when it returns home, but the metal ring stays where it is throughout the pigeon's life. There ought also to be a number stamped on the underside of one wing. As mentioned earlier, the governing body of the world of racing pigeons is the Royal Pigeon Racing Association, and if you do find one of these birds you should inform them. If the bird dies, return its ring to the Association but if you manage to save it tell them and quote the numbers on the rings. They will repay you any expenses incurred in feeding and returning the bird, and not only will the owner be pleased to have his pigeon back but this sort of information also helps the records that the Association maintains.

Injuries to reptiles and amphibians are rare and are usually of one of two sorts. The first is damage caused by one animal to another, such as a bite suffered by fighting. The second is a skinned nose which happens when an animal persists in trying to get through a piece of glass which it cannot see. It keeps knocking its face against the glass until the nose becomes bloody. The best thing to do in both cases is clean up the damage and leave the animal strictly alone, after removing the cause of the injury. Reptiles and amphibians can recover from horrendous physical injury and trying to treat them generally increases the problems. Remove aggressive animals from the tank and paint the inside of the glass with white emulsion and let it dry and you ought to find that all is well thereafter. The only objection to painting the glass is that you can no longer see your animals, and one of the reasons you bought them is so that you could enjoy watching them. There is an answer to that but it does not work every time by any means. What I do is to wait till the injuries are healed and then I run something like a screwdriver blade down the painted glass at about 2.5 cm (1 in) intervals. This removes very thin strips of paint. A week later I do the same thing in between the first lot thereby increasing the bars of transparency. A week after that I draw horizontal bars and I keep on repeating these steps until eventually all the paint is removed. Sometimes the animals become so used to the front wall that they do not notice that it is slowly disappearing and they do not thereafter try and get through it. But they are not very intelligent beasts and the only real answer might be to put them in an enormous enclosure with all the branches and other cage furniture well away from the glass and an opaque panel where the glass meets the floor. Skinned noses on reptiles and amphibians take forever to heal, especially when the atmosphere is very humid, so you have to pay particular attention to hygiene at this time.

If one animal has suffered a bite from another, think very carefully about the community in that tank, as most reptiles and amphibians regard any moving object of suitable size as edible, and the first bite may be a sign that one animal is growing faster than you had realised. I knew a pair of sibling monitor lizards that started life at the same size at the same time. They lived happily in the same tank. The person who owned them saw them every day and the fact that one was growing far faster than the other had not really registered, until one day I noticed the large one eyeing his cage mate in a speculative manner. On my suggestion the two were separated and immediately the small one started to bloom. He became confident and glossy and grew far bigger in a very short time.

The other common injury to lizards occurs when tiny cuts on the feet become infected with bacterium of some sort, which results in abscesses on the bottom of the foot and to the toes. If scrupulous hygiene is observed and branches and cage floors are carefully and regularly disinfected these lesions will usually clear up, though they will frequently result in lost or deformed toes. Disinfect the injured feet regularly and, as soon as the abscess bursts, clean it well and pack the cavity with wound dressing powder. The same treatment can be used for abscesses on other parts of the body, though I have found that these usually occur only on the feet. When they do they are usually on a particular animal that must be in some way susceptible to attacks by the infective micro-organism, and if this is the case that lizard will probably continue to come out in bumps throughout its life.

Invertebrates are rarely injured, and the injuries only take two forms. The commonest thing to happen is that an animal loses a leg. If that is the case do not worry about it as many invertebrates shed legs easily as a defence mechanism and will often regenerate them. Other injuries can be avoided by taking extreme care when handling your animals. Don't drop your spiders on the floor, for example; stick insects are another animal that can come to grief through careless handling. Little ones should be moved using a soft paint brush. Larger ones should not be picked up by a leg, or it will shed it, and it is very tempting to grasp them gently between finger and thumb around the body. DO NOT do it. Invariably the body begins to shrivel below this point until after a week or so it is completely dried up and useless. The only way to pick up a stick insect if you really must is to lower your hand over it and close your fingers beneath it so that where the two of you are in contact it is because the stick insect is touching you with its feet rather than you touching the insect. This way it is enclosed in a cage of fingers, but the best way of moving them is to get them to climb onto a twig and move that.

DISEASES

Detailed information on diseases is far beyond the scope of this book and, in any case, if you ever feel worried about the condition of a pet, or you think that something serious is wrong, take the animal to a vet without delay. As you gain experience you will feel far more confident about what to do when your pet is ill and you will not feel guilty about consulting a vet on what might turn out to be a minor problem. Before you ever start keeping animals, you should ask around among your friends for their opinions on local vets. When you have found a practice that sounds right, go along and have a look at it and, if you are still happy, ring up and make an appointment to see the person who will be treating your stock — it is as well to get to know your vet. You can also find out about your local RSPCA inspector.

You have now made sure that you have available back-up in the event of an emergency, or when your animal falls ill. The risk of disease can be reduced to a minimum by scrupulous attention to hygiene, and putting thought into looking after your animal.

Some diseases to which animals are prone can be passed to humans, elementary care and hygiene is therefore vital. Always clean feeding bowls and other equipment well — and not in the bowl you use for washing up the family's plates, and do not use the same dishcloths. Wash your hands well after handling animals, litter trays and the like, and again, not in the washing-up bowl. Children and pregnant women ought never to touch dog or cat faeces, as they can transmit all sorts of nasties, and if you get bitten or scratched make sure that your tetanus injections are up to date, and disinfect the site of the injury, and never, ever let your dog lick your face. Periodically, comments of this sort provoke some dog or cat owners to anger, but all responsible pet keepers take these precautions anyway and understand that they must be seen to be responsible. For this reason they prevent their dogs from defecating on pavements and public places.

Get yourself a good book on your particular pet and read through the chapters on diseases so that you know where to look when your animal is sick. In time you will find that much of what I am saying is common sense and that many illnesses can be prevented. Frequently, all that is needed when something goes wrong is warmth and peace and perhaps little or no food for a day or so, but plenty of clean water. But, if your patient is a small bird, do not ever skimp on his food. Birds have a high metabolic rate, which means that they convert food into energy much faster than other animals and consequently they have to feed more often to replace the expended calories. If you do not feed a Labrador for 24 hours it will not matter too much except that you will have a hungry dog. Do the same to a small bird and it might very well die.

A new owner of any animal sometimes becomes over-anxious or panics when the pet seems not to be its usual happy self, and if you are aware of the symptoms of common ailments it will give you confidence to deal with them, so it might be a good idea to look at them quickly. As far as cats and dogs are concerned, before you read through the next bit, I must stress that you should check the regular vaccinations are kept up to date. That sounds so obvious, but you will be surprised how often it is neglected.

SPECIFIC COMPLAINTS

DOGS

Obesity. If your dog is fat it is almost certainly your fault, for if you feed your pet on a normal diet and exercise it sufficiently it should not get fat. Be honest with yourself, and list all the tidbits and treats that you feed your pet during the day. You are being just as cruel to the animal as if you were deliberately mistreating it. Obesity can lead to and aggravate heart problems, hip dysplasia and can complicate matters when your dog needs an anaesthetic — so

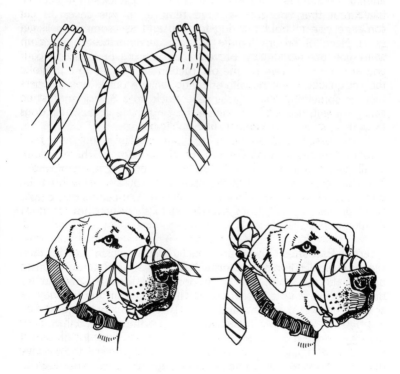

Even the most placid dog might bite when in pain. A simple muzzle will prevent you being injured while you administer first aid.

throw away the chocolate drops and the biscuits, and start to feed your pet properly and become a responsible pet owner.

Dental Problems. You know how miserable you feel when you are suffering from toothache, so if you suspect that your dog is feeling the same way take it to your vet. Canned food is so soft that there is almost no chewing necessary, so tartar soon begins to build up on the teeth. Once this has happened, your vet can remove it but if you start a programme of dental hygiene when your dog is really young you can get it used to having its teeth brushed. Do not use toothpaste but otherwise do it just as you do yours, keeping a special toothbrush strictly for the dog. Broken teeth can lead to infection, and dental abscesses are not infrequent.

Coughs and Sneezes. If the condition persists, take the animal to a vet but before you do, have a look inside the mouth if the animal is coughing — it might have something stuck in the back of the throat that you can see and remove. In this case, do get someone else to hold the dog for you and use something like a short piece of broom handle to slide gently between the teeth while you are working to prevent them closing on your hand. If you are unable to remove the obstruction easily, give up and go to the vet quickly. Similarly with sneezing, have a quick look to see if there is something like a grass seed stuck up a nostril and if you can get it out, do so. If the sneeze is a single one, there is no need to worry.

Impaction of the Anal Glands. On either side of the anus are small glands that sometimes become swollen and uncomfortable. The dog will constantly lick the area and may also slide his back end along the floor to relieve the condition. You can usually empty these glands yourself, but get your vet to show you how to do it the first time.

Internal Parasites. These are usually worms which can be conveniently divided into roundworms and tapeworms. Roundworms are usually about 1–2 cm ($\frac{1}{2}$–$\frac{3}{4}$ in) long and look like thin, white maggots. You may see them around the anus or in the faeces. Get some roundworm tablets and administer them according to the instructions on the pack. But do note that the tablets will not kill the eggs inside the dog, so they will hatch into a new lot of worms if you do not give a second dose a few days after the first as directed. It is very easy to neglect this stage when you find that the first dose has got rid of the worms. Tapeworms are amazing animals. They have heads with lots of teeth that lock onto the wall

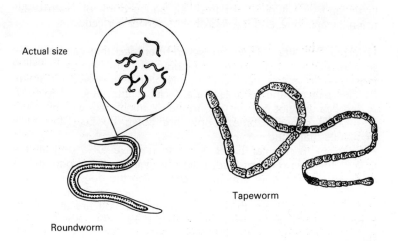

Actual size

Roundworm

Tapeworm

Parasitical roundworms and tapeworms, common in many animals.

of the gut so that they can extract nutrients therefrom, and then they start to grow. A good healthy tapeworm can grow to a length of many metres (yards). The body is white, segmented and flat, and you might find short, broken-off bits around the anus or in the faeces and again the treatment is by using tablets — tapeworm tablets in this case. Roundworms are easy to see but frankly one does not often find tapeworm segments despite my description of them. The easiest way of diagnosing worms is to keep an eye on the quantity of food the animal eats. If he becomes abnormally hungry for no apparent reason and if he also acquires a narrow, pinched look around the flanks there is a good chance that you are feeding worms as well as dogs.

Vomiting or Diarrhoea. Provided that your dog is otherwise well and neither of these symptoms persist, nor do they occur together, it is likely that the animal has only picked up a mild infection or become overexcited. In the case of diarrhoea, a dose of kaolin and morphine should help and for the vomiting, refrain from feeding the dog until the next day and then give it a small meal. However, if the whole messy business continues or there is blood in the vomit or faeces, call your vet.

Heatstroke. This is almost invariably caused by leaving a dog in a car during hot weather, despite the annual warnings not to do this. You will rightly be accused of cruelty to your pet. Let the dog cool down and give it plenty of fresh air and a drink of clean water when it wants one, and it will probably recover perfectly.

External Parasites. There are several parasites that can cause all sorts of skin problems for dogs. Undoubtedly the one that worries most people is the flea. Owners visualise themselves becoming infected as well, and there is still a social stigma attached to fleas. A dog flea will not live on you, though it might very well bite you, and oddly enough some people are bitten by fleas far more frequently than others.

Contrary to popular belief, fleas do not live on a dog all the time — they jump on to feed, then off again to their home in the dog's bed or favourite armchair, so spraying the dog will only get rid of the fleas that are actually on him. I have found that if you put up Vapona blocks throughout the house, you are unlikely to have flea problems: every new lot that is brought in by the dog soon dies off.

During the summer when your dog goes for long exciting walks through the long grass he might very well pick up the odd sheep tick. These little animals embed their tiny mouth parts in the skin and sit there happily sucking blood. They look like a white or grey lump about the size of the nail on your little finger, attached to the dog by a fine point. If you try and pull it off you will almost certainly leave the very small head embedded in the dog and this might cause an infection and, if the tick's body bursts during the operation, you will find it full of blood from your pet. There are various ways of getting rid of the things, such as painting them with alcohol or oil and waiting a day for them to die whereupon the mouthparts relax, but by far the best way is to pull them off with a quick jerk. But, do not attempt to do this unless someone experienced shows you how — there is a knack to it that is impossible to describe — or you will leave the head behind.

One frequently sees dogs scratching, especially in the summer, and sometimes this is in response to eczema or mange caused by lice or mites. This sort of parasitism is really annoying because not only do you have the problem of the parasite but you also have the possibility of secondary conditions caused by the dog scratching away at the site of the irritation. Do not bother with creams and potions — take the dog to your vet because the causal organism has to be destroyed. Some mites cause ear problems which again require veterinary treatment.

The other condition which causes a fair bit of distress through the summer is caused, unbelievably, by vegetable matter such as the awns on some grass and corn seeds. These awns have microscopic barbs, which sometimes penetrate the soft skin between the toes during a walk in a field or a park, or even enter a nose while the animal is having a good sniff at an exciting smell. Once an awn has dug itself in, it is virtually impossible to remove as it snaps into segments. Those that are left slowly bury themselves deeper, and every movement causes them to travel further, often causing infection as they go. They eventually work their way out again through the skin but sometimes this might not happen till the seed has travelled right up a leg. They are nasty things and the wounds refuse to heal until the awn is out. The only thing to do is to take the animal to the vet; in the meantime, be aware of the danger and keep your dog away from fierce looking grass seeds.

CATS
Many of the ailments suffered by dogs are also suffered by cats, so read through the section on dog diseases before you go any further.

Poisoning. Some cats are great hunters and forever bring home trophies. They are often rodents or birds and if these have been eating poison, your pet can be affected. Cats sometimes accidentally consume other poisons when they eat plants in gardens that have been sprayed with toxic chemicals and the results are horrifying and distressing to watch. The symptoms vary according to what the poisonous compound is but vomiting, diarrhoea, convulsions and paralysis are common. The vomit is often of a green, frothy consistency, but whatever it looks like, if you suspect poisoning call the vet first. In the meantime wash any trace of poisonous substance from the fur to prevent the cat ingesting more of it, and if you know what the poison is, tell the vet when he arrives or give him a sample so that he will know what action to take.

Coughing. A cat may cough for a variety of reasons but the commonest of all is because it has swallowed a quantity of fur while it was grooming itself and it wants to get rid of this hairball. This is perfectly natural and nothing to be alarmed about but if you are not used to it, it looks dreadful. The cat sounds as though it has been smoking 50 cigarettes a day for 40 years and its sides heave violently. Luckily it does not last long and afterwards the animal is fine.

HORSES

Colic. Colic means stomach ache, for whatever reason. A horse with colic looks unhappy and keeps looking around at his sides.

105

He may try to lie down or roll about and he may sweat, all because of the pain. You must keep your horse warm and quiet — walk him around if he cannot keep still, but do not let him lie down even if he wants to or you may have problems with the bowel. Administer an enema to relieve constipation and if things do not improve and you are worried, call the vet.

Laminitis. Laminitis is an inflammation of the foot and, if allowed to continue unchecked, the leg, and is the result of insufficient exercise and too much greenfood. It is not the easiest thing to treat and causes much pain to the animal. The answer is to ensure that it does not happen in the first place.

Conditions of the Leg and Foot. Some of these foot and leg troubles are not injuries but if you suspect something is wrong because the horse is favouring one leg when it walks or because it rests one foreleg on the tip of the hoof (as opposed to a back leg which is perfectly normal), see if you can find the trouble. Very often it is simply that a stone or something equally uncomfortable has got stuck underneath the hoof and removing this will resolve the lameness. Another cause of lameness might be a small cut in the same place; treat this as you would any other wound. But if there is swelling somewhere along the leg or it feels hot, leave it alone and call a vet.

External Parasites. Two insects that can be a considerable nuisance to a horse are the Warble Fly and the Bot Fly. A female Warble Fly lays her eggs on the horse, often just where the saddle goes. When they hatch out the larvae burrow just beneath the skin and settle down to grow. As they get bigger they eat a hole in the skin; at this stage they can be squeezed out and the resulting cavity cleaned and disinfected. Bot Flies lay their eggs from the knee to the top of the foreleg and the horse licks them off and swallows them after which they are very difficult to get rid of. The eggs look like yellow specks and the only effective way of dealing with them is to scrape them off with an old, blunt knife blade.

RABBITS, GUINEA PIGS AND RODENTS

Luckily all these animals rarely come down with disease, though of course they can. Older animals can develop tumours, in which case you should talk to your vet.

Disorders of the Gut. These conditions occur sometimes but this is usually due to incorrect feeding. Inexperienced owners soon discover that these animals like fresh vegetables and before long the quantity of cabbage leaves and tomatoes is being increased at the expense of the seeds and corn and the other hard ingredients. The result is that the animal starts to suffer, so keep the greenstuff in proportion, and make sure that it is absolutely fresh with no mouldy bits, frost free and completely dry. Hay is often overlooked as a food for rabbits and guinea pigs but it should be given to them.

All these small animals have black or blackish hard droppings, so if you find that the faeces have become a funny colour or are of a loose consistency and the animal's anus is a mess, you know something is wrong. Correct the diet and check the hygiene, and if you still cannot solve the problem talk to your vet. I should add that rabbits pass soft faeces at night only, which they eat to produce hard pellets the following day.

Overgrown Teeth. Another thing that can go wrong if a diet has far too much greenstuff is that the two long incisor teeth at the front of the mouth can become overgrown. If this happens, ask your vet to clip them but do not try it yourself — just imagine if an inexperienced person tried to cut a chunk off your front teeth.

Heatstroke. Guinea Pigs can suffer from heatstroke so do not site their cages where this might happen, and never keep them in a garage as car fumes could kill off your Guinea Pigs. They are not the easiest of animals to treat when they have infectious diseases because, unlike many mammals, they can be killed by doses of some of the common antibiotics.

Myxomatosis. Myxomatosis is a horrid disease that was introduced, by people, to Britain in the 1950s, specifically to reduce the wild rabbit population. It was initially very effective, but what a nasty way of killing rabbits. It still flares up sometimes and is transmitted by fleas so during the summer your rabbit in the garden can become infected. Some years ago several local rabbit owners asked me to look at their sick pets, all of which turned out to have myxy. I discovered that the local waterboard has been scything the long grass from the sea walls and it was left to dry for some days before being carted away. In the meantime someone had discovered this marvellous supply of hay and had started selling it to local rabbit owners. Originally rabbit fleas lived in rabbit burrows but as the disease killed off all the rabbits the fleas no longer had a food supply and some of them had adapted to living in long grass where they could jump onto any passing animals. Some of these would be rabbits and some would be other species that subsequently visited rabbit warrens which meant that this new strain of fleas was able to survive. Anyhow, this free hay was riddled with myxy-carrying fleas. This is a splendid example of the unforeseen consequences of interfering with nature.

If your rabbit contracts myxomatosis, have it killed by your vet for the suffering is protracted and awful. The animal looks generally unwell, the eyes look as though they are going to pop out of their sockets, there is a runny nose and the whole head swells and the skin between the ears might split.

Ear Canker. Canker is caused by a small parasite that results in brown sticky muck partially filling the ear. It can be treated with a powder from the vet.

BIRDS — CAGED

If you have a sick bird, treat it fast. Due to a bird's high metabolic rate and body temperature, a sick bird usually either recovers or dies quickly.

Colds and Chills. Put the bird in a hospital cage — if you are quick enough it ought to recover. Move the original cage in the meantime to a draught-free place.

Diarrhoea or Constipation. Probably due to incorrect feeding or poor hygiene. In the case of the former add finely powdered charcoal, cuttlefish bone or grated yolk of hard boiled egg to the diet. For constipation, add a couple of drops of oil to the food. Put the bird in the hospital cage. If there is blood in the droppings see the vet as you might need an antibiotic for the bird.

Scaly Face or Scaly Legs. This disease of budgies is caused by a mite and looks as the name suggests. If caught early enough the infected parts can be dabbed with turpentine (not white spirit) on a soft paintbrush, but do be careful not to get the stuff in eyes, nostrils or mouth.

Feather Plucking. I am convinced that feather plucking is most often due to boredom or stress. It can also be due to parasites, for which your vet will give you sprays, or a lack of vitamins A and D in the diet, in which case a suitable supplement should be added to the food.

Egg Binding. If a hen cannot pass an egg for some reason she needs help fast or you will lose her. The first sign is the bird simply looking extremely miserable. If you suspect egg binding, pick her from the perch very carefully and, as gently as you can, feel the abdomen. You will probably feel the egg. Whatever you do, do not break it or you can end up with all sorts of nasty things happening inside the bird. Having said that I know someone who took an egg bound budgie to a nameless vet who told her that the cure was simple. He crushed the egg through the abdominal wall and told her that the bird would soon pass it. It died.

Hold the bird with her vent over a bowl of hot water so that the steam rises and softens the skin. Warm a bit of cooking oil so that it is tepid, and using a soft paintbrush, dip it in the oil and gently insert it into the cloaca to lubricate it. Put the bird in a hospital cage and hope. Do not keep on with the paintbrush operation or the trauma can kill a small bird, and furthermore all the feathers become covered in oil however careful you are and when the bird preens she will ingest all this oil which will be no good to her. Any clean cooking oil will do, except for mustard oil which is an irritant. If the bird is a fairly large, tough one you might be lucky and she will pass the egg, but to be perfectly honest a very small bird is most unlikely to survive all this.

Anaemia. If you are feeding your bird correctly and it becomes anaemic you are probably having trouble with parasites of some sort. The bird will look unwell and any visible skin will appear pale and the bird might scratch itself frequently. If the bird is in a cage, the culprit is likely to be red mite, which are only red when they are full of a host's blood. At other times they are whitish grey. They do not live on the bird but in cracks in the cage from which they emerge at night for a feed. If you suspect red mite, cover the cage front one evening with a white cloth. In the morning most of the mites should be sitting on it. Remove it quickly and burn it, and repeat the operation the following night to get rid of any remaining mites.

Mouth Fungus. Some of the nectar-feeding birds sometimes develop a nasty fungal growth inside the beak that can grow so large as to prevent the bird from feeding. Gently and carefully remove the fungus with cotton buds and tweezers and ask your vet for something to treat it with. This usually works but sometimes it is recurrent. The only thing to do is to repeat the treatment and eventually the fungus simply disappears.

Eye Troubles. Eye troubles are usually the result of injury from another bird, a sharp piece of wire or something similar. However, if the eyes start to go opaque and the bird cannot see very well, try dipping a clean soft paintbrush in some halibut liver oil and, gently opening the bird's beak, rub the bristles against the sharp edge of the bill so that the oil trickles down the throat. Repeat the next day, and often you will find that the condition improves. Do not repeat it again, or the bird will end up with digestive troubles.

Transit Disease. If you buy a newly imported bird it might be suffering from what is called Transit Disease in the trade. There is no such thing really, but it is a convenient way of describing the condition of freshly imported birds that will be suffering from stress, due to fear and overcrowding, colds and chills, sneezes from breathing dust in a confined space, lack of food, dehydration and gastric infections from contaminated food. Keep the bird warm and quiet in quarantine, and treat each condition separately as it occurs.

BIRDS – WILD
It is against the law to keep native birds in captivity unless they have been bred in captivity from captive-bred parents, and they have been close-ringed shortly after hatching. Similarly, it is also an offence to sell native species unless they are aviary bred and close-ringed (ABCR). The only time native birds may be kept in captivity is while they are recovering from accident, disease or injury, after which they must be returned to the wild.

The following information, therefore, is designed to help on those occasions when an injured bird or orphaned chick is brought to you for treatment.

Chicks of all Species. Each spring many people find little feathered chicks sitting all by themselves on the ground and cheeping plaintively. If you discover one, move it out of danger if it is somewhere like the middle of a road but otherwise leave it strictly alone. If someone brings such a chick to you, tell them to put it back. The mother bird will almost certainly find it and continue to rear it successfully. If it is known for certain that the parents are dead you can try and rear it yourself, but it will probably die: little chicks are extraordinarily difficult to rear. When very young, bald chicks are found, put them back into the nest and, if the nest is damaged, repair it as best you can and replace it.

On the occasion that you do have to hand rear a baby bird it is essential to discover what species it is, and what it eats. After identifying your orphan, put it into a makeshift nest to prevent it flapping about all over the place, inside a hospital cage heated to 32°C (90°F), or failing that, somewhere that will provide similar conditions. You will also need to study the feeding behaviour of the species in question so that you can duplicate it as far as possible. Some baby birds shove their heads down the parent's throat to extract semi-masticated food, whereas others peck around on the ground behind their mother. Do not imagine that you can rear everything on bread and milk; it will not work. If a bird eats insects, feed it insects: if it feeds on mashed-up fish, offer it mashed-up fish. Sometimes, holding a morsel of food above the chick's beak in a pair of blunt ended forceps and waggling it about will stimulate the bird to take it, whereas if it is held motionless it might be ignored. Sometimes tapping the bird's beak gently with the food might encourage it to gape for food. It is useless to imagine that you can get away with two or three large meals a day — baby birds feed almost constantly throughout daylight, and this is what you will have to duplicate. It is a thankless task, and almost certainly doomed to failure.

A chick that is determined to starve itself can be gently force fed but the added trauma is not conducive to success. To force feed a bird, carefully open the beak while you hold the bird still, poke the food in and gently push it down beyond the back of the tongue. Let the beak close and massage the lump of food down the neck, otherwise the chick will vomit as soon as you release it. Sometimes, if the bird will not swallow, a few drops of water trickled down the throat with an eye dropper will encourage it to do so. Throughout the time you are hand-rearing the bird you will have to gently clean the plumage of spilt food, and remove any faeces, for if the bird is allowed to become matted and horrible it is less likely to survive. A general all-purpose rearing food is hard boiled egg mashed up with wholemeal biscuit to a crumbly consistency.

Once the chick has grown a bit you will need to put dishes of food in the cage and help it to learn to feed for itself. At the same time slowly reduce the temperature of the hospital cage until it is the same as the ambient temperature, and when you are positive that the orphan is self-sufficient, release it into the wild. You will soon discover that big, tough birds like gulls are the easiest to rear. If you have to hand-rear any birds of prey, do not feed meat on its own — the birds need roughage and if you do not have access to chicks or mice, you can snip bits of hair from dogs, cats or friends, or sometimes find sheep's wool on barbed wire fences. A little bit of any of these added to butcher's meat will make the difference between death and survival.

Injuries. Virtually all the injuries that you will come across in wild birds will be of one of four types. The commonest is a broken limb; for treatment see the chapter on first aid. The next most common injury is concussion, caused by the bird flying into a car or a sheet of glass. The latter happens frequently during the summer when to a bird, houses that have long rooms with windows in both the front wall and the back appear to be a through flyway. The concussed bird usually shows no sign of damage though the head might flop about as though it is too heavy for the neck to support. The eyes are often half closed and the bird usually sits quite still, though sometimes it scrabbles about in unco-ordinated fashion for a few seconds.

Treatment is simple: put the bird in a warm, quiet box and leave it in semi darkness. Usually it recovers in a few minutes and when it is completely well you can let it go, though if all this happens late in the evening I prefer to wait till the morning to release the bird. If a bird does not recover from this type of injury it almost always dies quickly.

The third type of injury, which is not as common as one might think, is holes caused by cats' teeth. They are quite distinct and readily identifiable. When the injuries are in muscle tissue, clean the surroundings well with an antiseptic and put the bird in a quiet hospital cage to recover, using some antibiotic from your vet to prevent infection. You might be lucky and the bird will survive, but if the teeth have entered the thoracic cavity, the abdomen or the skull, the only thing to do is ask your vet to kill the bird painlessly. When you start to clean up the tooth holes, make sure you do not miss any of them. There will be four of them but some might be hidden by feathers. You can work out where each should be if you visualise the position of the cat's mouth.

The fourth type of injury is that inflicted by fish hooks and tangles of nylon that have been left hanging about by thoughtless anglers. A hook that has penetrated the skin has usually gone in and out again. Cut it off below the barbs and carefully pull it out. Cut away all nylon line and treat cuts made by it with antiseptic, and if infection has set in, with antibiotics from your vet.

Oiled Birds. Birdy people who live by the sea will at some time be brought an oiled bird to save. If the bird is completely covered in the stuff, the chances of recovery are virtually nil. If only half the bird is contaminated, it might recover if the accident has only recently happened; but if the bird has been flopping about in a glued-up state for a week, unable to feed, and preening itself until the gut is full of the foul, black substance, its chances are slim. A fat, healthy bird that is not too oiled stands a good chance of recovery.

Before you start to handle an oiled bird, make sure you are

wearing some old clothes and a waterproof apron: crude oil is disgusting stuff that gets everywhere. In addition to cleaning your patient, the important thing is to clear any oil from his gut, so wrap him up in an old piece of thick cloth so that he can neither preen nor spread oil all over your furniture, and feed him some long, thin strips of white fish. You might need to open his beak and push the fish past the back of his throat to start with, and massage his neck to encourage him to swallow. By the way, when you are handling birds such as gulls and herons, watch your eyes. They can stab faster than you can move when they set their mind to it, and they always go for the eyes.

After some feeds, your patient should have evacuated all the oil from his gut, as you can tell by keeping an eye on the faeces. When all traces of black have disappeared, if the bird is fit and strong when you received it, you can clean it immediately. Gently put it into a large bowl containing a one per cent solution of cheap washing-up liquid in tepid water: expensive liquids are not so good as they contain more perfumes and dyes and other chemicals which are not good to ingest. You would not believe the mess you are going to get into during the operation, so set up all your equipment somewhere that will not suffer. Gently wash the bird, using a toothbrush where necessary, and open the tail and wing feathers so that the detergent penetrates everywhere. When you have removed as much oil as you can, rinse the bird in clean, tepid water. A shower attachment is good for this if you can be sure that the temperature is not going to fluctuate between freezing cold and far too hot. When you have finished, put the bird in a box and clean the bowl out and re-fill it with the detergent mixture and start again. You might well need three of these baths in succession before the bird is clean, and when you have finished release the patient into a small pen where it can wash as often as it likes in a container of clean water. I use my greenhouse for this. A week or two later the plumage ought to be waterproof once more and the bird fat and well, and ready to be released. Take him somewhere suitable before you let him go, and check to see there is no crude oil in the vicinity. The satisfaction of watching the bird fly away is enormous.

Whenever you have an avian patient to treat you should first of all feel the breast bone. You know from your supermarket chicken how the breast should look — a hard ridge down the middle with a plump muscle either side. If it has been a while since the bird has eaten properly these two areas of muscle will be wasted and concave and this means that the bird is very weak. At this stage further trauma could be fatal, so unless there are overwhelming reasons for handling the bird or commencing treatment immediately, it is far better to keep the patient warm and quiet while you fatten him up for a few days.

Birds are not easy patients, and you might find that, despite all you do, a time will come when apathy sets in. No interest is shown in anything, nothing is eaten and the head slowly sinks to the floor each time you lift it up. Once a casualty is at this stage there is no chance of saving it and you should ask your vet to kill it.

If you ever need any help or advice on wild animals of any sort that are brought to you for treatment, or if you feel that you cannot handle them yourself, contact your local wildlife hospital. There is sure to be one in your area and the people there will help all they can. If you do not know where it is, ask your vet or RSPCA or PDSA inspector, or the police station or library might be able to tell you whom to telephone.

REPTILES

Newly imported reptiles frequently carry a good load of internal parasites. In captivity, the internal parasites seem to cause no problems and frequently disappear after a while. When reptiles first arrive from abroad they almost invariably are crawling with external parasites as well. There are all sorts of ways of dealing with these, but the method that causes least distress to the host and is the most effective of all is to keep a suitable sized block of Vapona in your animal room, or cut one into pieces — while wearing rubber gloves as they are highly toxic — and put a piece in each tank protected in such a way that the reptile cannot touch it. That will soon get rid of your parasites.

Abscesses and Bumblefoot. Bacterial infections are common in some lizards, but a vet should be able to sort them out for you with a little Betadine. Both these conditions start as soft lumps which continue to grow until they burst or are treated, though it must be said that individuals occasionally seem to be prone to frequent fresh eruptions.

Respiratory Infections. Infections of the breathing apparatus can be the result of a variety of organisms and need treating by your vet.

Gout. Reptiles must have adequate sunlight. Failing that (and in Britain there is not usually enough), tanks should be fitted with ultraviolet light tubes such as Phillips CSR O24 Black Light U/V tubes. Ultraviolet rays are essential for the assimilation of vitamin D3 which serves as a vehicle for the proper uptake of calcium and phosphorus. Dietary supplements such as Vionate or SA 37, which can be obtained from your vet, should be given regularly together with calcium carbonate and vitamin D3 in the proportions two parts calcium carbonate to one part D3.

Mouth Rot. Snakes sometimes suffer from a fungal infection in the mouth that can cause considerable distress, and grow to such an extent that the whole shape of the mouth is distorted and the snake cannot feed properly. The condition seems to be related to the eating of mice. If you see a snake in this condition at a dealer's premises leave it where it is. If one of your snakes develops mouth rot, clean it gently as well as you can, removing the cheesy fungus, and treat the mouth with Betadine from your vet.

AMPHIBIANS

Red Leg. The disease most feared by amphibian keepers is red leg which will wipe out a whole collection in no time. Early symptoms are red flushes on the abdomen and back legs. It is thought to be caused by a bacterium and is a direct result of dirty conditions. Improve your hygiene and take infected animals to your vet.

Skin Lesions and Disintegration of the Mouth Parts. These distressing conditions are caused by lack of hygiene and can be treated by your vet if caught early enough. Whatever you do, do not let your amphibians sit around in frog urine. Amphibians absorb chemicals, including toxins, through the skin and you are asking for trouble if you leave puddles of urine in the tank.

INVERTEBRATES

External Parasites. The only common condition that you are able to do anything about in invertebrate pets is infestations of mites. Beetles are particularly prone to having quantities of these animals attached to the underside where the legs join the thorax. You cannot employ an insecticide or you will kill the host as well, but I find that if you carefully touch each mite with the hairs of a soft paintbrush dipped in cooking oil it will drop off in a day or two. Take care you do not cover the beetle in oil, or you might kill it.

6
CONSERVATION AND BREEDING

CONSERVATION

Years ago when I used to give talks about wildlife, I was sometimes asked why it mattered whether the Giant Panda disappeared or the Mauritis Pink Pigeon became extinct. That was the point at which I put on a serious face and muttered platitudinous remarks about morals and aesthetics. My answer was adequate, but I always felt that it was incomplete. Luckily, in the last 20 odd years, considerable amounts of scientific work have been done so that anyone in the same position can now give a positive scientific answer to a question on the need for conservation. Whenever a species of animal, or plant for that matter, is removed for ever it leaves a gap in the ecosystem, so the chances are that the animals which depended on its existence will also be affected. The now extinct animal might have been the major prey of another species. It might also have been the host to parasites that lived in its fur or laid eggs in its nest. There are all sorts of ways in which it might have had a relationship with other animals, so as soon as it was exterminated these creatures with which it had such a relationship would be affected as well. Before long their populations could start to decline so that animals relying on their existence would be in trouble too. Eventually a whole chain is affected and the whole balance of the environment would be altered. Ultimately, humans too can start to suffer and if you doubt that, look at specific examples of how people's interference in nature has resulted in distress or tragedy for them.

There are signs that our thoughtless exploitation of wildlife is beginning to have a deleterious effect on the planet. Weather patterns are changing and if the destruction of rain forests continues it would seem as though the oxygen levels in the atmosphere

116

could start to fall. Today, more and more people are becoming aware of the need for conservation, not just on moral and aesthetic grounds but for practical reasons as well. Sadly, the greater part of the profits from all this senseless destruction goes to a comparatively few extremely wealthy companies which make such colossal sums of money that no one can possibly convince them to stop. I know the whole argument is so complex that there are no facile answers, but the points of discussion will soon be nothing more than academic. Unless the destruction is halted now, and quickly reversed, it will be too late.

So if you keep a species of wild animal, or a dying breed of domestic animal, do please keep a pair or a breeding group and do what you can to encourage the animals to reproduce. Far sighted people have been setting up gene banks for a number of years of varieties of domestic animals that have fallen from favour. Apart from the pleasure they give, in the future when a technologically produced hybrid begins to weaken or prove to be susceptible to some pathological condition, new vigour can be bred into it from one of these gene banks. I might add that if it was not for such enthusiasts, these breeds would have been lost for ever in some cases, as no official stocks were maintained.

As to imported exotic animals, I am convinced that the day will soon come when the importation of wild animals will be forbidden. Even if that does not happen, many species that fanciers now take for granted are going to become scarce in captivity as they disappear from the wild, mainly because their habitats are being destroyed at such a rate. It seems to me imperative, therefore, that strenuous efforts must be made now to breed every species in captivity. In the early 1960s, you could buy Spice Birds at a pet shop in Britain for seven shillings (35 pence) a pair. They are now about £12 and I think that this can only be a good thing as it restricts impulse buying considerably.

BREEDING

Before we begin to talk about how to encourage your animals to breed, if you are keeping a pet of a type which is already abundant, then do think very carefully before you embark on a breeding programme. The world is full of mongrel dogs and cats and gerbils and rabbits and very often it is literally impossible to give them away. It is not responsible to produce baby animals if you are going to have to get a vet or the RSPCA, or the PDSA, to kill them, and it is even less responsible if you allow your pet to wander free to breed promiscuously. If you have a single pet dog or cat, have it neutered; it is not being kind to neglect having the

117

operation performed, and one can disregard in confidence all the old wives' tales about an animal getting fat. Nor is there any truth in the supposition that an animal ought not to be neutered until after it has had a first litter.

Some animals in captivity will breed so readily that they require no special conditions, others will be rather more demanding and some need highly specific conditions before they will even think of mating, and some have never been known to breed in captivity. Twenty years ago this last was true of many animals, but as we learn more about their requirements many species are breeding ever more readily in captivity these days.

Whatever you are breeding, you ought to keep records. If you don't, you are bound to regret it the following year when you need to check something, and keeping records makes the whole business so much more interesting. When you can look back over ten years of record keeping, you will be surprised at how much you would otherwise have forgotten, and how much you have learnt. There is no reason why the storing of information should be a chore if you get a book and divide each page into appropriate columns. Each day all you need to do is scribble one or two words in each column, and maybe a sentence in the general remarks section. This way, as an animal keeper, you will gain experience and acquire considerable knowledge. Much of it is taken for granted, and it is often not till years later that you might come across an article in a journal questioning or neglecting some fact that you thought everyone knew. If all your information is readily available, you can write and add your expertise to the general knowledge on the topic. If you subsequently write articles or books, or give talks, all the accumulated information will prove invaluable. Some months ago somebody was writing a book about snakes and grumbled to me that he could find no information on the seasonal fluctuations in a snake's appetite. Luckily I had kept such records and from my data the author was able to prepare a table for his book. Astonishingly, there was no published information on the topic.

Watch your animals, write down what they do however trivial it may appear at the time, and your hobby will become infinitely more rewarding and enjoyable, but if you forget to record anything for a few days, when you get around to the job leave a gap for the missed days, unless you can honestly remember what happened. Your record will be more valuable than if you make it up or write what you think may have occurred.

Dogs
Never let the breeding of your dog be an accident. If you do not

want puppies, have your dog neutered, but assuming that you would like your dog to breed and you know positively that you have homes for the puppies, if your dog has a pedigree, check that the other prospective parent has one also. Unless both dogs are registered with the Kennel Club, you will not be able to register the puppies. If your dog is a mongrel, pedigrees are not going to worry you.

When a bitch is mature she will be ready to mate twice a year when she comes into season. You can tell when this happens by watching for the few drops of blood that she loses from her vulva for two or three days. At this time you will notice that her genitals are swollen. If you have had your bitch since she was little it is as well not to mate her at her first season as this could result in a small litter of not too healthy puppies, but her second or subsequent seasons are perfectly all right. She will be most fertile ten or twelve days after bleeding has started, and at this time take her to the home of the male dog who is to father her pups. Before taking her to be mated, you should have had her wormed and cleared of all fleas and other parasites as these can be passed to newborn pups. Keep an eye on the two of them while they are together, in case the female acts aggressively towards the dog, but all being well, a short time after meeting each other the male will mount the bitch. After a minute or so they might separate or the male may dismount and the two will stand facing in opposite directions like a pair of bizarre bookends. The penis of the male is still inside the female but do not try and separate them: this is quite normal and by interfering you could cause damage. Twenty or thirty minutes later when the penis has relaxed, the two dogs will separate and you can take the bitch home.

Do not be surprised if there is no sign of pregnancy — plenty of bitches go right through to birth without revealing their condition, but after about a month take your animal to your vet who will confirm the pregnancy for you. The puppies will be born about 63 days after conception, and from about halfway through the pregnancy the bitch will require more food — up to half as much again as she normally eats. Give her lots of small meals full of good quality protein, together with a vitamin supplement from your vet.

As the time of the birth approaches, keep an eye on your dog. Some bitches show many more signs that birth is imminent than others. Leave her alone to get on with it — lots of people fussing about will only create stress for the dog. All you need to do, if she is a long haired variety, is to gently trim the hair away from the vulva and the nipples, and prepare a suitably quiet, peaceful place for the birth, and line it with lots of newspaper. Do make sure that you introduce the dog to it well before the puppies are due or she might give birth on your favourite armchair, and that can be messy. A cardboard box of the right size is often the best place: it is secluded and warm.

Try not to worry when your dog is about to have a litter, or you may transmit your concern to the dog — she has enough on her mind without wondering what you are going to do next. If she is a mongrel there are likely to be fewer problems than with a pedigree dog, but if things get out of hand all you have to do is call your vet.

All the books about breeding dogs will tell you the signs to look for: a lowering of the bitch's temperature, persistent panting, development of the mammaries, refusal to eat during the final 24 hours and a green discharge a couple of hours before the birth. I daresay that the professional dog breeder does keep a check on all that lot, but I find the reality is that one minute your dog is sitting in her box quietly licking herself, then five minutes later the first soggy little puppy is scrabbling about, while the mother licks it clean, and soon afterwards it is fighting its way to the nearest nipple. Over the next few hours the rest of the litter will be born. Each baby will have a separate placenta and the mother will probably eat them. When it is over, keep an eye on all the dogs for the first few days to make sure they are well. Do not be surprised if the mother has diarrhoea or vomits, nor if she is crotchety and protective, and for this reason keep small children away from the litter. You may find that you have up to a dozen fat furry 'sausages', but they put on weight very quickly, and to enable the mother to produce sufficient milk she will need up to three times her usual food intake. Before too long you will be taking the puppies to the vet for their injections.

Cats

Some years ago not very far from my home, an old woman living alone, died. She left behind 69 very wild cats which had to be killed because they were flea-infested, worm-ridden, scrawny savages which their owner's next of kin did not want. There had originally been one, which had kittens ...

Cats breed so prolifically that it is almost impossible to give them away these days and it is not nice to have to kill litter after litter of healthy babies; so, unless you are deliberately breeding pedigree cats, have your pets neutered. If you do not, however careful you are, before very long your cat will be fathering, or giving birth to more unwanted kittens. A cat's pregnancy lasts about 60 to 70 days. After the kittens are born there is a period of lactation which lasts six weeks or so, and less than a month later the female is ready to breed again, and a female that is not allowed to mate will drive you crazy until she does — you will have no doubt at all that she is in season. Her mate will recognise the female's mating posture and will copulate with her, repeating the operation many times during this period if the cats are not separated by circumstances. You may notice your cat's nipples becoming pink at about the third week of pregnancy; later on you may observe a weight gain, but you are just as likely to miss it, especially with long-haired varieties. You should now make a suitable place for the cat to have her kittens. A cardboard box is fine for this and it should be thickly lined with newspaper and put in a dark warm spot which is a favourite of the cat so that she can get used to it well before the birth.

You are unlikely to have any problems with the actual birth, though sometimes the whole business does seem to go on a bit as baby after baby comes tumbling out. Each one is licked clean and before long they are all fighting their way to a nipple, squeaking loudly the while. If you have any worries, contact your vet; but even if all went well, talk to him about injections for the kittens, which are essential.

Rabbits

Be warned that baby rabbits are impossible to give away, and when you remember that a doe can have 70 offspring in three years you will begin to appreciate the problem. Unless you really feel that you want your rabbits to breed, keep does together. If you keep bucks together, they will fight, if you keep both sexes in the same enclosure, you will soon have an awful lot of rabbits. Does become ready to conceive as a direct result of attention from a buck rather than through seasons, as do dogs, so if you are going to breed from your rabbits, take the female to the male and it is likely that they will be mating in a short while. After a second copulation take the doe back to her own home. If she is pregnant she will give birth about a month later. Give her peace and quiet and leave her alone with plenty of soft hay as bedding and she will take care of everything herself. Do not be tempted to investigate or she may abandon her kittens or even eat them but you will soon be aware if she has given birth as you will hear the babies squeaking.

While the female is feeding her litter give her as much food as she can eat and keep the place clean, but do leave the nest strictly alone. After a week and a half the kittens' eyes will open and a few days after that they will leave the nest. When the babies are about seven weeks old they are ready for weaning, which you can achieve by removing the doe. Check the sexes of your offspring before too long as rabbits can begin breeding at the age of six weeks, though it is best to wait until they are a few months old.

Guinea Pigs (Cavies)

One of the reasons that Guinea Pigs are so popular as pets is that they are inexpensive; the reason they are inexpensive is because they breed so easily; this in turn means that it is really difficult for a breeder to get rid of any baby Guinea Pigs — so before you think about breeding from your animals, find homes for the babies. A female could have 20 offspring during her life, and it might be easy to get rid of one animal, but have you really got twenty friends who desperately want a pet cavy?

To sex a Guinea Pig, examine the genital region closely. Unlike many mammals there is not much difference in the distance between the anus and the genitals, but the female cavy has a genital slit while the male's opening is round. Males, which are called boars, sometimes fight so it is not a good idea to keep them together but one of them can be kept with up to five sows if their enclosure is large enough, and he will serve all of them. A sow may well be sexually mature after a month but she should not be mated until she is at least three months old, and the male should also be no younger than this.

If your Guinea Pigs live outdoors they are unlikely to breed during the colder part of the year, but if you keep them in a warm building they will breed throughout the winter. The length of the pregnancy is about 63 days, and I feel that if both parents live in a small enclosure, it is best to remove the father when the female becomes pregnant, though if there is a community of animals in a large pen there is no reason to disturb it. Guinea Pigs have a surprisingly long pregnancy for rodents but when the young are born, they are well furred, their eyes are open and within 48 hours they can eat solid food, though they still need milk from their mother. Baby Guinea Pigs are sweet, just like clockwork toys, but they grow fast and by the time they are four weeks old they are ready to be weaned and the mother should be removed. During the pregnancy you should feed the female plenty of hay and vegetables but do not increase the quantity of cereals as otherwise there can be difficulties with the actual birth. All pregnant animals should have peace and quiet to get on with making babies and this is especially true of Guinea Pigs, which are rather nervous animals.

Hamsters

Hamsters will fight savagely if they are kept together. This means that if you are thinking of breeding from your hamster you must either have a lot of cages or a lot of hamster-loving friends with a single cage each.

Young hamsters are very difficult to sex, but adult hamsters in breeding condition are no problem as the testes of the male are prominent and the female has two rows of teats along her abdomen. It is best not to mate hamsters before the female is 14 weeks old and the male about six weeks older, and hamsters are not long lived so that by the time the animals are a year old their useful breeding life is about over. A female comes into season every four or five days but unless a mating is timed just right, you will have a fight on your hands. Some people suggest putting each hamster in the opposite cage for a while so that they can get used to each other's scent, and then replace them in their own cages which should be stood alongside each other in order that the two animals can get used to each other. Whether you swop them over or just put the cages together you are wasting your time when the female is not in season, but if she is and there is no apparent animosity between the two hamsters, lay a pair of stout gloves beside the cages and put the female with the male — do not even think of doing it the other way around — and hope. If the female attacks the male put a glove on and take her out again, and try again on the next evening since most matings take place at this time. If she stands perfectly still with her tail in the air, the male can mount her. Separate them after 15 minutes. Hamsters do not bite very often but they might do so at this time, when they are nervous and excitable, which is why I suggested the gloves. But if you use them, do be aware that you cannot handle an animal so sensitively when you are wearing gloves.

Four days after the first mating put the cages alongside each other once more. If the female is aggressive to the male you can be pretty sure that she is pregnant, whereas if she indicates that she might want to mate again, the whole performance was unsuccessful and you will have to repeat the mating. If she is pregnant the female will give birth 16 days later.

Halfway through the pregnancy clean the mother's cage and give her plenty of extra bedding including hay, and ample supplies of food. After that leave the cage alone apart from removing any wet floor-covering each day. A litter consists of between six and twelve babies which are born blind and bald. Leave them alone for the first week and then just have a brief look to check that all is well. Throughout the period during which the mother is nursing her offspring she should be given plenty of milk to drink. This should be supplied in a water bottle clipped to the front of the cage; a dish soon becomes filled up with all sorts of rubbish and it might be tipped up by the hamster standing on the edge or trying

123

to burrow underneath it. The babies will leave the nest at about two weeks and they can be weaned by removing them from the mother a week later. A week after that the males must be separated from the females or you might end up with another generation. It is not a bad idea to isolate each animal anyway at this stage because before long they will realise that their role in life is to hate each other.

Chipmunks

Chipmunks are very active little animals that need a lot of room; surprisingly, they have bred in cages, but a pair is more likely to do so in an aviary. A male in breeding condition has prominent testes, but at other times chipmunks can be sexed, as with other rodents, by the greater distance between anus and genitals in the male.

A good warm, draught-free nest box, big enough to take a lot of nest material should be supplied and a separate sleeping compartment must be provided for the male who will be removed while the female nurses the young. Chipmunks mate in February or March, and a pregnancy lasts from between 31 to 40 days. A litter of between four and eight baby chipmunks will be produced. They are blind and pretty well hairless at birth though even then one can see stripes on the little bodies. It is important not to disturb the nest or clean out the nest box until the youngsters are at least four weeks old.

Mice

Rats will tolerate other rats but if you put a new mouse into an existing community it will be attacked, so if you must do this put the newcomer's cage alongside the community cage so that he can be examined and sniffed before he is introduced.

Mice can be sexed by examining the distance between the anus and the genital opening. In an adult male this is about 12 mm ($\frac{1}{2}$ in) and only half that in the female. This distance is covered with fur in the case of the former, but not in the latter. Females come into season every fourth or fifth night. If they are mated at this time they will have between four and ten babies about three weeks later. It is best to keep the pregnant female on her own, but do not handle her during the last two weeks of pregnancy or you can do her a lot of harm. Give her plenty of nesting material and plenty of food, and if she will take it a little milk in a container that cannot be tipped up or filled with rubbish from the cage floor. Baby mice have no hair at birth, and they are blind but they grow fast and ought not to be handled until they have left the nest. They can be weaned between three and four weeks by separating them from the mother. Separate the males from the females before the age of six weeks, or they will start breeding, and it is better to wait until they are ten weeks old.

Rats

Baby rats are not the easiest animals to find homes for, so do think hard before you breed any.

Rats are gregarious animals and are perfectly happy to live with other rats, so they can be kept together in any combination provided that you do not overstock a cage. Rats can be sexed from birth by looking at the distance between anus and genitals: in males this is about half as much again as in females. Rats will breed throughout the year so that females are pregnant pretty well all the time. If you have two or more rats living together you can leave them to get on with breeding on their own, which they will do enthusiastically, but the best way might be to remove a pregnant doe to another cage so that she can have some peace during her pregnancy, which lasts about 21 days, at the end of which she will produce between four and ten babies which are naked and blind when they are born. It is best not to disturb them until they leave the nest, and they will be weaned after about four weeks.

Gerbils

Baby gerbils are difficult to find homes for, so before you start to breed from yours, check that you can get rid of the babies to suitable homes. Sexing adult gerbils is not difficult. The back end of the male is more tapered than the rounded rump of the female, and the distance between the anus and the genital opening is much longer in the male.

Breeding gerbils is an infinitely less harrowing business than breeding hamsters provided that you remember one thing and that is that a pair ought to be introduced to each other before they are six weeks old. They will then live happily together for life and you ought not have any difficulties. Try and introduce them as adults and they will fight, but if they have been together since they were little you can leave both parents to get on with breeding and raising the offspring without worrying.

A female comes into season every six days right through the year, and when mating has taken place she will be pregnant for about 24 days. She will probably have five or six babies which are hairless and unable to see. As with all animals, leave the mother in peace to get on with things. If you disturb her or handle the babies she might eat them. By the time the young gerbils are about three weeks old their eyes are open and they are properly furry. When they are nearly six weeks old remove the youngsters and ask their

125

new owners to come and collect them. The female meanwhile is probably pregnant again; she comes into season shortly after a litter is born and will mate at this time, but gerbils are capable of 'delayed implantation' which means that while she is suckling one lot of babies a female will not begin her next pregnancy, so to speak, until they are out of the way so that her second litter will not appear until six weeks after she was impregnated.

Goats

If you have a female goat and are thinking of breeding, and you will certainly need to have her mated periodically if you want the milk, you should be aware that if the kids turn out to be male you are probably going to have to ask your vet to kill them. You cannot keep lots of billies together, which is why nobody wants them.

Goats ought not to be mated until they are over 18 months old, and when a nanny is old enough she will have regular breeding cycles of 21 days. Mating will take place about the middle of one of these cycles, usually in the autumn. When she is ready to mate, your goat will let you know by bleating and twitching and wandering about unable to settle. If you look at her vulva at this time you will find it swollen and reddish.

Few nannies look progressively more pregnant, so all you can do is hope, and while you are waiting, give her plenty of food and exercise. When she is about to kid, make sure that she has ample clean bedding, and beyond that you are unlikely to have to do anything else. Goats will generally give birth to two kids which must be left with their mother for at least the first few days so that they can stock up on antibodies via their mother's milk. After that you can leave them where they are, or you can hand rear them which will result in tamer kids and more milk from the nanny, but I can promise you that hand rearing goats is no fun.

Bushbabies

Captive breeding of bushbabies is increasing but it would be wrong to think it is common. A pair or one male and two females should be kept together, but these animals are notoriously difficult to sex. Mature males fight like mad, if that helps! Gestation is about 16 to 18 weeks and if you think your female is pregnant it is wise to remove the father until after the babies are born. There are usually two, which are born furry and able to see. The mother carries her family around with her for some weeks though, as they grow, the babies will leave her for an occasional short trip of exploration. They are eating more or less the same food as their parents by the time they are two or three months old, when they reach adult size, although they will still suckle from the mother for a while after that. They are sexually mature at nine months old.

Budgerigars

A cock Budgerigar has a blue cere which is the bare skin situated between the top of the beak and the front edge of the feathers. A hen's cere is brown, and the time to think about breeding is when these ceres are brightly coloured, the birds are healthy and tight-feathered, and should be at least eight months old. Breeding starts any time between December and early spring. You can certainly breed from budgies if you keep them in a large flight cage, but they will do better if you have an aviary. The first essential for a successful breeding season is a nest box, or if you have an aviary, several nest boxes — more than one for each pair of birds — which should be situated as high as possible, sheltered from the weather and placed in such a position that the sliding door can be opened without disturbance. A budgerigar nest box is about 23 × 13 × 13 cm (10 × 5 × 5 in) and is made of plywood with an entrance hole at one end. The other end consists of a sliding glass panel and also a sliding wooden panel. The floor of the nest box is fitted with what is known as a 'concave', a thick slice of wood with a shallow concave cut into the top, which is where the eggs are laid. No nesting material is added.

When the birds are in breeding condition put them together if they do not already live in the same cage or aviary flight. They should start to court by snuggling up together on the perch and rubbing beaks. The cock will also feed the hen with regurgitated seed. However, if the two birds just do not get on, you can do one of three things; replace the cock and try again, house the birds where they can see another breeding pair which should stimulate them, or failing that put a mirror or two in such a position that the birds can see one or more reflections of themselves. Budgies are gregarious birds and will breed more readily if they are part of a flock.

Budgerigar breeders pair up their birds to breed offspring of a specific colour and if you are interested in this aspect of the fancy, you will find relevant information about the genetics involved in a specialist book about breeding budgies. If you just want your pet budgies to breed, it does not matter what colours you pair up and you can match green and blue or whatever you like. You may be interested to know that some breeders have been trying for a lifetime to breed either a pink budgie or a black one, and in fact some years ago someone put up a lot of prize money for either of these; it was never won, though there have been several claims relating to pink budgies. On investigation they have all been found to be frauds. It is rather strange because there are violet budgerigars and violet is made up of two pigments, red and blue. You can breed blue budgies but not, as yet, pink ones. Similarly, when you consider the vast number of these birds that are bred each year it seems surprising that a melanistic (black) specimen has not been thrown up somewhere.

Anyway, whatever colours you put together, provided that the birds are happy with each other they will copulate and the first egg will probably be laid between seven and 14 days later. The hen starts incubating immediately but she will continue to lay an egg every day until the clutch is complete, which can mean anywhere between three and seven eggs. The eggs take 18 days to hatch and while she is sitting the hen is fed by the cock, and when the chicks hatch they are fed on regurgitated, partly digested seed by both parents. The chicks will leave the nest box four to six weeks after hatching and they will continue to be fed for a few days after that, so if you want to remove the youngsters wait for a good week until after they have left the nest. The parent birds will probably start nesting again, but after a third lot of chicks have flown, remove the nest boxes and clean them for next season otherwise your budgies will wear themselves out.

It is not always easy to sex young budgies from the colour of their ceres and you may need to wait a while to be sure about whether the birds are cocks or hens. Young birds are known as barheads from the dark, pencilled edges to the feathers on the forehead as opposed to the clear heads of adult birds.

Canaries

The canary is the domestic form of the wild serin from the Canary Isles, and although many people think that canaries are inevitably yellow that is far from the case: there are brown, green, khaki, red, orange and white canaries, and some varieties have crests or frills. As with budgies, specialist fanciers breed their birds for colour and type, but, again as with budgies, you can put any two birds of opposite sex together and try and breed from them. But be warned, canaries are extraordinarily difficult things to sex and you may be sold a canary in good faith that turns out not to be the sex that it was thought to be. Some fanciers are pretty good at sexing canaries but all will admit to making mistakes sometimes. If you have a cage full of canaries it is usually possible to pick out one good butch male simply because he 'looks masculine' and an equally sylph-like feminine canary; but it is all a matter of experience.

During the breeding season life becomes easier. Only the cocks sing while the hens merely utter plainful cheeps, so it will be obvious which is which.

If both birds live together in an aviary, or in a large box cage indoors, you should see the cock starting to feed the hen in February and this is the time to put up a nest pan in the cage, or several in an aviary, high up in a secluded corner, protected from the rain. You can make a wooden nest box or buy plastic canary nest pans which I prefer. Line it with a piece of thick felt or something similar, or a purpose made nest pan felt liner, and supply a quantity of moss, meadow grass, cat hairs and similar nesting material. At this stage start to add a bit of niger seed to the basic diet and make sure there is plenty of mineral grit available to the birds. Unlike budgies, which nest inside a closed box, canaries use an open nest so that you can see what is going on.

From the time the birds start to feed each other until the first egg is laid is between one and three weeks. The eggs are laid at daily intervals and the incubation lasts for about 14 days, and the hen starts to sit after laying the first.

Canaries cannot rear their brood on seed alone and throughout the time the parents are feeding the chicks you should make available to them a mixture of grated hard boiled egg yolk and wholemeal biscuit or bread crumbs mixed together so that it is not sticky, rather of a crumbly consistency, or you can buy a commercial canary rearing food. This must be supplied from about the thirteenth day of incubation and continued until the chicks are ten days old, but it must be mixed fresh every few hours and old food thrown out and the pots scrubbed clean as it goes off very quickly. When the young are able to feed themselves on cracked hemp, canary seed and soaked teazle start to introduce them onto the diet their parents feed on, which is primarily a canary seed mixture and fresh fruit and vegetables.

Canaries will continue to breed throughout the season, but it is better to remove the nest pans after two or three broods or the birds will wear themselves out.

Zebra Finches

These delightful little birds are very easy to sex in the wild grey form. The cocks are far more colourful and boldly marked than the hens and in most of the colour varieties this continues to be so, though the difference might be less marked than in the grey form. With white Zebras the only way of sexing the birds is to look for the vivid red beaks of the cocks and the rather more orange beaks of the hens.

Zebras will breed readily in a large box cage or in an aviary. Keep only one pair in a cage but in an aviary it is best to have at least ten pairs: if there are only two or three the birds squabble continuously. In the spring put a foreign finch nest basket in the cage, or if you have an aviary put up plenty of them — far more than you have pairs of birds — as high as you can and protect them from inclement weather. A foreign finch nest basket is a wicker construction about the size and shape of a coconut with an entrance hole in one side near the top. When you have put up your nest boxes fill them almost to the top with hay or grass and moss. Zebra Finches have a hobby; they make a nest in a suitable basket, lay a clutch of eggs, build another nest on top of them, lay a second clutch, build another nest and so on till they get to the top. Then they will happily incubate the top clutch. By now, though, the hen is so worn out and the season so far advanced that often the chicks do not do at all well. However, by filling the nest to the top so that there is only room for a single clutch of eggs you can overcome this problem.

Zebras may well lay large clutches of eggs but they may find it difficult to incubate all of them, or feed great hordes of famished chicks. If you keep Bengalese Finches in the same aviary try getting them to incubate the Zebra eggs — it is worth knowing that Bengalese are great foster parents. Both birds take turns to sit for twelve days, and the chicks leave the nest after 20 days, after which they continue to be fed by the cock for a while. It is a good idea to provide extra food such as sprouted seed, millet sprays, seeding grasses and wholemeal bread in milk for the chicks. After a pair has reared four broods, remove all the nest boxes and clean and disinfect them for the following season.

Cockatiels

The wild form of the Cockatiel is grey but today all captive Cockatiels are captive-bred and many colour forms are available. With most of them the cock can be distinguished by the brighter yellow and orange on the head. Cockatiels are not difficult to breed but individual birds can be a bit pernickety. They will breed in a cage but it has to be a fairly big one as the birds are quite large. They do better in an aviary and are far more peaceable birds than budgies. They need a large, deep, vertical nest box and if you are making one it is a good idea to fix a strip of weldmesh to the inside of the front wall so that the birds can use it as a ladder to climb out. A layer of slightly moist peat should cover the floor of the nest box. Correct humidity is important; if the eggs are too dry the chick will die inside the shell, and if they are wet fungal infections could result that again would mean the death of the chick.

The birds should be left strictly alone to get on with breeding since they can be very twitchy at this time and ready to abandon the eggs at the slightest disturbance. Extra food, such as soaked seed and wholemeal bread soaked in milk, should be given for the chicks, and other foods such as fruit or insects may also be taken. During the day both parents take turns at incubating but only the hen sits during the night.

Pheasants

The breeding of pheasants is a topic about which several books have been written, but briefly one should keep a pair or one cock and two hens to a flight. It is generally simple to sex the birds as they are often completely different. Eggs are laid from the end of April until the end of July. If the aviary in which the birds live is a large one with plenty of cover and you feel that it would be nice if your pheasants breed but you are not too interested in producing large numbers of chicks, I would be inclined to leave the birds to get on with things, only keeping an eye on them to check that the hen and her eggs are being left in place by other birds. When the chicks hatch they should be fed on commercial pheasant rearing pellets, though if you care to supplement them with mealworms, maggots and, after a few days, a little chopped chickweed or lettuce, the pheasants will be delighted.

Remember, though, that baby pheasants cannot stand the wet, so you must make sure that the top of the flight is covered with something to keep out the rain.

Once your pheasant poults are self-sufficient you should remove them to a separate flight or fighting will break out.

Alternatives to letting the hen pheasant incubate and rear her own offspring, are putting the eggs under a bantam or in an incubator. If you intend to use a bantam, you need a separate set-up so you can breed these birds as well as the pheasants, and a number of arks to contain the foster mother and her brood.

Incubators are complicated pieces of equipment in which eggs must be maintained in a correct temperature — about 38°C (103°F) — for three weeks in a critically humid atmosphere, and turned daily. Hatching eggs in an incubator is a science in itself.

Waterfowl

All the commonly kept ornamental species of ducks and geese will breed readily in captivity. Suitably sized nest boxes, from which the tops can be lifted to inspect the nest, should be placed around the birds' enclosure, and a layer of straw put into each. For some species the nest boxes must be on posts 75 cm (30 in) above the ground and supplied with slatted planks so that the birds can reach them. Ducks will soon find the nest boxes during the season and start to lay. If you are sure that they are not going to become waterlogged or taken by predators such as rats, leave the eggs where they are, otherwise remove each one as it is laid and replace it with a dummy until the bird starts to cover the clutch with down. This is the time to replace the proper eggs and clean and disinfect the dummies till next year.

When the ducklings hatch, special care has to be taken to ensure that they are not eaten by predators. Their food can be supplemented with boiled potato and wholemeal bread, but as with pheasants, ducks can be reared by bantams or in an incubator.

Quail

Quail are lovely birds that are useful on the floor of an aviary, but breeding can present problems. The two important things to remember are that the birds are very nervous, and therefore extensive cover and complete privacy is essential; and that only one pair (or trio) of birds can live in each flight. Then if you are lucky the hen will dig a scrape in the ground, lay her eggs and sit tight. But do keep an eye on the cock: if he bothers her or the chicks, put him somewhere else until it is all over. When the chicks hatch, depending on their size, feed them on small insects, an egg-biscuit mixture such as is used for canaries, sprouted small seeds and anything else that might seem appropriate.

If you are keeping Chinese Painted Quail you should be aware that the newly hatched chicks are no bigger than bumblebees and will get through 1.25 cm ($\frac{1}{2}$ in) mesh, so some sort of protection must be provided along the bottom of the wire panels of the aviary.

Other birds

There are so many species of birds that it would be impossible to give details in a book of this size on how to breed all of them, but there are plenty of specialist works for you to consult. However, if you cannot find the information you want, try to reproduce as accurately as possible the conditions under which the animals live in the wild, so if the bird is a parrot which nests in a hole in a tree (and all do except for one species, the Quaker Parakeet from South America) then the nest box should be enclosed, and so on. If you are not sure what food to offer the chicks, supply as wide a variety as you can in separate dishes and see what they take; and in every case leave the birds in peace and always be aware of hygiene.

Snakes

Until a fairly short time ago it was uncommon for snakes to breed in captivity but fortunately the picture is changing and more and more species are being captive-bred, as we discover more about

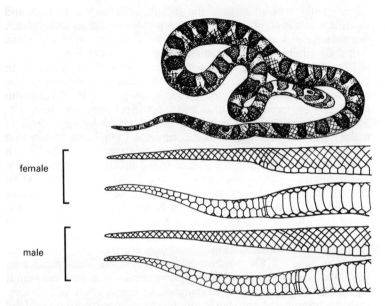

How to sex snakes: the female has a distinct 'step' at the point where the genital opening occurs, when the snake is viewed from the side. The male has a much more even profile. The feature is exaggerated in the drawing.

their requirements. There are so many species of snake, all with specific requirements, that in a book of this nature it is impossible to treat the subject in detail. By joining the herpetological societies, and reading the excellent magazine, *Snake Keeper*, and other literature, you will soon begin to pick up a variety of useful tips.

If you are lucky, you may find that when you buy a snake it is already gravid (pregnant), in which case half the hard work has been done for you. Some snakes give birth to live young and if this is the case your only problem is to persuade the babies to feed. What they eat will depend on the species but, remembering that all snakes are carnivorous, it is worthwhile providing a variety of suitable prey to see what they will take.

Some baby snakes will refuse to feed at first and as a last resort they might have to be force fed, but this is very stressful to the snake and can be dangerous for it, so do not try it until you have been shown the technique by an experienced herpetologist. However, sometimes it is possible to start a snake feeding with a little persuasion. Mouse tails are useful as a starter food. All that is necessary is to remove the tails from dead adult mice and chop them into short lengths. If the snake is gently held and the piece of

133

tail is gently pressed against the mouth, with luck the snake will open it whereupon you insert the tail just inside the mouth, release the snake, and hope it might swallow the food.

If your adult snakes are egg-layers, and it is most likely that they will be, they may be of a species that incubates the eggs, in which case let them get on with it; or they may leave the eggs for you to deal with, in which case they should be placed in a container which can be maintained at a suitable temperature and humidity. The latter is critical, but a careful watch has to be kept on it to make sure that the eggs do not contract a fungal infection, which will be fatal. See Lizards below for further details.

Perhaps the most difficult part of snake breeding is inducing the adults to mate in the first place. Sexing snakes is not the easiest task for the novice, but an experienced herpetologist will be able to help. However, as a rough and ready guide, have a look at the snake from the side in the region of the vent. At this point there is a sudden change in the outline of the female while a male tends to taper evenly towards the tail. When you are sure you have got a true pair, wait till the autumn and try reducing the temperature gradually over the winter. When spring comes and you increase it again this ought to act as a stimulus, in conjunction with photo-period − in the wild, the day length increases in the spring and I am sure that this increase in the hours of daylight is just as important as the temperature, so, depending on your snake room, you may have to fake an increase in day length with artificial lighting.

Typically, with snakes such as Corn Snakes, mating will take place in early spring and a clutch of about twelve eggs is laid six to eight weeks later. Incubation is also six to eight weeks and the young, when they hatch, are between 20–25 cm (8–10 in) long.

Two final points about breeding snakes are worth remembering. The first is that all snakes − babies are no exception − are escape artists, and can escape through the tiniest holes. You might well have small holes somewhere in the vivarium that you have taken for granted since you knew they were too small for the adults to escape through. You probably do not notice them any more but I can promise that your new babies will find them. The other point to watch is that snakes are carnivores and big snakes might eat little snakes, so take care to remove the babies to their own tank.

Lizards

Most lizards lay eggs, a few give birth to live young, and if conditions are right and you have a true pair, many species will breed in captivity. Some lizards such as the Common Iguana are easy to sex but in most species both sexes are alike. Some lizards glue their eggs to the wall of the vivarium and they should be left alone as they can be easily damaged. Other eggs are laid on the ground and these should be incubated in a dish of vermiculite, available from garden centres, in a temperature of 26°C (80°F) to 32°C (90°F) at a suitable level of humidity, which may need to be as high as 90 per cent. The eggs should be contained in such a way that the adults cannot tread all over them or they will be damaged. Unlike birds' eggs they should not be turned — keep them the same way up as you found them, and illuminate them with ultraviolet light for two hours each day to prevent mould. Snake eggs should be similarly treated.

Most lizards are carnivorous and many will happily eat smaller lizards, so remove any hatchlings to a separate tank. And look out for the tiniest of possible escape holes. Baby lizards are very fast and watch that one does not shoot up your arm when you have your hand in a tank or it may escape.

Young lizards will take most moving prey of suitable size, so depending on how big they are you can try them on greenfly or baby crickets or Fruit Flies.

Tortoises

It is now illegal to import the traditional 'pet shop' tortoise so if you are lucky enough to have a pair you should do your utmost to breed them; if you have a single specimen, give it to someone with one of the opposite sex. In fact, the most frequently imported tortoises belonged to two species, Hermann's Tortoise and the Spur Thighed Tortoise. The males of both species have concave undersides to the shells and females are flat. After mating the female will lay her eggs in peat or loose soil and they should be kept in a temperature of 25-30°C (80-85°F) for ten to twelve weeks, or even longer. During incubation they should be treated like lizard's eggs (see above).

If you go into a pet shop and see for sale a Box Tortoise, and are told that it is kept in the same way as other tortoises, do not believe it; they are not tortoises at all, they are terrapins.

Terrapins

Terrapins of breeding size are somewhat large animals, ranging from 20-30 cm (8-12 in), so for any success you will need a fairly big tank with land and water. When the eggs are laid, they should be treated as lizards' eggs (see above), and when the young hatch they will need plentiful supplies of aquatic animals such as *Daphnia* to eat.

Frogs and Toads

You will really need a fairly big tank for breeding frogs and toads, since a tiny volume of water becomes foul so quickly that eggs are likely to die. Female frogs and toads are frequently a lot larger than males and mating is generally in the spring, when the eggs are laid in the water. In a short time they hatch into tadpoles which are vegetarian, eating algae and perhaps other plants. As the legs start to appear they become carnivorous and will take small aquatic animals such as *Daphnia*. Some people suggest feeding them on meat or chopped earthworms but this is not a good idea as the water becomes polluted very fast. Amphibians absorb toxins through their skin, and if you have to keep changing the water all the time the additional stresses will not help the tadpoles to survive. Keep tadpoles and newly metamorphosed animals away from the adults or they may well be eaten. And provide islands in the tank; the metamorphosing frogs can climb on them.

Newts

Most newts are easier to breed in captivity than frogs and toads. During the spring they become completely aquatic and the male grows a crest along its back. The mating is preceded by an elaborate courtship dance and the eggs are laid singly on aquatic plants. The tadpoles will require small aquatic animals as food until they metamorphose and leave the water. The adults and the tadpoles must be kept separate or the young will be eaten.

Salamanders

Treat as newts, except that mating takes place on land and the young are born alive, complete with four legs and gills. They are amazing, exquisite little animals.

Axolotls

Axolotls are really giant tadpoles of a Mexican salamander but the odd thing is that they can breed even though they are immature. Males are more slimline and have a longer tail than the more chubby females. They will breed in the spring if you deprive them of food for a short while and reduce the water temperature from 22°C (71°F) to 12°C (53°F) and maintain these conditions until after mating. Suspend a piece of muslin or bandage in the water and leave the tank alone in subdued light. The eggs will stick to the cloth which should be removed and placed in another tank where they will hatch at room temperature if you keep the tank out of direct sunlight. There may be up to a thousand eggs so when the tadpoles hatch two weeks later you must be aware of the possibility of overcrowding. As with other amphibians the young should be fed on small aquatic animals such as *Daphnia*.

Tropical Fish

The breeding of tropical fish is such a complicated business that if you are seriously interested in it, you ought to read one of the specialist books, but if you are keeping a community tank of mixed fish you might well find that some species lay eggs. When the eggs are laid, they should be moved to a separate tank without removing them from the rock or wherever they have been laid, or better still, if two fish look as though they are ready to breed, move them to another tank till the eggs have been laid and then return them to the community. The reason for this is that most fish regard newly hatched fry as food, and it is virtually impossible to catch the babies to take them to safety without damaging them. The hatchlings should be fed on infusoria (see the chapter on Livefood) until they are big enough to take larger animals like *Cyclops*.

If you keep Guppies you will soon discover that they breed like proverbial rabbits without having to do anything as long as you start with a true pair. Males have flamboyant, flowing colourful tails and fins and females are drab fish, larger than the males.

Goldfish

It is extremely difficult for a novice to sex Goldfish so to be sure you have a pair, get several fish. If your fish are in a large pond with plenty of cover and not too many predators, they will probably breed without any help from you; however, if you want to breed Goldfish in a tank you will need to maintain the water at below 11°C (60°F) throughout the winter and then warm it gradually to 20°C (68°F) and in the spring start to feed your fish with plenty of livefood to bring them into breeding condition. After prolonged courtship the female will lay up to 10,000 eggs which will slowly sink and stick to aquatic plants, such as *Myriophyllum*. Remove the eggs on their plant or the fish will eat them. Keep them at 21°C (70°F) for five to seven days and they should hatch, though at the first sign of fungus on the eggs — if they turn white and furry they are infected — get a bottle of methylene blue from your aquarist shop and add it according to the instructions. Feed the fry on infusoria or Brine Shrimp (see the chapter on Livefood) and eventually a tiny fraction will grow up to become Goldfish. Losses are very high and do not be surprised when you find that the babies are not gold — the colour comes later.

Tarantulas (Bird Eating Spiders)

These super arachnids are not easy to breed and if you are seriously interested in the subject join the British Tarantula Society and talk to the experts. The first obstacle is trying to find a male.

They are not often imported and when adult they do not live long. If you have got a pair, introduce the animals to each other very carefully and keep watch the whole time. If a fight develops, separate your spiders immediately or the male will be killed. If they mate, remove the male immediately afterwards anyway or the female will kill him. Hopefully the mating will result in eggs that will eventually turn into tiny little spiderlings which must be separated from the mother or they will be eaten. Spiderlings feed on any suitably sized livefood, such as Fruit Flies or baby crickets. The BTS maintains a directory of what breeding stock is available through its membership.

Stick Insects
If you keep stick insects properly they will breed without help. All you need to do is to collect the eggs as they are laid so that they are not thrown out with the faeces when you clean the cage. Do not handle baby stick insects — they are very fragile. To move them, let them walk onto a piece of food plant, and move that.

Butterflies and Moths
The important thing about breeding Lepidoptera (butterflies and moths) is to discover the food plant of the particular species. Provide a constant fresh supply of this in a large cage made of soft nylon mesh and the adults will lay eggs on the leaves. These hatch into caterpillars and in late summer they will pupate, either on the plant, the side of the cage or in a dish of peat on the floor. Collect the pupae and lay them in labelled rows in the corrugations of a piece of cardboard in an open topped box for the winter. Spray them gently each day (but do not let them become too damp or warm) and in the spring put the box in a butterfly cage with pieces of twig resting on the floor and propped against the side so that the newly emerged insects can climb up them to inflate their wings. If you put a shallow dish containing a piece of sponge rubber soaked in a sugar solution on the floor of the cage, the adults will drink this nectar.

Giant Millipedes
Provided these fascinating animals are kept properly they will reproduce without any help.

Giant Land Snails
Provided these snails are kept properly they will breed without help, though high humidity can cause mould on the eggs.

138

7
ANIMAL CLUBS
AND
ORGANISATIONS

There are animal societies and clubs galore, but which type of club you join depends on your interests. It is handy to divide animal clubs into three broad groups though inevitably their fields overlap on occasion, and in fact if you go to one of the major animal shows you will often find fanciers wearing badges from all three groups.

FANCY CLUBS

First of all are the Fancy Clubs. They are legion, and while some have a broad appeal, such as the local cage bird society which will welcome you whatever birds you keep, others are very specific. They may be a breed society like the Siamese Cat Club or the African Lovebird Society or related to a sport, like the Royal Pigeon Racing Association, but whatever your interest you will find it worthwhile joining one of these groups. There is no better way of learning about animals than joining a Fancy Club. Club meetings are held at regular intervals where you meet other pet keepers with whom you can exchange information and ask for advice. If you are new to the Fancy, do not be afraid to ask questions because most club members will be delighted to help. At first, you might feel that the membership consists of a number of cliques from which you feel excluded, but persevere and introduce yourself and you will soon discover a number of friends. And once you are an accepted member of the club, and feel at home, if you see a nervous newcomer at a future meeting, remember what your first time was like and go and make friends. It will make such a difference and if others follow your lead the club will slowly gain a reputation for being friendly and more people will join. Another point in favour of these organisations is that they arrange outings

139

to shows, collections and other venues which enable you to broaden your perspective considerably. As you meet other fanciers, whether they are in your own club or another part of the country, you will be able to buy, sell and exchange stock and equipment with confidence, knowing that you are unlikely to be ripped off. One of the great joys of going on a club's coach outing to visit a similar organisation elsewhere is coming back with exciting boxes of stock.

Some of the bigger, older established societies such as the Kennel Club, the Avicultural Society or the British Herpetological Society can offer other advantages like extensive libraries, pathological investigations and specialist members who may be solicitors or live abroad and whose advice you can call upon. But what is almost certainly the most important aspect of any Fancy Club is the show season. This will begin with little local shows from which the class winners will progress to county and regional shows until the whole business culminates in a National Show with thousands of entries, trade stands galore selling everything from feeding pots to animals, and more fanciers than you ever imagined existed. Experienced animal keepers try to get there early on the first day. It does not matter whether or not you are exhibiting, but if you are, your first call must be to see if your entry has won the red ticket that denotes a first prize. After a few minutes spent checking the competition, make for the trade stands to buy what you have been yearning for all year, then relax and look through all the exhibits. When you are really experienced, you make another visit shortly before closing time on the last day. The place will still be crowded, the reason being that all the trade stands will sell off any stock that remains at knock down prices. You can really pick up bargains if you are crafty and pushy enough to get served before anyone else.

The only sure way of finding out about the dates and venues of most Fancy Shows is by being involved, though some of them are so well-known these days that they are extensively promoted on television and in the press. Crufts, the national dog show run by the Kennel Club is one such. Each Fancy has a most stringent set of rules regarding showing. Check them out first, since generally a newcomer who has a specimen that he thinks will stand a great chance of becoming a national champion will not get a look in at a National, simply because he is not aware of all the pernickety little rules. A perfect show specimen may in some Fancies be rejected, not because it is not shown in a regulation cage, but perhaps because the bars have not been painted the approved colour.

Some of these Fancy Clubs are much more show orientated

than others while some, though still holding shows, are far more interested in breeding, conversation and the dissemination of knowledge.

If you are interested in joining a local society, your library will probably keep a list of local organisations. Alternatively, you could try looking it up in one of those free local guides that arrive through your letterbox once a year, or failing all that write to one of the relevant addresses at the back of this book which should be able to help.

CONSERVATION ORGANISATIONS

The second type of animal organisation that might interest you is the conservation body. Since you are reading this book you must be aware of some of them already, and which ones you join depends on your interest. The Royal Society for the Protection of Birds is self explanatory. Most of their work involves species on the British list but they do cover exotic birds to an extent. The RSPB do a great job in mounting events for birdy people, from local film shows to huge international birdwatches. The society produces super magazines full of information and advertisements. It also has a sister organisation for young people, known as the Young Ornithologists Club (YOC).

The World Wildlife Fund's headquarters are at Godalming in Surrey, but they have 280 supporters' groups around the country. If you want to find the one nearest to you, contact headquarters who will have the information you want, and you can ask at the same time about national membership. The benefits of national membership vary according to the level of subscription, but they include newsletters, gift catalogues and copies of the BBC Wildlife magazine which is worth getting whether or not you join WWF. It is a superbly produced magazine and the only one of its kind in Britain. Young people can also join WWF at either a local or national level.

The Royal Society for Nature Conservation is the umbrella organisation for a national network of what used to be known as County Naturalists Trusts but are now called Local Wildlife Trusts, so look up both in your phone book if you wish to join.

Young conservationists are catered for by WATCH, the junior RSNC organisation. This seems to be one of the best of such bodies. Members get the chance of joining in an astonishing variety of conservation projects from clearing ditches to monitoring pollution, counting insects and all sorts of things. There are 800 local groups around the country which organise camps and days out.

There are groups to care for hedgehogs and spiders, marine animals and bats; there are groups for all sorts of things; and if none of those that I have talked about are of interest, have a browse through the addresses at the end of the book.

ANIMAL WELFARE ORGANISATIONS

The third sort of animal organisation is that devoted to animal welfare. There can be no doubt that in Britain the best known by far is the Royal Society for the Prevention of Cruelty to Animals, and whatever your age you can join that and help in the society's fight against cruelty. A smaller organisation is the People's Dispensary for Sick Animals and, as with the conservation organisations, animal welfare organisations are legion and range from the British Union for the Abolition of Vivisection to Chickens' Lib. One body that is constantly in the news is Compassion in World Farming which exists to try and educate people to the horrors of battery cages, the dreadful plight of veal calves and other abuses to farm animals. One of their current campaigns is against the eating of frogs' legs. Most of these welfare organisations will be delighted to welcome you. Some need only the support that your subscription brings but quite a lot of them encourage practical support as well.

Many national societies, whether they are Fancy Clubs, conservation organisations or animal welfare bodies have a presence around the world, and even where that is not so one can frequently find members in other countries or at any rate sister organisations. This is rather useful, as it means their members can set up meetings for when you go on holiday.

The list of addresses in this book is by no means comprehensive but, by using that list as a starting point, you ought to be able to find any other that you might want. The most comprehensive directory of conservation addresses is the Sierra Club's *World Directory of Environmental Organisations Conservation Directory*. In Britain there is a pretty comprehensive one to be found in 'The Conservation Review' which is published by The Conservation Foundation. It contains well over 500 addresses.

8
FREE PETS

In an age when an understanding of the need for conservation is becoming more common, many people are beginning to question the taking of animals from the wild in large numbers for the pet trade. This attitude is reflected in changes to the legislation concerning the export and import of wild animals and my guess is that in a few years the trade in wild animals will have almost ceased, except under special licence. In addition, Western life styles and housing are changing which means that many who would like to keep pets are precluded from doing so through lack of space or the close proximity of neighbours. With the new awareness, though, people with an interest in natural things can do their utmost to encourage plants and animals around their homes and in the towns in which they live. By deliberately encouraging wildlife into your garden or window box, you can enjoy animals just as much as if you had an animal room full of cages.

There are several books on the subject of wildlife gardening and nowadays one can buy packets of seeds designed to attract animals. Garden centres frequently stock nest boxes and bird tables, and at the Chelsea Flower Show in 1987 there was a wild garden for the first time. It may seem obvious, but it is worth saying that if you wish to attract animals to your garden, you must provide the conditions that they require — in the most simple terms this means food, water and shelter. In the traditional British formal front garden which consists of a square of mown lawn surrounded by a flower bed full of rose bushes interplanted with bedding annuals throughout the summer, you are not likely to find much in the way of wildlife, and if yours is like this and you would like to encourage animals, why not spend the winter evenings with a pad of graph paper and a pile of seed catalogues working out the best way to turn it into a nature reserve. If you are interested in gardening you will already know how satisfying it is to replan a garden and dream about how it is going to look when you have finished.

MAKING A POND

Start your planning by thinking about a pond. It might not be practical in your garden, but they are marvellous features if you can include them and they are even better if you can incorporate a stream and a bog garden. If you can include this feature the ideal would be for slow moving water and a small cascade or waterfall. Slow moving water in a garden is a better habitat than a rivulet that rushes along so fast that all the animals have to hang on tightly to avoid being swept away, though there are some that thrive in this environment. I suggest the cascade because the humidity around it is great for some ferns and other plants that appreciate these conditions. The pond itself should not be of even depth and most books suggest a shallow shelf around the edge and a deep bit in the middle, which is fine, but I think that an ideal

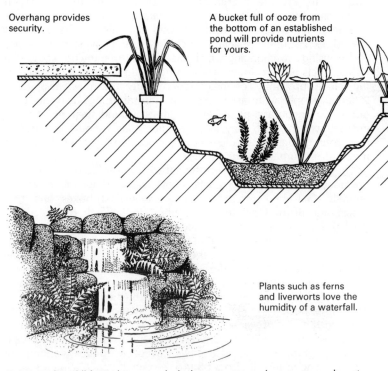

Overhang provides security.

A bucket full of ooze from the bottom of an established pond will provide nutrients for yours.

Plants such as ferns and liverworts love the humidity of a waterfall.

Features of a wildlife garden: a pond which incorporates a boggy area, and varying depths of water will accommodate a greater variety of plants and animals. A waterfall will provide a humid environment for some species, and a hibernaculum made from old brick rubble enables animals to hibernate beneath the frost.

arrangement would be for the stream to end up running through the bog garden before entering the pond which slopes from a depth of a few cm (in) at this end to 60 cm (2 ft) at the other, with maybe a marginal shelf at the deep end.

Nowadays the choice of materials for pond making is larger than ever before, but if you can afford butyl rubber, use that, though it is more expensive than some of the other options. The great advantage of polythene is that it is cheap but even the thickest grades will not last long before a leak appears, and it is almost impossible to seal even if you can find the hole. The laying of concrete is a difficult business and, although it can be undertaken by a novice, it is better for a professional to do the job. It is not a cheap undertaking for, in addition to the materials and labour, wooden shuttering has to be built to hold the concrete in place while it is drying.

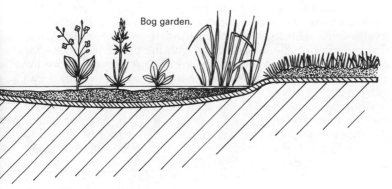

Bog garden.

Plastic tubes provide entrances to the hibernaculum, disguised by the rockery.

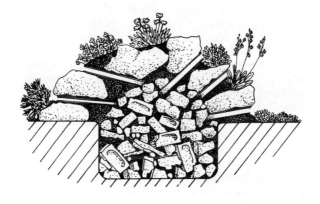

145

If you have opted for a pond liner, this should extend beyond the pond to cover the bottom of the bog garden or the water will simply soak away. When you have dug the hole, you should find and remove every sharp stone on the bottom, and if you come across any roots do make sure you get rid of them rather than saw them off, because if they start to grow they will make a hole in your pond. Plants are amazingly strong things that on occasion even force their way through tarmac and pavements. When the inside of the hole has been cleared it is a good idea to coat it with a layer of damp sand that acts as a good smooth surface on which to bed your liner. If you are using butyl rubber the next thing to do is to line the hole with the fibrous matting that is supplied as a base and then lay the rubber on top. There should be a fair bit of excess rubber above the edge of the hole as when water is added the rubber will settle deeper into the depression. I have assumed that you will not want a formal pond. If you do, you have to ensure when you are digging the hole, that the top edge is level, using a spirit level to check, otherwise you will inevitably find that on one side the water is flush with the top of the hole while on the other you have several cm (in) of bank exposed above the surface. With an informal pond a bank at one side is not a bad thing at all.

When you have reached this stage put a few bricks or lumps of rock on the edges of the rubber to hold it down, drop the end of the hose into the hole, and turn on the water. It takes far longer to fill even a small pond than most people realise, but eventually, perhaps even a day or two later, the water will reach the brim. Cut off the edges of the butyl rubber to leave about 30 cm (1 ft) lying on the ground all the way around, and start to landscape the new area by placing suitable rocks around the edge to overlap the water a little. There should be spaces here and there so that little animals can get between them to the water's edge and do provide lots of holes and crevices. If you are fortunate enough to have a heap of builder's rubble and broken bricks, put them into a pile and cover them with soil; but leave a few lengths of drainpipe protruding as entrances which can be concealed with plants or by placing a rock over them. This pile of rubble is an excellent place for amphibians, reptiles and even small mammals to shelter beneath the frost during the winter. When everything is to your satisfaction shovel soil over everything to make it look natural, adding any topsoil, peat or whatever as necessary.

The pond itself is now ready for attention, and you can start by putting something in the bottom. Pea shingle is a good idea and you can buy this from a builder's merchant, but rinse it thoroughly to remove any pollutants such as petrol residues. At this stage I like to add a couple of buckets of sludge from the bottom of a natural pond to the bottom of a new one. It may look like a foul black slime but it is a rich biological soup which is packed solid with living things — which is why you should not tip it into a new pond until a couple of days after you have filled it with water since tap water contains chemicals which kill small life forms. The sludge from the natural pond will act as a starter culture for the new pond. If the water looks absolutely awful when you first tip it in, do not worry, the sludge will settle and the water will clear in a few days, and soon you will discover that it is full of *Daphnia*, protozoans, diatoms and other animals. If the pond is large enough and you know someone who keeps native species of fish from whom you can get a few, introduce these into the pond. It is not a good idea to put in any Goldfish; these grow to such a size and will soon eat every living thing in the pond, unless the volume of water is very large.

PLANTS FOR THE WILDLIFE GARDEN

At this stage your garden is ready for planting and this is where you can really have fun. You can visit the garden centres and nurseries for your plants and seeds, or you can go and see all your friends who have gardens. I find that plantsmen are always only too happy to give away plants; you will almost certainly find some in this way that are suitable for your needs. Bring and buy sales, Women's Institute markets and the like are other fruitful sources and, in some areas, conservation agencies such as the County Naturalist Trusts and the World Wildlife Fund hold annual plant sales. But, wherever you get your plants do buy a tree or two if you have room, and lots of shrubs. Any type of tree will do, as long as it has dense cover for nesting and roosting. I have a magnificent Twisted Willow in the front garden but nothing ever nests in it as it is just too open to provide any security. If you are choosing a tree it is worth bearing in mind that some provide berries in the winter which will attract birds, while others are the food plants of certain insects — the Lime is the food plant of the Lime Hawk Moth for example.

The same sort of thinking has to go into selecting shrubs for your nature reserve. Buddleia is well-known for the attraction that the flowers possess for insects, and in fact it is frequently referred to as the Butterfly Bush. Roses are good provided that you choose one of the old fashioned varieties that are richly perfumed and have a good supply of nectar to attract insects. The other advantage of the rose is that you might be lucky and find that it becomes covered in aphids which in turn attract ants, that you can

147

watch as they milk the aphids for their honeydew, and predators such as ladybirds and small insectivorous birds. Honeysuckle is a great plant to have in the garden and mine, which covers most of the front of the house is rich in wildlife particularly throughout the flowering period in early summer. Blackbirds regularly nest in it and last year one of the nests was just below the bedroom windowsill so that each time I opened the window and peered down between the leaves I could see eight little black eyes peering up at me and as soon as they realised someone was there the yellow beaks would open wide and the fledglings would screech frantically in the hope that I would drop caterpillars in to them. This honeysuckle is packed full of insects and on a warm summer evening just as it is getting dark the whole thing is alive with moths of all sizes buzzing and whirring before it while they hunt through the richly scented blooms for nectar. At dawn the day shift takes over and it is not at all uncommon to find dozens of bees and other nectar feeders hard at work and completely oblivious to a human being only a few centimetres from them.

Fruit trees and bushes are alwys good for attracting animals. Currants and gooseberries attract Magpie Moths; apples and pears attract birds as well as insects right through till the autumn, when the fallen fruit might be visited by hedgehogs who love fermenting fruit. If you plant Broad Beans and some of the brassicas, you are bound to find plenty of blackfly which in turn attract small birds, and white butterflies.

A good variety of native plants in your garden will soon become the homes of all sorts of things. Bistort flowers are much loved by bees, and wild thyme when it is in flower is covered in insects busily working the deep purple flowers; and these insects attract other animals to the garden to feed on them, from small inverte-brate predators like the fast moving, undulating centipedes to hosts of spiders whose webs you will soon find everywhere. Thistles and teazles are marvellous plants to have in a garden; they attract Goldfinches.

Wild Foxgloves and Primroses and Lavender all have a place in a wildlife garden and, if you have room, leave part of it actually wild and watch how Fat Hen and Rosebay Willow Herb and Groudsel grow first on a patch of bare soil, later to be overtaken by grasses, brambles and nettles, which are vital to some insects, such as Red Admiral Butterflies. And did you know that cloth used to be made from the fibrous stems of nettles?

You should also try to find space somewhere for a compost heap, not only so that you can recycle all your unwanted vege-tation and turn it into excellent compost, but to attract animals as well. The decaying vegetation is home to a wide range of little creatures and the heat generated by the decomposition enables the life cycle of some of them to continue when it might otherwise be arrested. Slugs, snails, woodlice, centipedes and spiders all love compost heaps and, if you are very lucky, you might even end up with Grass Snakes laying their eggs in your compost heap.

Grow some Sunflowers; each huge seed head will contain dozens of different insects which in turn will be eaten by several species of birds, and later in the year as the seeds ripen, other birds will come to feed from them and perhaps the odd squirrel as well. Someone else who will be after your sunflower seeds will be any neighbourhood pet keeper, who will try and beg them from you for his collection.

Once your garden is established introduce some frog and toad spawn into your pond — but not if you have fish in the pond, as they will eat the eggs and the tadpoles. Don't try introducing the adult amphibians because they will try and return to their original spawning pond and you will lose them, but those that grow up in your pond ought to regard your garden as home and you will occasionally come across them in other parts of your garden.

In order to encourage the greatest number of variety of animals as possible one should try to grow plants that will provide flowers, fruit and seeds from very early spring until winter; so the season might start with Primroses in February or even earlier if the weather is not too cold until the flowers of Pink Sedum in the autumn, and the hips and Holly berries and the nuts last you through until nearly Christmas. Like all the best wildlife reserves yours will need a certain amount of management or you may find that one particular plant is so successful that all the other prize specimens in its neighbourhood start disappearing as the first takes over. Some naturalists maintain that everything should be left strictly alone. While I can see the arguments for this point of view, I prefer some management in a garden reserve, so at the end of the year I carry out some careful clearance, but I am very aware that I should not remove seedheads simply because they might look untidy. Those seeds are a valuable source of food through the winter, and odd bits of leaves, grass stems and the like are eagerly snapped up as nesting material in the spring.

A good wildlife garden is a great place for taking photographs of animals and, if you have suitable equipment, it is full of insects and other small creatures which tend to be overlooked by the photographer in favour of the more obvious birds and mammals. Wildlife gardening is a rewarding operation and, unlike conventional pet keeping, once you are over the initial outlay, costs are minimal — which is not a bad plus point these days.

BIRD TABLES

The end of autumn is a good time to think about a bird table; as it gets colder the insects die off and all the cold-blooded life forms bury themselves until the spring, and most edible berries and virtually all the nuts have been eaten by Christmas, so available food supplies for birds are much reduced. The mammals do not fare so badly as many hibernate and those that do not often survive with the aid of a food store that they laid down in the autumn, but birds have a really difficult time especially after snow starts to fall and covers what little food is available. Furthermore, a bird converts food to energy more quickly than other animals which means that it needs to replace it more frequently. On a cold night, a small bird can lose a third of its weight just keeping warm and staying alive. When morning arrives, it has to go out and find food quickly just to get back to where he was the night before. In Britain, we spend far more than anyone else on keeping our birds alive but, as a result, a far higher percentage of our resident birds survive the winter than in other countries with a similar climate. So there is certainly a place in your garden for a bird table.

There is no ideal design for a bird table, and it is certainly never big enough, but all of them ought to incorporate a few standard design features. The most important of these is that it should be cat proof. Probably the best way of ensuring that cats cannot get at feeding birds is to put the table at the top of a 1.5 m (5 ft) metal, or at any rate metal covered, pole, but mine hangs from the branch of a tree that is too thin to support a cat. I have never actually seen a cat catch a bird on a bird table but their very presence prevents the birds from feeding. You ought also to include a few drainage holes, or you can end up with a soggy lump of decomposing food if the water does not run away readily. Thirdly, a roof over part of the bird table is a good idea so that however much snow is coming down at least some of the food is uncovered. If the whole bird table is roofed over, it takes the birds longer to find the food if they cannot see it as they fly overhead, and in the enclosed space they feel nervous and therefore keep interrupting their feeding to fly off for a while. The final standard feature is that the bird table should be situated fairly close to a shrub or a tree which birds can use as a sheltered base between feeds. It is far easier to land in a tree, hop to a convenient branch and fly a few lengths to a bird table than to dive straight onto a squabbling flock of starlings that seem to inhabit most bird tables during the hours of daylight.

Provided it incorporates all these ideas it really does not matter whether you buy a bird table or make it yourself, but if you set it up close to a window, you can watch your feathered visitors at really close quarters. An excellent way of feeding small birds, such as tits, is to suspend their food inside a cage of 2.5 cm (1 in) square weldmesh, which prevents bigger birds from hogging the food.

One thing that is really difficult to provide actually on the bird table itself, but which is just as necessary, is a container of water for the birds to drink and bathe in. It ought to be fairly large, rough bottomed, shallow edged and no more than 5 cm (2 in) deep. As if those criteria were not difficult enough to fulfil, you have to work out how to stop the water freezing over. Just as I have never seen a perfect bird table, neither have I ever seen a perfect winter bird bath, but the best one I came across was an inverted metal dustbin lid that had been painted with several coats of emulsion into which had been mixed a couple of handfuls of aquarium gravel. This refinement prevented the birds' feet from sticking to the bare metal of the rim during really cold weather, and the texture provided by the gravel meant that a bird entering the water would not slip or feel insecure. The whole thing was mounted on four bricks laying on their sides and there were a couple of nightlights underneath which had to be replaced periodically whenever they went out or burnt down. Being virtually on the ground this bath was placed in the middle of a lawn, well away from the nearest cover, so that cats could not creep up and pounce suddenly from behind a wall.

During the winter you can put almost any foodstuff you like on the bird table and someone will come down to take it, and any leftover scraps of your own food are ideal, though it is best not to put out large pieces as they will often be removed by a gull. If you do have any bones for the birds to peck at, hang them one by one from the branches of a tree.

In addition to household scraps you can supply all the usual birdy things like half coconuts on strings, cylindrical wire feeders full of peanuts, bits of bacon rind and a few kilos of wild bird food. The plastic bags full of peanuts are not such a good idea, as the birds cannot extract the nuts easily and sometimes the plastic tears so that all the nuts end up on the floor whereupon they are wolfed in a few seconds by the starling mafia. I would also not recommend threading lots of individual peanut shells one by one on a piece of string. It takes less time for a few tits to extract the nuts than it did to thread them, which is absolutely maddening, and it is difficult to see, unless you go right up to them, when all the nuts have been removed. The shells are left on the string and from the warmth of your kitchen they look as though they have not been touched.

Seed balls go down well and the best way to make them is to stack a whole pile of yoghurt pots inside each other and push a hot skewer through all the bases. Separate the pots and cut as many 30 cm (1 ft) long pieces of string as you have pots. Tie one end of each piece of string round the middle of a dead match and push the other end of the string through the hole in the bottom of a pot, leaving the match inside the pot. Now put a good smear of lard round the hole to seal it and put all the pots in the fridge. While they are cooling, melt some lard in a pan and pour in a quantity of wild bird food to which you have added some sultanas and stir the whole lot together and leave it to cool. When it has, put 1 cm ($\frac{2}{5}$ in) of the mixture in each pot and pull the string from the outside so that the match is resting on this layer, and then fill up the pot with the mixture. When all the pots are full put them back in the refrigerator overnight to harden. If you take them out too soon they will fall to pieces. Next day, push the bottom of the pot to release the seed bell and flap it up and down for a minute or two till it drops out, and then, feeling very pleased with yourself because it has worked so well, go and hang it on a tree by the string.

I tried a variation on this system last winter that worked even better. Instead of using a match I tied a 15 cm (6 in) piece of twig to the string. I filled the pots in one go and pulled the string tight from the bottom so that the twig rested across the rim of the cup. When the bell was turned out the twig provided a perch for a feeding bird. One of the delights of feeding birds during the winter is that they can become so tame and if you can supply them with mealworms some of them will learn to take them from your hand.

NEST BOXES

Come early spring, the birds start to nest, indeed Rooks are already busy in February, by which time you should be putting up nest boxes if you expect birds to use them that year. Some books go into considerable detail, but in fact you do not need a lot of complicated diagrams or instructions. All you want is a box made from 2 cm ($\frac{3}{4}$ in) thick wood. The base should be about 15 cm (16 in) square, with a couple of drainage holes, and the sides should be 20 cm (8 in) high at the front and 25 cm (10 in) at the back. Fix the whole thing to a backboard which extends above the top and bottom so it can be fixed firmly to a tree and hinge a sloping roof so that the rain does not sit on it to rot, and so that you can clean the thing out before each breeding season. The hinged roof is not there so that you can keep lifting it to see what is going on. That is a sure way of encouraging your birds to nest

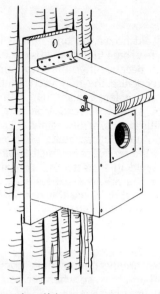

A simple, well designed nest box. If this is to be used in an aviary it might be a good idea to fix a metal plate around the hole to prevent damage by birds that are prone to chewing wood.

elsewhere. The only variable feature of the nest box is the front panel. If you want it for tits or birds of similar size, drill a 30 mm (1⅛ in) entrance hole. For larger birds use a 40 mm (1½ in) hole and if it is intended for Robins or flycatchers make the front wall only 12 cm (4¾ in) high so that there is a gap at the top. If you would like Robins to nest the box must be situated fairly low down, as in natural conditions they nest in banks.

When you are siting the nest boxes, if you put up only one the chances are that you will be unsuccessful in attracting birds to it. Put up a dozen and you immediately improve your likelihood of success. Site them in all the attractive places you can find, being careful not to position them so that the entrance holes face the prevailing wind.

A further encouragement to nesting birds is a ready supply of suitable nesting materials, and lumps of hay, combings from the cat, and even the dog if the hair is short, should be stuck in forks of trees or holes in walls or anywhere suitable for the birds to find. Long horse hair or sheep's wool should be cut into short lengths before being offered, or it can become wrapped around a bird's leg and a fracture can result, or occasionally a bird can be hanged by its leg until it dies.

BATS

If your home is an old house, go and have a look in the loft and you might find a few bats hanging upside down in the rafters. Look closely though because if you are not familiar with them you might not at first recognise the nondescript little black bundles as sleeping bats, which are far smaller than many people realise. If you cannot see any at first, have a look at the joists and if you come across any little heaps of droppings it could be that a bat is sleeping above. You can buy or make bat boxes for your garden but I find that it is harder to persuade bats to use these than to persuade birds to build in a nest box. You are probably wasting your time anyway if you are in a batless area, but keep your eyes open at dusk and you should see the occasional bat hawking for insects.

FOXES

In some areas foxes are becoming more common, and they are also moving into urban areas, so wherever you live you might very well find a fox in your garden. They do like nice private places to dig out an earth and if you have a garden shed with a raised floor so that there is a space beneath, you might find a family of foxes taking up residence. They are super animals and if you want to encourage them you can put out food. It need not be only meat, because foxes will take all sorts of things, and you can certainly leave out anything that is left from dinner.

The best way to enjoy a fox is when it is a regular visitor to your garden. I know they look like very cuddly dogs especially when they are little, but they really are very bad as pets: only rarely do they remain tame but you do not realise this when you first take one on as a cub. As they mature they become increasingly less tractable. You cannot possibly keep them indoors after this, as they will rapidly wreck everything and, if the animal is a male, it will spray the whole place with an extremely pungent odour. About this time a pet fox will withdraw from you. Where a dog will willingly come up to meet you, a fox will cringe into the furthest corner away from you. If you leave it alone it will not bite — it will just keep as far away as it can, but as soon as you try to stroke it or put a collar on it will have a go, and a determined fox can leave the most painful bites. So, the best advice I can give you is — don't keep a fox as a pet.

154

9
THE PET KEEPER AND THE LAW

The laws relating to animals exist for several reasons and it may be useful to look at why they are there.

1. Prevention of cruelty.
2. Conservation.
3. Prevention of disease.
4. Protection of humans.
5. Prevention of damage to the environment in the importing country.

There can be few countries nowadays that do not have laws covering these five aspects of animal keeping, and in Britain and the USA they are for the most part effective, but in many places in the world the law is completely disregarded, especially when it concerns cruelty and conservation.

The animal welfare organisations spend a lot of time and money trying to educate people so that they are not thoughtlessly cruel to their animals. When all else fails they bring prosecutions but this is in a way a negative course of action. If the case is successful the offender will probably be fined but magistrates rarely see animal cruelty cases as meriting more than a small penalty. Subsequently it is quite likely that the criminal will be anti animal welfare and may take out his resentment on his other animals to show he does not care.

Often a case of cruelty comes to light as the result of a complaint from a neighbour, but when an inspector follows this up unless he can see cruelty the case could rest on the evidence of the complainant, and often this person will back down rather than go to court over it, and who can blame him. Another difficulty in cruelty cases is that in Britain one cannot be found guilty of causing pain or distress to a wild animal — it has to belong to somebody before such an accusation can be brought to court.

Conservation legislation is even more complex. It exists to prevent exploitation of wild animal stocks abroad, and native wildlife. The first is pretty well covered by laws based on the Convention of International Trade in Endangered Species (CITES) but the results sometimes work against conservation. Two or three years ago a consignment of illegal Monitor Lizards arrived in Britain, and the animals were confiscated. The reason the importation was illegal is because monitors are becoming scarce in the wild, and the reason for that is not because they are collected for people who wish to keep them, but for them to be made into fashionable boots, handbags and the like. Once the animals were in Britain, a disgracefully half-hearted attempt was made to find homes for them and when this did not succeed, because hardly any of the responsible collections were asked if they would like them, the whole lot were killed. Have you ever heard anything so ridiculous? The USA has considerable problems with illegal consignments of birds being brought into the country across the border from Mexico. Much of their information about these consignments comes from caring bird people who tip off the border patrols. Until comparatively recently such intercepted birds were, just like the Monitor Lizards, killed — a course of action which horrified the informants who were trying to save the birds. Large numbers of birds were destroyed and suddenly all the tip-offs ceased and the number of captured smugglers dropped abruptly. People were simply not willing to pass on their knowledge if the birds were to be killed as a result, so the government changed its policy. Intercepted birds are now held and cared for until after the court case and then auctioned. This is by no means a perfect solution and open to much abuse but at least the birds live and some of them end up with caring collectors who are doing their best to breed them.

The picture that many people still have of a wild animal is of a proud, fearless beast roaming through jungles, picking occasional fruit from the trees in between periods of sleeping the day away with a smile on its face. The reality is that the animal may have a constant battle with thirst and hunger, predators and parasites, disease and injury, and on top of that it has to fight off intruders into its ever decreasing territory caused by you and I wanting cheaper hamburgers and mahogany coffee tables. In between all these activities it also has to raise a family.

A great number of wild animals are probably suffering from a disease of some sort or a load of internal and external parasites, or any combination of these factors, so when they arrive in another country, either as pets or as migrants, they bring their various conditions with them. Some of these diseases can be transmitted to humans. Such a disease is known as a zoonosis and the obvious ones are rabies from any mammal, but especially canines, virus B which causes encephalitis and is carried by primates, bubonic plague from rats, and salmonella infections from terrapins and the like, while birds can be infected with ornithosis, a disease that was thought only to affect parrots at which time it was known as psittacosis.

In theory a single infected animal that gets through import control could infect the human populations with any of several zoonoses, or it might equally infect other livestock with a variety of pathological conditions. There is ever a risk that someone is going to smuggle an infected animal into a country, and it is surprising how irresponsible some pet owners can be about taking risks with rabies. One of these days rabies will enter the United Kingdom; I do not see how it can be otherwise, and once that happens life will never be the same again. I feel strongly that courts do not come down heavily enough on dog smuggling, and what is going to happen if a channel tunnel is ever built I have no idea; I just cannot see how efficient controls can be set up to prevent a fox trotting through the tunnel one night.

To some people pets are more important than humans, and most of us feel at least some degree of interest in animals. One of the great problems that pets pose, though, is when they escape and become established in the wild for that can lead to a multitude of complications. The newcomers can oust existing species, they can frighten the human residents of the area, and they can eat their way through millions of pounds or dollars worth of crops and native wild plants. If you feel that I am overstating the case, just look at some of the escaped or deliberately released animals that have become established in a foreign land: there are American Grey Squirrels in Britain, and rabbits in Australia. There are Coypu and Mink and sparrows and mongooses on the loose in parts of the world where they are not native species.

In a democratic attempt to do what is best for everyone, legislation affecting keepers of all sorts of animals has come into being. There is a great deal of it, and I have spent a long time sifting through it trying to make sense of it all. In the end I decided that the best thing to do was only to list that legislation that is likely to affect pet keepers in one way or another, even though the likelihood of some of them being relevant to all pet keepers is small. So some of the laws concerning the importation of exotic species will affect people who keep parrots, while legislation on riding stables will be of interest to equestrians. Having arrived at this

157

stage in my researches I added one or two odd pieces of legislation that are unlikely to be of any use to you at all but that struck
me as interesting, but hopefully you will find in the following lists
all the law you as a pet keeper are likely to want.

Most pet keepers will never come into contact with the law
regarding animals but it is as well to know what there is, and
knowing that and having a comprehensive insurance policy to
cover your stock and equipment should ensure a lifetime of peaceful animal keeping. When you are talking to your insurance broker
insist that your hobby is covered aginst theft and vandalism.
Animals are valuable items these days and thefts are common, and
as an old animal keeper at Whipsnade Zoo said to me once, locks
will only keep out honest people.

If you are a keeper of a collection of exotic animals it is useful
to have a list of which species are legal and which are not and if
you contact the Department of the Environment in Bristol they will
send you one. Do make sure it is up to date, though, as it is
constantly being amended. CITES, and the legislation that covers
it, deals with most species of exotic animals.

The Wildlife and Countryside Act on the other hand is
concerned with British Fauna and Flora and nowadays it is illegal
to trap or keep native animals that were commonly kept before the
advent of this legislation. Despite all the legislation, we continue to
exploit animals quite blatantly and illegally and it really needs
caring people like you to try and educate the rest of the world.
You may care to join the Association of Responsible Animal
Keepers or one of the other groups that specialise in your kind of
animal.

A fairly recent piece of legislation in Britain is the Dangerous
Wild Animals Act, which says that if you want to keep one of the
animals listed as being dangerous you must first obtain a licence.

Table 1: UK Legislation

Legislation is listed in chronological order, and where appropriate the licensing authority is shown together with brief notes regarding the scope of each Act where this is not obvious from the title of the legislation.

Title of Legislation	Licensing Authority	Scope of Legislation
Cruelty to Animals Act 1876	Home Office	Covers experiments on animals.
Dogs Act 1906		Stray dogs
Protection of Animals Act 1911 (and amendments)		Refers to domestic and captive animals only.
Performing Animals (Regulations) Act 1925	Local Authority*	
Control of Dogs Order 1930 (and amendments)		Requirements regarding collars and control.
Destructive Imported Animals Act 1932		Controls importation of potentially destructive animals.
Protection of Animals (Cruelty to Dogs) Act 1933		Allows a court to disqualify an offender under the Protection of Animals Act 1911 from keeping a dog.
Protection of Animals Act 1934		In effect, prevents rodeos.
Cinematograph Films (Animals) Act 1937		To prevent cruelty being used on animals while filming. If you ever want to read a silly piece of lawmaking, try this one.
National Assistance Act 1948 in conjunction with The National Health Services Act 1946		If a hospital (or other) patient cannot make arrangements for the care of his pets while in hospital, the local authority must make arrangements to look after them till his return.
Docking and Nicking of Horses Act 1949		Prohibits these activities, and importation of animals treated in this way.
Dogs (Protection of Livestock) Act 1953		Permits a farmer to shoot marauding dogs under certain circumstances.

Protection of Animals (Anaesthetics) Act 1954 and 1964		Covers the use of anaesthetics for castration, tail docking, etc.
Dog Licences Act 1958	Post Office	A licence is required to keep any dog.
Abandonment of Animals Act 1960		Covers not only abandoning and dumping animals, but also such things as going on holiday and leaving an animal to fend for itself.
Highways Act 1959 as amended by The Criminal Justices Act 1967		Animals straying on the highway.
Animal Boarding Establishments Act 1963	Local Authority*	Deals only with cats and dogs.
Riding Establishments Act 1964 and 1970	Local Authority*	Deals only with horses.
The Markets (Protection of Animals) Order 1964		
The Markets (Protection of Animals) (Amendment) Order 1965.		
Veterinary Surgeons Act 1966		States what may be done by persons who are not veterinary surgeons.
The Agriculture (Miscellaneous Provisions) Act 1968		Covers cruelty to animals kept on agricultural land.
The Theft Act 1968		Covers the theft of animals.
The Criminal Damage Act 1974		Makes it an offence to kill or injure another person's animal.
Live Poultry (Restrictions) Order 1971		Restricts poultry movements to and from shows.
Pet Animals Act 1971	Local Authority*	Licensing of pet shops and market stalls.
Breeding of Dogs Act 1973	Local Authority*	A licence is required if an owner breeds commercially from more than two bitches.

160

The Rabies (Importation of Dogs, Cats and other Mammals) Order 1974	Ministry of Agriculture, Fisheries and Food	
Transit of Animals (Road and Rail) Order 1975		Regulations concerning the transit of horses within the country.
Dangerous Wild Animals Act 1976	Local Authority*	A licence is required to keep any animal listed as being a dangerous wild animal.
Importation of Captive Birds Order 1976	Ministry of Agriculture, Fisheries & Food	Covers the importation of eggs and birds.
The Rabies (Importation Control and Quarantine for Rabies Susceptible Animals) Amended Order 1977	Ministry of Agriculture, Fisheries & Food	
The Animals Health Act 1981		Refers to agricultural livestock.
Wildlife and Countryside Act 1981	Department of the Environment	Very wide powers covering many animals and plants.
Control of Trade in Endangered Species (Designation of Ports of Entry) Regulations 1985 Statutory Instrument 1154	Department of the Environment	
Control of Trade in Endangered Species (Enforcement Regulations) 1985 Statutory Instrument 1155	Department of the Environment	

*The Local Authority is the local Borough Council or similar body.

Common Law Negligence: Common law says in essence that a person may be guilty of negligence if he does, or fails to do, an act which is likely to injure another, and does injure that other, so for example an owner allowing an animal to stray onto the highway can be sued in the event of an accident, though it should be noted that cats are privileged here — it is understood that their nature is to roam. Similarly, the act of walking a vicious dog in a public place without a muzzle could come under common law if someone is bitten as a result.

Anyone who keeps valuable animals or animals that could be held likely to be involved in a common law negligence suit at some stage ought to be insured. Not all

161

insurance companies will insure an animal, but plenty of them do, and it is well worth hunting around till you find one.

It should also be noted that separate local by-laws concerning pets may exist in your area and you should check with your Local Authority.

If you are interested in importing or exporting animals, even if it is a single dog when you go abroad, you should be aware of the International Air Transport Association (IATA) guidelines regarding suitable crates. See the end of the USA legislation table for further details.

Table 2: USA Legislation

As in Britain, there is national legislation in the USA covering the keeping of animals, but individual states have their own laws and these should be checked by contacting the local police station. Most national legislation is embodied in the Code of Federal Regulations and these are abbreviated throughout the table as CFR. Addresses for permits are listed at CFR part 42/71.50.10/21 and law enforcement addresses are listed at CFR part 42/71.50.10/22. That sounds very complicated but when you actually look it up, it is much easier to make sense of than British legislation.

Title of Legislation	Scope of legislation
Lacey Act 1900 (USC 42-44) and amendments of 1908, 1969 and 1981 (16 USC 3371 et seq)	Prohibits importation into the USA and from one State to another of animals taken illegally in the exporting country or State.
Migratory Bird Treaty Act 1918 (16 USC 703-711)	Prohibits the taking of listed migratory birds.
Tariff Act 1930	If a country restricts the taking of a wild animal, a permit must be obtained from the local US consul before that animal may be imported into the States.
Convention on Nature Protection and Wildlife Preservation in the Western Hemisphere 1940	Though not fully implemented in the USA, the Convention provides a variety of protection measures to animals and plants.
Fish and Wildlife Acts 1956 (and amendments)	Incorporated in the CFR, see below.
Marine Mammal Protection Act 1972	Covers not just whales and dolphins but also such species as sea otters, sealions, etc.
Endangered Species Act 1973 (Statute 87, part 884, 16 USG 1531 et seq.)	In essence, prohibits trade in endangered and threatened species except under permit.
Convention on the Conservation of Migratory Species of Wild Animals 1979	Covers all migratory animals including birds. Not ratified in the USA but should be noted.
Fish & Wildlife Conservation Act 1980 (160 5C 2901)	

Nongame Act 1980	Lists animals which are not considered to be game animals and therefore subject to other legislation.
Bald Eagle Protection Act (16 USC 668-)	
Code of Federal Regulations:	
part 9/1 c-q	Definitions.
part 9/2	General information.
part 3/3	Standards of facilities required for keeping animals including such details as feeding, watering, sanitation, employees and transportation.
part 9/3.1	The humane handling and other requirements for dogs and cats.
part 9/3.25	Requirements for keeping guinea pigs and hamsters.
part 9/3.50	Requirements for keeping rabbits.
part 9/3.75	Requirements for keeping primates.
part 9/11	Requirements for keeping horses.
part 9/12	General information.
part 9/53	Information on diseases.
part 9/75	Communicable diseases in horses.
part 9/82	Communicable diseases in birds.
part 32/232, 3/c 3	Fish and wildlife management programme procedures.
part 32/232, 3/C 4	The removal of predatory or undesirable animals.
part 38/22015 August 15, 1973	
part 39/1159 January 4, 1974 and amendments	
part 42/71	Foreign quarantine to prevent the spread of disease within the US.
part 42/71.53	Primates: they cannot be imported except by a registered importer, and in any case can only be imported for scientific purposes or for exhibition or education — never as pets.
part 42/71.54	Prohibits the importation of any animal capable of transmitting disease.
part 42/71 50, 10/1 Sub chapter B	Covers the taking, possession, transportation, sale, purchase, barter, export and import of wildlife.

part 42/71 50. 10/12	Defines 'taking' as: meaning to pursue, hunt, trap, kill … or attempting to do any of these.
part 42/71 50. 10/20	Lists protected birds.
part 42/71 50. 10/21	Lists addresses for permits.
part 42/71 50. 10/22	Lists law enforcement addresses.
part 42/721 50. 11/2	Details of scope of the regulations.
part 42/71 50. 12	Useful information.
part 42/71 50. 13	Useful information.
part 42/71 50. 14. 12	Allows the importation of animals only through designated ports.
part 42/71 50.14/17	Concerns personally owned pet birds. Any pet owner can import a single personally owned pet bird.
part 42/71 50. 16	Injurious wildlife.
part 42/71 50. 16/12	Birds that are forbidden. These are Rosy Paster, Red Billed (and other forms) Quelea, Java Sparrow and Red Whiskered Bulbul.
part 42/71 50. 16/14	Covers amphibians.
part 42/71 50. 16/15	Covers reptiles.
part 42/71 50. 17	Lists threatened and endangered species of wildlife.
part 42/71 50. 19	Useful general information.
part 42/71 50. 20	Information on migratory birds.
part 42/71 50. 21	Useful general information.
part 42/71 50. 22	Bald Eagles and other eagles.
part 42/71 50. 23	Incorporates CITES into the national legislation.
part 42/71 50. 27	Useful general information.
part 42/71 50. 30/11	The control of feral animals.
part 42/71 50. 31	Fish and wildlife conservation.
part 42/71 50. 90	The feeding of depredatory migrating waterfowl.
part 42/71 50. 91	Covers export requirements
part 42/71 50. 92	Covers import requirements.
part 42/71 50. 97	Covers overtime limits for people working with animals.
part 42/71 50. 151	The recognition of breeds, pedigrees and studbooks.
part 42/71 50. 313	Humane regulations involved in handling and slaughtering animals.

part 42/71 51.　　　The importation of dogs and cats.

part 42/71 52.　　　The importation of turtles, tortoises and terrapins. Briefly, one cannot import these animals if they have a shell length of less than four inches unless they are not to be used in commerce, and even then, only up to a maximum of seven specimens. On admission to the USA they become subject to the Food and Drugs Admin. Regulations (21 CFR 1240.62) and require other permits as detailed under 50 CFR 17 and 23.

The Live Animal Regulations of the International Air Transport Association (IATA) state in considerable detail what is necessary for the import and export of animals. In themselves they are not legally binding, but much of their contents have been incorporated into national legislation, and members of IATA ought not to accept a consignment that does not comply with these guidelines. If you are shipping your pet dog to another counry, it is no use putting it into any suitably sized box — you will not get away with it. Ask IATA for a copy of their guidelines instead.

10
WORKING
WITH
ANIMALS

A great number of people who started keeping animals when they were children have grown up to work with animals. Others might have wanted to be involved with animals from an early age but were prevented from doing so through circumstances. Usually this means that parents were unsympathetic or that the family home or income precluded any pets. It certainly seems to be the case that most adults who keep animals began doing so as children.

The interaction between people and other animal species is endlessly fascinating and I am delighted to see that at last the psychological benefits of keeping pets has been given scientific respectability. Animal keepers themselves have always known this instinctively — there is nothing more satisfying than going into the animal room, closing the door and pottering about for a couple of hours. I suppose that one might divide pet keepers into three groups. There are those who want a friend or two in the house. There are those who keep animals for a specific purpose, such as showing or racing, and there are those who keep the animals to study and breed, although perhaps not in any academic way. Pet keeping gives all three groups an interest which can sometimes fill their lives, and have you ever noticed how much more interesting are people who have an absorbing interest of some sort. Unless they become obsessive, they are fascinating to talk with even if their own subject is not yours.

What I find really interesting about animal keepers is the huge stock of information they accumulate. Few of them are the sort of people to write books, and even if they were, a book on their topic might not be commercial, but in conversation with such folk I have frequently come across snippets of scientific observation that I have never seen written up formally. This is even the case with species so common that one would be tempted to think that they

167

had been studied ad nauseam, but because of their ubiquity some aspects of their lives have been overlooked through familiarity.

Equally it must be said that in a multitude of ways humans have abused animals. Many have been taken from the wild for the pet trade, and large numbers of specimens have died before they reached a final purchaser, but despite the cries from certain organisations, there are few wild populations that have been threatened by this activity. Far more damaging is the daily destruction of the animals' habitats.

What does worry me is the number of animals being taken from the wild and then completely lost from the gene pool by being used for research. Some species of primate that were in the past exceptionally common have become decidedly scarce, and whereas this is not the place to become entangled in an argument about animals for research I consider it indefensible to take wild chimps for this purpose since their populations have been severely depleted.

Certainly, science has learned much from animals, and, however indirectly, that information affects all our lives. And for those people who have kept animals and would like to work with them in some way, the options are greater than might be supposed. That is not to say that it is easy to find an animal job in the present economic climate, but if you are persistent and able to think laterally there are more opportunities than becoming a vet or working at a zoo as a keeper.

The specific information in this chapter is geared to work opportunities in Britain. For readers in other countries, the general information is equally as valid, and will suggest starting points for looking for work with animals.

VETERINARY SURGEONS

Opportunities in Veterinary Medicine:

General Practice	Armed Forces, Customs &
Consultancy	Excise and Police
Teaching	Research
Pathology	Government Departments
Zoos	Horse Racing

I do not know if it is still true but a few years ago when fictionalised autobiographies of vets started to become popular in Britain, the number of applications for places at veterinary colleges grew to an extent where veterinary medicine became the most desirable choice of all university courses. It has been popular for a long time

Working with animals: veterinary surgery and pathology.

but at the moment it is not easy to become a vet. The only way to do so is to obtain a B VetMed degree from one of the colleges that offer this course. It involves many years of hard work, but if you are to be accepted for a place you have to obtain fairly high grades in three A level subjects which have a relevance to the course, such as chemistry, biology and physics. And, although no one officially admits this, it is even harder if you are a woman.

Unfortunately, many teenagers at college who feel that they would like to go on to become a vet have an unrealistic view of the job. No animal job consists of posing for the camera with a wide smile on your face and a cuddly lamb in your arms, yet it is surprising how common is such a view. Most animal jobs are hard, mucky and smelly and can involve considerable physical work and antisocial hours, for animals need looking after 24 hours a day, even on Christmas Day.

Similarly, a lot of youngsters visualising a career in veterinary medicine think only in terms of general practice, and even more specifically in terms of treating cats and dogs and budgerigars, which in the profession is known as small animal practice. The reality is that vets do all sorts of things. When he is qualified a vet can either join the armed forces or work for a company, or he can apply to work in a general practice as an assistant, or, if he has the funds available, he can either set up his own practice in an area that needs one, or sometimes buy into an existing practice that is looking for an additional partner.

General Practice

In a general practice, the partners are usually employees of the company though they might be self employed, or take on freelance consultancy work in addition to their position in the company. Salaried assistants who are also qualified vets may be employed if the workload warrants it. A general practice can be a small animal practice which deals mostly or entirely with pets, or it can be a farm animal practice or more usually a mixture of both, in which case what happens is that those partners who are interested in farm animals concentrate on those and leave the pets to partners who would rather work with them, though inevitably someone has to do both jobs on occasion.

A veterinary surgeon who is a partner in such a practice needs to be an astute businessman as well as a vet and to know all about the problems that running any business involve.

Consultancy

Any business to do with animals is going to require the service of a vet at times and it could be worth its while to employ one or more on a salaried basis. However, if the company is not large enough to do that, or if the veterinary work is not full time or of a sporadic nature, a vet in general practice may be contracted to act as a consultant to the organisation. This means that he is paid a flat fee on the understanding that he makes himself available when required, and when he actually does some work for the company he is paid for that separately. Some examples of the sort of places that use veterinary consultants are circuses, animal welfare organisations, race meetings and local authorities. Kennels and other breeding establishments will probably have a consultant vet as well.

Teaching

All the veterinary colleges or veterinary departments of universities employ vets as lecturers.

Pathology

The big zoological bodies employ veterinary pathologists to help keep the animals fit by working on disease organisms. Teaching colleges and some suppliers of food animals also use veterinary pathologists.

Zoos

Not many zoos are in the fortunate financial position of being able to afford full time veterinary staff, but some do and these posts are much sought after. What is not realised by many young people who wish to take up veterinary medicine as a career is that the B VetMed course has very little to do with wild or exotic animals. It is primarily geared to those industries in which animals equal money, such as horse racing, poultry breeding and dairy farming. Consequently those vets that go on to specialise in zoo animals, in their own time and frequently at their own expense, are at a premium.

Armed Forces, Customs & Excise and Police

The services and the police use animals and consequently need vets. The animals concerned are chiefly horses, which today are almost entirely used for ceremonial purposes — although until just recently the British army still had a mule unit in Hong Kong — and dogs which have to be versatile beasts as they are used on the one hand in riot control and the apprehension of criminals, and on the other for public relations purposes such as tournaments and other displays where they jump through hoops of fire and retrieve scented handkerchiefs on command. They are also being increasingly employed in the detection of drugs and explosives at airports and in warehouses.

Research

Veterinary science like all else is forever advancing, and all the teaching colleges have research vets working on all sorts of projects, but they are also to be found in a variety of companies. Firms that produce meat or other animal products such as eggs or milk for human consumption employ vets to keep their animals more healthy than those of their competitors, and to find ways to make sure their product gets bigger and fatter faster on less food than anyone else's.

Other companies that test their products on animals all use vets for controlling disease, conducting autopsies and finding ways of reducing the damage that their product may cause to animals.

Local Authorities

Local Authorities such as borough councils have a statutory obligation to provide vets to oversee the slaughtering of animals at

abattoirs within their jurisdiction. This is always done on a consultancy basis and vets are required to attend each day whilst animals
are being slaughtered, to make sure that legislation concerning the
welfare of the animals is complied with and that the meat is of a
quality that is suitable for human consumption.

Government Departments
The Ministry of Agriculture, Fisheries & Food employs many vets
in a variety of research and administrative posts.

Animal Welfare Organisations
Bodies such as the RSPCA and PDSA frequently use vets, generally as
consultants, in animal treatment clinics and to provide professional
evidence in prosecuting cases of cruelty.

Horse Racing
There is so much money involved in horse racing, that the industry
now has its own vets to research into equine disease and genetics
and to treat injured animals.

ZOOS, SAFARI PARKS AND CIRCUSES
Opportunities in Zoos, Safari Parks and Circuses:

    Keepers
    Research zoologists
    Education officers
    Ancillary staff such as drivers, gardeners, secretaries and caterers

Zoos and Safari Parks
Zoos are always overwhelmed with requests for employment,
especially by young people, many of whom have no real idea of
the work involved. Respectable zoos make sure that they employ
knowledgeable, caring people but some of the less responsible
establishments seem to take on people that are totally unsuitable
for working with animals and, given the fact that so many people
are just longing to work with animals, I cannot understand why
they do this.

The better zoos employ a few zoologists on research work, and
during the summer a good number of people in all sorts of
capacities, and even selling ice-creams or directing cars in the car
park can lead to the opportunity of someone becoming a keeper.
There are nowadays acknowledged examinations for zoo keepers
and advancement frequently depends on a combination of exam
results and experience. There are no special requirements for

Working with animals: zoos and dolphinaria.

potential trainee keeper posts but the person who can show knowledge and enthusiasm on the one hand and who looks neat and is articulate on the other has an immediate advantage. It must be remembered that caring for animals is only part of a keeper's job, for while the public is in the zoo he must also police the collection in a firm and friendly way and pass on all sorts of information about the animals. Keeping can be very rewarding: equally it can be miserable, and the pay is poor and in the summer the hours are long.

A fair bit of strength is called for in a keeper in a zoo — carrying a hundredweight sack of flaked maize on your back when the weekly delivery of food arrives is part of the job. The other thing that an aspiring zoo keeper must accept is that even if his passion is for antelope, he might be given a job in the reptile house. If he can accept this he is in a good position to end up with his antelope

173

when someone leaves or is promoted to a different section.

Some zoos have a policy of changing their keepers from one section to another every two or three years. My opinion is that this is counterproductive since if a keeper is absolutely dedicated to elephants he is not going to be happy and so will not work as efficiently if he is transferred to the bird section. Incidentally, when a zoo divides its keeping staff into sections it might either make the divisions zoologically, as for example an ungulate section, or it might do it geographically so that all the enclosures along the west wall belong to one section.

Quite a few zoos offer accommodation to single keepers as part of the conditions of employment, but it is often pretty grim and is not infrequently an ancient caravan set in a secluded corner of a muddy field. Rarely is accommodation offered to married keepers. Another unattractive feature of the job is that many zoos do not offer a reasonable system of promotion to their keeping staff and someone might do the same job all their working life. Even in those zoos where one can join as an assistant and graduate through the various keeping ranks to end up as a head keeper, promotion to this last position almost always happens when an incumbent retires so the chances of filling it are very slim. Keeping is not for the ambitious.

The better zoos realise that they have a duty to educate the public about the natural world and to enable them to do this they employ education officers. If you are fortunate enough to land one of these posts in a zoo that will leave you to get on with things it can be a great job. Most of your time will be taken up talking to groups of children and showing them around the zoo.

Everybody who works in a zoo has something to do with animals, simply because they are there. Even if you spend your time selling ice-cream, the atmosphere is all around you and, as I said, you might be lucky enough to be there when they want a temporary keeper.

People who are interested in working in a zoo often do not think broadly enough. They contact the best known establishments, like London Zoo and the Jersey Wildlife Preservation Trust, and forget that the country is covered in small zoological establishments which are often of a specialised nature. There are butterfly farms and falconry centres. There are children's zoos run by local councils and there are aquariums. There are wildfowl collections, and plenty of parks and shopping precincts have aviaries that all need looking after.

Circuses
Circuses need keepers too, but in a circus the day must be

arranged around the evening performance so the evening feed must be given at a time that will not interfere with it. Virtually all circus animals are large mammals which means a fairly hefty mucking out job each morning. Unlike a zoo keeper, one employed by a circus is unlikely to be involved in public relations but on the other hand he will have to groom and prepare the animal for its performance. Circuses take a lot of people on a casual basis at each town where they are playing and this is a great way of getting in, but only a skeleton staff is kept on over the winter. Animal keepers are paid very badly.

THE ARMED FORCES, THE POLICE AND CUSTOMS & EXCISE

Opportunities in the Armed Forces, the Police and Customs & Excise:

Troopers in the Household Cavalry as riders and grooms
Gunners in the Royal Horse Artillery as riders and grooms
Soldiers in other units as riders and grooms and dog handlers
Police constables as riders and grooms and dog handlers
Royal Air Force police dog handlers and falconers
Customs & Excise dog handlers and animal inspectors

If you visit one of the military spectaculars you will be able to watch horses and dogs performing in the arena. Nowadays, nearly all the horses belonging to or attached to the armed forces are used for ceremonial purposes. Police horses by contrast are for crowd and riot control although they do appear in displays at public events from time to time. Some of the dogs belonging to the armed forces and police also become part-time performers but the greater part of their numbers are used in guard duties, in the arrest of armed intruders and in crowd control.

Customs & Excise use their dogs to detect illicit drugs and explosives at airports and seaports, as well as in warehouses where consignments of imported goods are temporarily stored. What is often overlooked is that the airforce and some airports also employ falconers whose birds are flown to discourage gulls and other wild birds taking up residence on the airport.

Airports are also where consignments of animals arrive from abroad and whether a plane has come in from New York carrying a single pet dog, or from Bangkok with several thousand birds, the animals will need to be inspected and given clearance before they can be released. At one time customs officials who had no knowledge of animals would clear such consignments but today those with specialist knowledge are in demand for this work. One customs officer in New York, when opening a container load of furs, asked me how he was supposed to know the many different animals from which they came, and whether they were protected or not. Specialists are needed.

FARMS

Opportunities in Farming:

Farmhands on:

Dairy farms	Turkey farms
Beef farms	Maggot farms
Sheep farms	Fur farms
Rabbit farms	Deer farms
Quail farms	Guineafowl farms
Duck farms	Pheasant farms
Chicken farms	Trout farms
Salmon farms	

Farming might not appeal to everyone since the whole point of farming animals is to kill them, but it is surely better that while they are alive they are looked after by someone who cares about them. It is undoubtedly hard work involving long hours, bad pay and conditions, and often a tied house.

I am sure that when most of us hear of a farm we visualise a rosy cheeked farmer's wife serving frothing milk to her children while a border collie lies before a crackling log fire and lambs inevitably gambol in crisp spring sunshine outside the window. First prize goes to anyone who actually knows a farm like this, but there are farms where the animals live for most of their lives in the open. Cattle are invariably farmed in this way, whether they are being kept for meat or milk, and sheep too generally live on open pasture, either wandering about on the moors, or far more commonly in fields. Most other farming today is carried out in what most people call factory farms but which the trade prefers to refer to as intensive farms. This is not the place to discuss the morality of the system, and factory farms do need staff to look after the animals. In some of these farms the animals are confined in small cages for most of their lives and in others they live in large, tightly packed communities on deep litter in a huge shed. The amount of work that is left for a farm hand to do varies according to how automated the process is, so in a broiler unit raising chickens for supermarkets, one man can look after tens of thousands of birds. All he has to do each day is to look at the stock, remove any bodies and keep an eye on the computer that controls food, water, light and temperature. When the birds are sent to the slaughterhouse at about seven weeks, he helps to clean and disinfect the buildings so that the next day they can be restocked with a new lot of day-old chicks and the cycle starts again.

It would be wrong to assume that there are only farms to produce cattle, sheep, pigs and poultry. Today, many kinds of animals are farmed, and while a gamekeeper would probably not think of himself as a farmer, the greater part of his work is the rearing of pheasants. The rest of the time he spends controlling pests and policing the estate on which he is employed. Guineafowl are farmed as well these days, and quail for which there is a growing market. There are deer farms, and the production of animals for fur: chinchillas, foxes and mink are all raised in this way.

The farming of fish is moving into the realms of big business and farmed salmon and trout can be found in any supermarket, but if you want to go for something really exotic, think about silkworm farms. The silk for the bridal dresses of the last two or three royal weddings was all produced in a British silk farm. And there are maggot farms, unpopular with their neighbours due to the smell, but they sometimes also produce mealworms and crickets which are sent all over the country to collections of animals to be used as livefood, and some of the maggots are sold to anglers as bait.

WELFARE AND CONSERVATION ORGANISATIONS

Opportunities in Animal Welfare and Conservation Organisations:

Inspectors (RSPCA)
Clinic attendants
Researchers
Writers
Office staff
Normal business personnel
Unpaid volunteers at local level

The animal welfare societies employ people who are interested in animals in two ways. First, there is the inspectorate and sometimes the staff in clinics, all of whom actually handle animals during their work. An inspector's work can be varied. During the course of one day he can visit a riding stable, rescue a swan with a fishhook in its mouth, destroy an injured dog, give evidence in court for an animal cruelty prosecution, and judge a pet show. The hours are erratic and involve shift work, the pay is not great, and although this is now changing one was usually committed to living in a tied house. There are opportunities for promotion and inspectors are moved around the country every two or three years.

The other people that are employed by such organisations spend their time working for animals but do not necessarily ever see a live one. Education is an important part of this work so many of them spend their time lecturing or writing booklets and reports, while others are researchers, press officers and secretaries. Such operations have to be highly sophisticated and competitive in today's society so all of them need computer operators, sales managers and graphic designers.

Some of these organisations have a network of unpaid volunteers who beaver away in their separate communities, raising public awareness of their work, together with much needed funds through endless coffee mornings and bring and buy sales.

COLLEGES, UNIVERSITIES, DRUG COMPANIES AND MANUFACTURING INDUSTRIES

Opportunities in Colleges, Universities, Drug Companies and Manufacturing Industries:

    Animal technicians
    Researchers

You would be amazed at the number of places that use animals for research, I hasten to assure you that very few are proponents of vivisection. Some of the pet food companies keep animals on which to test their latest recipe; pet food is such enormous business these days and mistakes are expensive. Processed animal feeds are also manufactured for farm animals and laboratory animals, and they all need animals to eat the things and therefore need technicians to look after the animals.

Many products must be tested by law on animals before they may be sold to the public, so the makers of cosmetics and medicines, pesticides and much else maintain stocks of animals. These range from rodents, through other domestic animals like cats and dogs, to various primates. Animal technicians look after the stock and there are recognised exams within the profession which is fairly well paid and often has decent working conditions. Educational establishments with biological disciplines keep stocks of animals for dissection and behavioural research, and you can find all sorts of beasts in these departments. There are the usual rodents, naturally, together with Fruit Flies and Clawed Toads, lizards, Guppies and stick insects. Animal technicians in such places are often not as well paid as in industry, but if you enjoy an academic atmosphere in which to look after your animals, it is an excellent job with which to combine research of your own. Due to educational system economics, such places cannot maintain large stocks of animals which means that you will have plenty of time during the day to get on with your own research.

All the places in this section have zoological researchers who are generally graduates, and although they are all working on something to do with animals, they may or may not actually come into contact with a live animal.

GOVERNMENT DEPARTMENTS AND LOCAL AUTHORITIES

Opportunities in Government Departments and Local Authorities:

Zoological researchers
Animal technicians
Environmental health officers
Meat inspectors
Clerical staff

The Ministry of Agriculture, Fisheries & Food and the Department of the Environment employ many animal people of one sort or another. MAFF are involved in many research projects with farm animals of all sorts. They do not simply try to build more meaty cows, they also conduct breeding experiments with lobsters, attempt to make sick oysters well again, do work on rabies and other animal diseases − in fact they have a whole animal health division − and oversee local authority slaughterhouses. The White Fish Authority is forever busy on a variety of fishy projects. All local authorities have a responsibility to ensure that meat from slaughterhouses is disease free, and to this end they employ inspectors who are present whenever animals are being slaughtered. Local authorities are also responsible for licensing pet shops and establishments like riding stables and boarding kennels, as well as for issuing dangerous wild animal licences. Usually someone who knows nothing about animals inspects these pet shops and the homes of ratepayers who want to keep a monkey. Consequently someone with an animal background is extremely useful for this sort of work, though it would be a mistake to think that such tasks would occupy the whole of the working week. For most of the time an environmental health officer is investigating complaints about noise, smelly drains and authorising loft insulation grants.

The Department of the Environment has a branch at Bristol that deals solely with the Washington Convention on International Trade in Endangered Species of fauna and flora (CITES). Officers handle the licensing of consignments of animals and plants for import and export. Pay and conditions for all these posts are what you would expect throughout the Civil Service.

WORKING WITH HORSES

Opportunities in Work with Horses:

Local authorities	Breweries
Racing stables	Heavy horse centres
Racecourses	Vets
Studs	Circuses
Riding stables	Children's zoos
Theme parks	Armed forces
Police	Holiday resorts
Royal Mews	Horse-drawn caravan holiday companies

The world is full of horses. I read recently that there are thought to be more horses in the British Isles today than there were a century ago before the motor car became so universal. Whether or not that is true, if you are looking for somewhere horsey to work, the choice is extensive. People who work with animals generally do so because they love the job, but it does put them in a vulnerable position and very often animal jobs are poorly paid, and this is certainly so in the world of horses. If the work is absorbing enough one can put up with low wages but what does seem indefensible is that the accommodation and working conditions associated with such jobs are often abysmal, but despite this there is never a shortage of applicants for the jobs.

If you want to work with horses the obvious place to start looking is the racing industry. All over the country there are racing stables and studs trying to produce next year's Derby winner, and racecourses where all the animals will run, while at Newmarket

Working with animals: the police and armed forces.

there is a museum of racing. At a more local level there is almost certainly a riding stable near you. If you are persistent enough you might be given some work, but sadly so many youngsters would do anything to work with horses that they are often taken on without pay, but merely for free rides in return for their labour.

The heavy horse is starting to make a comeback and it has been discovered that provided you do not want high speeds, heavy horse-drawn vehicles are more efficient and cheaper in towns than motor vehicles. At least two local authorities are using them to pull refuse disposal vehicles instead of using diesel dust carts. Heavy horses are also found on some farms and several breweries use teams of Clydesdales or Suffolk Punches to pull delivery drays during the working week and to attend country fairs and the like at weekends. And do not forget the current proliferation of heavy horse centres which the public can visit simply for the pleasure of watching these splendid animals.

181

Theme parks are very popular during the summer. Many of these have a Wild West Section where horses are used to pull stagecoaches, as mounts for the cowboys and Indians, or simply for giving rides to children. Jobs of this nature are frequently seasonal, though some staff are needed to care for the horses over the winter. Any holiday resort is a good place to look for seasonal work with horses for at many of them one can find pony rides for children.

Vets, circuses, the armed forces and some zoos, especially children's zoos, all have something to do with horses, so read the relevant sections. And, finally, the Royal Mews employs horsemen to care for the animals that are used in ceremonial processions.

WORKING WITH DOGS AND CATS

Opportunities in Work with Dogs and Cats:

Kennels	Foxhound and beagle packs
Catteries	Guide Dogs for the Blind
Quarantine stations	Armed forces
Dogs homes	Police
Kennel Club	Customs & Excise
Veterinary nurses	

Kennels and catteries are a sensible place to start if you are looking for this sort of work, and it might be worth having a word with the Kennel Club if only because they know everybody in the dog world. Quarantine centres are another good place to look. These have proliferated in recent years since the anti-rabies laws, and many can be found associated with veterinary practices. Advertisements for kennel maids can sometimes be found in local newspapers and it is worth contacting places like dogs homes to see if they are looking for anybody. If you are anywhere near the home of a pack of foxhounds or beagles you might find an opening and the armed forces, the police and Customs & Excise all use dog handlers, so read the relevant sections for more information.

The Guide Dogs for the Blind organisation spend a good deal of their time training dogs for blind people, and their kennel staff look after the animals from the time they arrive until they leave to start work with their new owner.

PET SHOPS AND ANIMAL DEALERS

Opportunities in Pet Shops and with Animal Dealers:

Pet shops   Bird dealers
Aquarist shops   Specialist animal dealers
Garden centres

Everyone knows what a pet shop looks like, whereas you might not have come across a dealer before. There are small, cowboy dealers who generally handle all the work themselves. The established dealers on the other hand tend to have fairly large premises where they hold comprehensive stocks of animals, which mean a lot of work. Most dealers tend to specialise in a particular sort of animal, so you get tropical fish dealers and bird dealers and reptile dealers and so on. The work can be very varied and its exact nature will depend on the type of place it is, but typically it involves packing and taking consignments to and from the airport or station, feeding and cleaning cages, making cages and treating sick animals. There are also the normal jobs involved in any business, such as secretarial work. You probably need to live near a dealer to be in with a chance because they almost always employ local labour.

Some pet shops are one man operations but with all the garden centres that have opened around the country in recent years there are now some fairly large establishments. If you know about animals and start to work in a pet shop no one will be happier than I, because they really do need knowledgeable staff. I am the first to admit that there are some with really great assistants who are knowledgeable and courteous, but many pet shops seem to specialise in employing unsuitable people. If you do work in a pet shop you will spend more time selling dog leads and millet sprays than you will pets, but there are usually a few common species of animals around to make life worthwhile. Pay and conditions are frequently poor.

VETERINARY NURSES

Opportunities in Veterinary Nursing:

Veterinary practices   Animal Welfare Clinics
Veterinary colleges

Whenever you take an animal to a vet you will find attendants who help to hold the animal, pass equipment to the surgeon and perform a hundred and one other jobs. They might be people just like you who wanted to work with a vet. They applied and if there was a vacancy and they had the right approach to the job, they were taken on and almost everyone will call them animal nurses. However, the Royal College of Veterinary Surgeons runs a specific scheme for training veterinary nurses. RVNs (Royal Veterinary Nurses) have to pass exams and it is exceptionally difficult to qualify and get a job as an RVN. Some practices have them and others do not, but be warned, for whatever the official line there is often much friction in a practice between the RVNs and the other animal nurses. Working conditions and pay scales vary enormously and depend on the practice. Sometimes the conditions are cramped and depressing and the pay insulting. At the other end of the scale the position has dignity, reasonable remuneration and a really pleasing working environment.

MISCELLANEOUS ANIMAL JOBS

Opportunities in Miscellaneous Fields:

Breeding establishments	Horticultural organisations
Wildlife hospitals	Animal agencies
Airline animal handlers	

This is the section for all those odd and ends that do not fit conveniently elsewhere. Let us start with airlines which handle so many animal passengers that the more responsible ones employ trained animal handlers. Some airlines are dreadful at handling live animals but those that care really do their best for the animals during a flight, and each time there is a stopover the animal attendant will check the stock, feed and water it if necessary and write a report which accompanies the livestock throughout the journey. The final attendant who moves the animals to the customs enclosure puts one copy of the report with the other documents accompanying the consignment so that eventually the importer can see what has happened throughout the journey.

One can find animal jobs in the oddest places; the Royal Horticultural Society for example, employs an entomologist and Queen Elizabeth II has her own pigeon keeper for her loft of racing pigeons. And who looks after the royal corgis?

Is it not odd that if you ill-treat a pet belonging to a neighbour you can be prosecuted for it, yet if you ill-treat an identical wild animal, unless it is one that has specific legislation referring to it, you cannot be taken to task?

This peculiar attitude to wild animals means that whenever a member of the public finds an injured hedgehog or seagull, he discovers that it is very difficult persuading anyone to look after it or even treat it since either one involves some expense, and without an owner to claim from, where is the money going to be found. This has led to a whole network of Wildlife Hospitals throughout the country. Some specialise in birds, some specialise in seals, and some, like the Wildlife Hospital Trust in Aylesbury, will take in any wild animal that is in distress and needs to be looked after, though even Les and Sue Stocker who run the Trust specialise in hedgehogs through a special hospital appeal known as St. Tiggywinkles. All these wildlife hospitals are desperately short of money but equally they are all overworked and as a result are delighted if someone is willing to give them a hand. You will not get paid for it, but it is a superb way of learning about animals, so that when you apply for a job elsewhere you can demonstrate that you know what you are talking about.

The last category in this collection of miscellaneous animal jobs is the breeders' establishments. There are people breeding all sorts of animals commercially and it is worth approaching them if you can discover where they are. They tend to keep a low profile, for two reasons. If it becomes generally known that they have several thousand pounds worth of pedigree cats on the premises sooner or later they will be visited by cat thieves during the night. Alternatively, if a business is breeding multitudes of rats for research it will not be long before animal liberators break in to release the rodents into the countryside, but with persistence you can discover their whereabouts and if you can persuade them that you are neither a cat burglar nor a rat releaser you might end up with a job.

You may not know that there are quite a few animal agencies which exist solely to supply animals for films, television programmes and commercials, and to advertising agencies for publicity purposes. Some of these are one man operations but not all, and some of them specialise. So if you want a hundred frogs for a pop video, or a cat that will scoop food out of a tin or even a dog that will bark on command, you ring an animal agency. Sometimes the people who work for these agencies have to play anonymous roles on screen when the macho film star hero really cannot bear to have a spider walking across his chest, or when the insurance company refuses to insure the leading lady if she has to fight a lion. In cases like these, the animal handlers, or wranglers as they are often called, stand in. Sometimes these agencies take on staff. They can be essential if one is asked to supply 500 assorted snakes for a scene. As the snakes warm up under the lights and start to wander off in all directions, believe me it takes more than one person to keep all of them in place.

FREELANCE WORK WITH ANIMALS

If you keep animals or if you are experienced with them in some way and already have a job, you may have sometimes wondered if you could not make some money on the side from your hobby. The answer is that there are all sorts of ways of doing so; but do not forget to declare it to the taxman. The most obvious way of making some money if you are breeding Zebra Finches in an aviary at the bottom of the garden is to sell off your surplus stock. You will not make any profit but the income will help to pay for your hobby. Similarly, if there is a long summer, you can grow rows of millet plants by using the seed from spray millet. Some of this can be fed to your own stock and the rest can be sold to other fanciers.

Many pet owners with a dog, a cat, or even a budgerigar that has some particular appealing mannerism, often never think of exploiting it. All the animals in commercials are only demonstrating their own mannerisms that have been cultivated by an astute owner. There will undoubtedly be people who exclaim that an animal should not be exploited, but I would say that if it enjoys scooping food out of a tin with its paw I see no reason why you should not be paid for it. So watch your pet and if it does anything that you think might be commercial, contact an animal agency, and remember to send some photographs when you do.

Similarly, if you are interested in photography and regularly take pictures of animals, do not put them away when they have come back from a processing lab. They are worth money provided they are good. Most publications will accept 35 mm colour transparencies, but if you want to sell your work to newspapers it is better to shoot on black and white print film and have some large glossy prints made from the negatives. But as with keeping animals research the subject before you dive in. It is worth looking at the Writers' & Artists' Yearbook which lists publications that might be interested in buying your work, and the Bureau of Freelance Photographers publish some useful books as well.

Writing articles is another way of making money from your animals, and you should not think solely of animal magazines as a market for your work. By thinking laterally one can sell pieces to all sorts of publications and, of course, if you have the strength you can write books about animals. But if you feel unable to face the discipline of writing, one really interesting way of making a little bit of money is to do slide talks about animals. Secretaries of societies are forever scratching around for speakers, and Women's Institutes, Rotary Clubs and the like will often welcome you with open arms. Public speaking can be really enjoyable and if you start off with a couple of jokes, you can generate a great atmosphere at evenings like these.

If you fancy the idea of earning money as a freelance there are three essentials to remember. One is to observe your animals the whole time, two is to record everything and three is to take lots of photographs. You will soon find that you have enough material to start marketing it.

GLOSSARY
OF PETS

COMMON NAME:
Axolotl

SCIENTIFIC NAME:
Ambystoma mexicanum (also
A. talpordeum and
A. subsalsum)

DISTRIBUTION: Mexico

HABITAT: Mountain lakes

ADULT SIZE: 30 cm (12 in)

General. Axolotls are the king-size tadpoles of a Mexican Salamander. The odd thing is that although they are immature, they breed freely. This condition, which is known as neoteny, is due to a lack of thyroxine. In the wild it sometimes happens that the waters in which the Axolotls live, dry up and the beds of the lakes become baked solid by the sun, but the Axolotls, instead of dying as one might expect, lose their gills and become adult salamanders.

Generally these animals are a dark greyish black, but there is another form, that is frequently kept in captivity, which is almost completely white apart from the bright red, feathery gills.

Food. In the wild Axolotls take tadpoles, insect larvae and fish. In captivity they eat earthworms, maggots and many kinds of other live food. Feed only on alternate days as digestion is slow.

Housing. The only way to keep Axolotls is in an aquarium. A large tank can house several, but they are better kept individually in tanks measuring 60 × 30 × 38 cm (24 × 12 × 15 in) as in a community they tend to bite off each other's feet and gills, although these usually regenerate eventually. A thick layer of gravel should be placed in the bottom and the tank filled with clean water which must be chlorine free, so if you are using tap water, do leave it to stand for a couple of days before introducing an Axolotl. A water temperature of not less than 20°C (68°F) is essential. The tank can contain water plants and rocks.

Breeding. Adult females are plumper than males and the latter have an enlarged cloaca. Though Axolotls will breed throughout the year, the spring is generally the best time and to induce breeding lower the water temperature slightly and introduce a male into a female's tank. The male will court the female with a dance that involves much tail swishing and after mating a collection of eggs will be deposited on stones and the leaves of plants. They should be removed to a separate tank as adult Axolotls will eat their babies. In the wild around 400 eggs are laid at a time, and even in captivity Axolotls produce large quantities which, in a water temperature of 21°C (79°F), will hatch in two to three weeks. The young animals should be fed with suitably sized livefood such as *Daphnia*, mosquito larvae, Brine Shrimp and tubifex.

COMMON NAME: Bird Eating Spider (sometimes incorrectly referred to as Tarantula)

SCIENTIFIC NAME: Many species, but typically *Brachypelma smithi*

DISTRIBUTION: The tropics

HABITAT: Various, from rain forest to savannah, parkland, marshland and beneath the floors and roofs of buildings

ADULT SIZE: 7.5–20 cm (3–8 in)

General. The most commonly kept spiders are the bird eating spiders. They are becoming ever more popular with fanciers, so much so that the Red Jointed Bird Eating Spider, or as it is sometimes known, the Red Kneed Tarantula, is now protected throughout its range in Mexico. Luckily there are numbers of captive-bred specimens available, and in fact the number of species that are bred in captivity is increasing all the time.

All spiders are venomous, but most of those that are commonly kept are neither lethal nor aggressive. The Red Jointed Bird Eating Spider is a very placid animal, as is the common Pink Toed Bird Eating Spider. A newly imported specimen or one that is upset will sometimes make a rapid flickering movement with the back legs.

191

Close examination of this behaviour will reveal that the spider is combing some of the hairs from the abdomen and throwing them at you. They stick in the skin and can be an irritant. Some people are not affected by them while others react quite badly. I have found that if you are attacked like this you can hold your arm up to the light and by looking closely you can usually see little clumps of the hairs standing vertically. Removing these carefully with a pair of tweezers soon ends the irritation.

A few of these spiders, such as the African Baboon Spiders, are aggressive, and as such are not for the novice. Some spiders can jump astonishingly well, and it can be fairly disconcerting if you are not expecting it. Handling them requires considerable care because if you drop one it will almost certainly die.

One tends to think of these spiders as fairly slow moving. This is a fallacy and in the wild they can run really fast when they wish. Periodically a spider will moult; it will lie on its back to do this, seeming for all the world as though it is dying. Do not turn it over, this behaviour is quite natural.

Adult males are rarely imported, and a male does not live long after reaching maturity so it is important to use him to fertilise as many females as possible while he can.

Food. Bird eating spiders will take any livefood of suitable size, such as crickets and mice, so they are not usually difficult to feed.

Housing. Spiders cannot be kept together; they will kill each other. They should be kept in individual small glass or plastic tanks, maintained at a temperature of 24–29°C (75–85°F). Special tanks, with fitted lids, can be bought for spiders in the better pet shops. If you use an ordinary fish tank, you can fit it with a plastic or glass lid with a small gap around the edge for ventilation, or you can cover the tank with plastic mesh of a suitable grade. Spiderlings are sometimes kept in plastic sweet jars.

Breeding. A suitable female should be introduced to a male and a close watch kept on the animals until the mating is over, since it is very likely that the female will attack the male and kill him. When they have been separated the male can be used to fertilise another female. Meanwhile the female, if she is pregnant, will lay her eggs which she will carry around in a specially created bundle. In due course they will hatch into a multitude of tiny spiderlings which must be separated from the mother or she will eat them. Newly hatched spiders require very small food items such as baby crickets or even Fruit Flies. There is always a ready market for spiderlings.

COMMON NAME:
Budgerigar

SCIENTIFIC NAME:
Melopsittacus undulatus

DISTRIBUTION: Australia, principally east of Perth, western New South Wales and along the Murray River

HABITAT: Inland grass plains

ADULT SIZE: 20 cm (8 in)

General. Budgerigars were first brought to Europe about 150 years ago, and since then have become ever more popular. In the wild they are green and smaller than domestic birds, but in captivity all sorts of colour forms have been developed by breeders. Those that one finds in pet shops are frequently the rejects from a show stud, which is not to say there is anything wrong with them — they simply do not conform to show standards. Budgies do sometimes contract a disease known as scaly face which is highly infectious, so that once it appears in an aviary it can infect a complete flock. So if you see a budgie you like but it looks a bit scabby around the eyes or beak, leave it strictly alone and go somewhere else for your bird, even if the proprietor tells you that it is a special breed.

The bare skin above the beak is known as the cere, and in cocks it is blue, brown in hens, but in young birds it is sometimes difficult to tell what colour it is going to turn into, so just use your judgement if you see a bird you fancy. If you want a single pet budgie, always buy a youngster. Baby budgies are called 'barheads' as the feathering above the cere shows lots of fine bars of dark colouring. An adult on the other hand has perfectly clear feathering with no sign of these markings.

Budgerigars are gregarious and are only happy with lots of friends and relatives around them, so if you are going to keep a single bird you must be prepared to be a flock of budgies to provide the companionship your bird needs. Which brings us to talking birds. Good talking budgies are uncommon. Get a youngster — some people say that cocks learn to talk better than hens but I have not seen any evidence that this is true, so take your pick. Then tame your bird so that it is completely relaxed with you

193

and make sure it cannot hear other birds. Once you have got to this stage you are halfway there — the rest is just patiently repeating a very simple, single phrase over and over till you get results, which can be rewarded with little treats and stroking, but finally, when a bird can speak, do not imagine that it will necessarily do so on command. Do not keep budgies with other birds — they can be aggressive.

Food. Budgerigars require a commercial Budgerigar Mixture of assorted millets and canary seed together with millet sprays. Good mineral grit is also essential, plus cuttlefish bone and a constant supply of fresh, clean water.

Soaked seed is an excellent addition to the diet, and when you can get hold of it greenfood and seeding grasses will be welcomed.

One of the commercial vitamin mixtures should be given regularly, and when Budgerigars are breeding, some fanciers supply them with little cubes of wholemeal bread soaked in milk with glucose sprinkled on top. It is not however, a good idea to give this to a single bird in a small cage as it is fattening. Some Budgerigars will take bits of fruit such as apple, tomato or grape but others refuse to touch such goodies.

In an aviary a bird will pick and choose the different items available to it and use up a lot of energy flying around, but sitting by itself next to the television it will get bored and might very well stuff itself silly on a particular item; so, if you are keeping a single bird, only give it a little greenfood or fruit. You are not being kind by giving it treats like this; it can be cruel and result in intestinal disorders. The majority of the diet must be the seed: do not change the brand of seed mixture.

Whenever you re-fill a seed pot always gently blow away the empty husks on the top before you add more food. From a distance the pot may look full of seed until the husks are removed.

Housing. An aviary is ideal, otherwise as large a box cage as possible. Do not use conventional wire budgie cages; they let in draughts and do not provide any security for the bird. Replace dowel perches with lengths of natural, fruit-tree wood — washed well to remove any pollution. If you can, let the bird out of the cage each day — it will get more exercise. But each time, make sure that all doors, windows and fireplaces are covered and that there are no predators in the room. Do not force him out of his cage and he will return when he wants, if you leave the door open.

Budgies are very fond of bathing and in an aviary you will naturally supply a shallow pond of some sort for them which must have a textured bottom and a slope at one end so that a waterlogged bird can walk from the water. If a budgie is to be kept in a cage, the best way of letting it bathe is to invest in a plastic enclosed bath that clips onto the door frame when it is open. The birds do fling water about with abandon, however, so make sure the cage is not near your television set.

Breeding. Budgerigar breeding is a fine art and each year many breeders go to considerable lengths to breed especially find birds, most of which are bred from a single pair in one of a number of cages in a birdroom. Only in this way can one be sure that your birds will breed true. If you are not interested in Budgerigar genetcs, it is perfectly possible to breed them on the colony system such as that described on pp. 208-9.

Nest boxes should be placed high up and out of the way, and in an aviary there should be more nest boxes than hens so that there is no squabbling over sites. If you happen to have a bad natured hen in an aviary, take her out or she will make life really difficult for everyone else.

Birds should not be allowed to breed till they are at least eight months olds, and though they will breed for most of the year, it is best to start the season about the beginning of March and remove the nest boxes again in August. A hen will usually begin to sit after she has laid two eggs, and as a result the chicks will hatch out at intervals. During incubation (18 days) the cock will feed his mate. The chicks will remain in the nest for about a month before they fly after which the cock will care for them while the hen will start to lay a second clutch of eggs.

Not infrequently a hen kept on its own in a cage will lay an egg. This will be infertile and will never hatch, even if you keep it in the airing cupboard.

COMMON NAME:
Bushbaby

SCIENTIFIC NAME: *Galago* species such as *senegalensis, demidoffi*

DISTRIBUTION: African tropics

HABITAT: Rain forest, gallery forest and savannah with trees

ADULT SIZE: 20-45 cm (8-18 in)

General. There are six species of bushbaby, but the most commonly available is the Senegal Bushbaby, though occasionally Thick-tailed Bushbabies or minute Demidoff's Bushbabies can be found.

Bushbabies live for ten to 15 years or more in captivity and can be kept in groups of females and young together with a single male. Mature males will fight savagely and such battles may even end in the death of the loser if they are not separated. All species are nocturnal and, because you might perhaps only have seen them during the day, it would be easy to think of them as slow moving — be warned, a bushbaby can cover 10 m (33 ft) in less than five seconds. Some people keep a single specimen and let it have the run of the sitting room each evening once it has been tamed; but the idea is not to be recommended. They are fairly fragile little animals and need to be handled sensitively and gently.

Never allow the animals or the cages to become damp, and clean the cage daily, but do not disturb nest boxes when there are young or new animals around. Tame a bushbaby by coaxing it gently with a favourite food such as a mealworm; never treat the animal roughly; and always remember that a bushbaby can give a painful bite. Bushbabies are marvellous animals but they are not good pets for a novice. You need plenty of experience as an animal keeper to look after bushbabies.

At night these animals frequently call loudly to each other and mark their progress along branches by 'urine washing', which is a fascinating bit of behaviour to watch if you are lucky enough to see it. An animal will balance on one foot while it deposits urine in the hollow of the opposite hand and foot. The scent of this urine then gets deposited on the branch when the animal repeats the whole operation on the opposite limbs. As it travels around it leaves a scent trail for others to follow. Each will go about its own business during the night, and in the morning, following a special rallying call they will all meet up again to sleep, usually all piling onto one nest box if they can. In the wild they will use a hole in a tree and sometimes they will make a nest of leaves in a suitable fork.

Food. These charming little animals are by no means easy to feed for they require chopped fresh fruit and vegetables, assorted livefood such as crickets, mealworms, locusts and waxmoths, baby foods and primate cubes. Multivitamin compounds must be provided as well, and clean water should be available at all times.

Housing. Bushbabies are active animals and need plenty of space, and a very minimum ought to be about 1.5 × 1.5 × 2.1 m (5 × 5 × 7 ft) high. The one condition of paramount importance is an absence of draughts, which are absolutely fatal. They need a temperature of 24°C (75°F): an infra-red dull emitter in a weldmesh cage (so that the bushbaby cannot burn itself) within the cage is ideal. The enclosure must be fitted with a nest box or two of adequate size and filled with sweet, fresh hay; a good supply of branches ought to be securely fixed so that the animal can perch, run about and jump from one to another. Faeces are very moist so a good absorbent floor covering such as newspaper or wood shavings should be laid and cleaned regularly.

Although Bushbabies are delightful animals, they are rarely seen to advantage since they are nocturnal, and there is nothing more infuriating than being kept awake night after night by an animal when you are trying to go to sleep. However, if you are determined to keep Bushbabies, I feel that the best solution of all would be to construct a cage in a dark place that could be fitted with electrical apparatus to enable one to reverse day and night, such as one can see nowadays in the better zoos. Timing devices and automatic dimmers are readily available these days so that anybody can set up such a system without the need for an electrician.

Breeding. Perhaps the best combination of animals to buy is one male and two or three females until you have built up a family group, but be warned, bushbabies are expensive. The male will impregnate all his females whenever they are in season, and this means that a female can produce twice a year. Gestation is about 130 days and usually either one or two babies are born at a time. Bushbabies, however, do not for the most part breed readily in captivity as they require highly specialised care.

COMMON NAME: Butterfly and moth. Many species, such as Small Tortoiseshell Butterfly and Cinnabar Moth

SCIENTIFIC NAME: Many, such as *Aglaia urtica* and *Callimorpha jacobaeae*

DISTRIBUTION: Worldwide, apart from polar regions

HABITAT: Almost everywhere that plants are to be found

ADULT SIZE: 0.5–23 cm
(¹/₅–9 in)

General. There are enormous numbers of species of butterflies and moths though, like many animals, the populations are decreasing, usually as a direct result of the intervention of humans.

Moths are usually nocturnal and have antennae of different forms, frequently feathery, and in repose they lay their wings horizontally on the back. Butterflies are generally diurnal, have antennae that look rather like matchsticks, with a knob on the end, and rest with their wings held vertically.

Many species of butterfly and moth can be maintained in captivity. Native species are easier than those from the tropics which need high temperatures and humidity. Lifespans of adults vary between a few weeks and several months. Some species hibernate.

Food. Adult butterflies and some moths feed on nectar from flowers. This can be supplied in captivity by soaking a piece of sponge rubber in a sugar solution and letting the butterfly stand on it whereupon it will usually feed. Some adult moths do not feed.

Larvae feed on the leaves of plants. Each species has its specific foodplant, or sometimes a choice of two or three, and they will not eat anything else. The best way of feeding the larvae is to put a potted specimen of the foodplant in the cage, but note that you may well need more than one. Do not buy a plant from a garden centre or nursery as they will have been treated with pesticides and your precious caterpillars will die. Grow the foodplant yourself without using any chemicals. This may well mean that you have to anticipate the purchase of your larvae by a year. Butterflies and moths are usually bought as pupae, or sometimes larvae. It is no use buying live adults — they are just too delicate.

Foodplants of some of the commoner British butterflies:

Brimstone	Buckthorn
Chequered Skipper	Slender false brome grass
Comma	Elm, nettle, hop
Large White	Brassicas
Orange Tip	Hedge mustard, sweet rocket
Peacock	Stinging nettle
Red Admiral	Stinging nettle
Small Tortoiseshell	Stinging nettle

Housing. Butterflies and moths are best housed in small cages made of nylon or terylene netting, or in a sleeve on a branch of a suitable tree. Do not keep them in a glass tank, as any moisture on the glass will cause the insects' wings to stick to the tank if they touch it and death will result from this accident.

Breeding. Some species of butterfly and moth breed far more easily than others and due to the large number of species involved it is impossible to be any more specific here, so it is important to read further on the subject if you are interested in breeding these insects. However, if you obtain a number of pupae when they emerge as adults in the spring you ought to find some of them mating soon afterwards. Very shortly after that the female will lay her eggs on the foodplant, and a week or two later the tiny caterpillars will hatch. They will probably eat the egg shells and then commence feeding on the edge of a leaf. They continue to grow until in late summer they pupate. Where they do this depends on the species, some bury themselves into peat on the floor of the cage, and others attach themselves to part of the plant or a suitable flat surface. In the spring the adults will emerge from the pupal cases and climb up a vertical twig to hang quietly while they inflate their wings.

COMMON NAME:
Canary

SCIENTIFIC NAME: *Serinus canarius*

DISTRIBUTION: Originally the Canary Islands. Now domesticated throughout the world

HABITAT: Wherever trees are found

ADULT SIZE: 13 cm (5 in)

General. Pet canaries are kept mainly for the song of the cock — the hen just cheeps. Most people think that canaries are always yellow, but they can also be brown, khaki, green, orange, red and white. You can even get crested varieties. Canaries are gregarious and should not be kept alone.

They are accommodating little birds that are easy to care for, they are truly domesticated and will breed in a suitable cage if you are interested in keeping a pair. However, sexing canaries is difficult and you may ask to buy a cock and be given a hen in all good faith.

Food. A Canary Mixture of seed from your pet shop forms the basis of the bird's diet, which should be supplemented with a variety of greenstuff. Mineral grit, cuttlefish bone and clean water are essential. Special food is required when the birds are breeding.

Housing. A good box cage is quite suitable for a single canary, and these birds will nest quite happily in a 90 cm (36 in) cage. The cage should be fitted with natural wood perches (never dowel) from a fruit tree or willow, that should be changed periodically. The best floor covering is several layers of clean newsprint. The birds also do well in an outdoor aviary.

Breeding. One of the interesting things about breeding canaries is that, unusually amongst cage birds, they nest in an open pan rather than a nest box. When breeding a special food is required. This can be made from a mixture of hard boiled egg and biscuit.

COMMON NAME: Cat

SCIENTIFIC NAME: *Felis catus*

DISTRIBUTION: Probably of North African origin, now worldwide

HABITAT: Originally savannah, nowadays around humans

ADULT SIZE: 45 cm (18 in)

General. The origins of the domestic cat are not entirely clear, but the bones of African wild cats have been discovered in caves that were normally inhabited by early humans. That is not to say that the cats were tame as the bones might be those of animals that were hunted as food. We do know, however, that by 3000 BC cats were being kept in grain stores by the Egyptians to control the rats and mice that invaded the buildings. Phoenicians took them to Italy whence they slowly spread across Europe. The earliest record we have of domestic cats in Britain is a law protecting them that was enacted by Howel Dda, a Welsh prince.

The long haired cats are thought to have evolved separately from species that inhabited the region around Afghanistan. It was not until the nineteenth century that cat shows as we know them came into existence (though David Taylor refers to one in 1598), when specialist Fancies relating to the different breeds of cats began to gain popularity. Today there are more than 100 breeds and varieties of the domestic cat.

Unlike dogs, of which there are many working examples, the cat is almost invariably kept as a pet, apart from farm cats which perform a valuable pest control service. Since all cats are much the same size and shape beneath their fur a prospective owner does not have to take into account the wide range of factors that face a dog owner. Cats are far less demanding as pets, but you must establish that every member of the family is keen on the idea of a cat before you go out and get one. You will then need to choose between a pedigree cat and a crossbreed. If you are not concerned about showing your cat I would recommend a crossbreed. Each cat leads an individual life style and yours will spend much of his time away from home. Pedigree cats are valuable animals and thefts are increasing. Crossbreeds are usually safe from theft, and in appearance they are so variable that one can find in them most of the characteristics of pedigree cats. Another advantage of the crossbreed is their price. Put the word around that you are looking for one and the chances are that you will not have to pay for it, or if you go to a local cats' home run by an animal welfare organisation you will have the added satisfaction of knowing that you might have saved an animal from a premature death.

Almost all pet cats are obtained as kittens, and until they have had all their injections — against feline enteritis, feline influenza, and rabies, if endemic — you should keep them in the house. Similarly, if you do take on an older cat, prevent it from going outdoors on its own until it has learnt to accept your home as its new territory or it might well return whence it came.

I have no idea how the idea arose that a cat needs to be out all night. On a warm summer night he might very well choose to go out, but it is quite wrong to put him out whether or not he wants to go, and during the winter such behaviour is irresponsible and cruel.

Much has been made of the difficulty of getting a cat to take tablets when the need arises. People hide the pills in food and get cross when the cat spits it out. All you need to do is to crush the pill and mix it with a little golden syrup or honey and smear it over the top of the front paws. A cat will not like the sticky sensation and will soon lick it off.

Food. Most domestic cats are fed on commercial diets which can be bought from your supermarket or pet shop. Do not feed canned dog food to a cat, as it is inadequate in its vitamin, mineral and fat content.

Breeding. If your cat is a crossbreed, have the thing neutered. Sackloads of unwanted perfectly healthy kittens are killed every year by vets and animal welfare organisations simply because people will not have their cats neutered. Don't add to this massacre; have your cat done before it is old enough to breed.

Owners of a pedigree animal might want to breed their cat. Make sure it is registered with the Governing Council of the Cat Fancy in Britain or the Cat Fanciers' Association in the USA, and that a potential mate is similarly registered. These bodies will put you in touch with breeders of the type of cat you are looking for to mate with your own so that you can make arrangements to pair the two animals.

COMMON NAME:
Chipmunk

SCIENTIFIC NAME: Many
species such as *Eutamias sibiricus* and *Tamias striatus*

DISTRIBUTION: Temperate
sub-tropical and tropical regions of the world, though the animals usually kept are from Asia and the USA

HABITAT: Originally, forest
underbrush and broken rocky ground with plenty of ground cover, bushes and trees. Being opportunists, they are also found in similar places in close proximity to humans and many gardens and parks have a population of chipmunks, or ground squirrels as they are sometimes known. They are abundant in many zoos where they take advantage of the food put out for the captive animals

ADULT SIZE: 25 cm (10 in)

General. Chipmunks spend much c. .ne day (and the night) rushing around being busy. They rarely stop except during brief periods when they freeze and peer in concentrated fashion into the distance for a few seconds. They seem to be looking hard at something neither you nor I can see. This habit is known as a 'ghost stare'.

They spend a good deal of time preparing for winter by stockpiling food, and sometimes you find little piles in their cages. If your animals are tame and live indoors, and are sometimes given the run of the room, you will discover odd sunflower seeds hidden down the sides of chairs, under mats and all over the place. It is a good idea to remove all these otherwise in time you will find that the chipmunks are becoming reluctant to return to their cages as there is plenty of food outside. They move very fast, and can, if they set their minds to it, bite very hard indeed.

Food. In the wild chipmunks eat nuts, seeds, insects, leaves and occasionally tree bark. Though they live on the ground they will readily climb trees for berries or nuts. They also take insects and fruit.

The best basic diet in captivity is a commercial hamster mix supplemented with chopped fruit and vegetables, and insects such as mealworms or crickets. Too many peanuts are not a good idea for caged chipmunks. You should also provide fruit-tree branches for the animals to gnaw so that their teeth are kept in good condition.

Clean water is essential and the best way to provide it is through a fountain attached to the side of the cage — an open dish of water will either become full with rubbish or be tipped over when an animal decides to see what lives underneath.

Housing. A metal or glass cage, which should be as large as possible if chipmunks are to be kept indoors, though they will do a lot better outdoors in an enclosure not less than 1.8 × 1.2 m (6 × 4 ft).

All chipmunks are escape artists, so every care must be taken to see that the tiniest holes are closed. The chipmunks must have sleeping/breeding boxes which ought to be draughtproof and warm with plentiful supplies of bedding, such as shredded paper. Chipmunks are active animals so lots of branches, hiding places and so on must be provided for them. In my chipmunk 'aviary' I have placed a giant bale of moss peat with a few holes cut into the plastic and they happily spend hours tunnelling through this.

Cage floors should be covered with wood shavings or shredded paper. Ordinary sheets of paper are of no use as the animals tear it to pieces to use as bedding, leaving the cage floor bare. In a cage a hamster wheel is a good idea if the animal will use one. A good ground covering in an aviary is peat and leaves.

Breeding. Although the sexes are alike, a male in breeding condition can be identified by its large scrotum. A male that is ready to mate lets out a short high pitched whistle every now and again. Chipmunks breed well in captivity and nowadays are almost always captive-bred. They seem to copulate throughout the year but the breeding season is in early spring. Successful mating takes place in February or March, and gestation is 31–40 days. A female will disappear into her nest box to have her babies at which time the male is removed to live elsewhere. Generally between four and eight young are born and at birth they are blind and almost without fur though one can see the stripes even at this stage. They grow fast and are soon independent. It is important to start taming chipmunks when they are tiny, but do not disturb the nest box nor try to clean it out until the offspring are a good four weeks old. Although chipmunks will live for several years the females cease to breed after four or five.

COMMON NAME:
Dog

SCIENTIFIC NAME: *Canis familiaris*

DISTRIBUTION: Probably originating in the Middle East, the domestic dog can now be found worldwide

HABITAT: Close association with man

ADULT SIZE: 45 cm–1.90 m (18 in–6 ft) in length

General. It is thought that domestication of some sort of wild dog first took place between 10,000 and 35,000 years ago. The first domesticated dogs undoubtedly served some specific purpose though no one is sure whether they were bred for hunting, to be eaten, or for some other purpose. In due course different types evolved and today there are about 200 distinct breeds available.

Though dogs, as pets, have many advantages they are by no means ideal and nobody should buy one without carefully considering the implications of adding a dog to the family. It is obvious not to take on a large, active dog if you live at the top of a tower block, as it will need far more exercise than most people realise. Equally, there is no point buying a tiny Yorkshire terrier if you are the sort of person who loves to spend the weekends tramping across hills. A final point to bear in mind is that dogs are pack animals and, as part of a human household, the family must be the rest of the pack. Most things that a dog does are directly related to its position in the pack and it is vital that members of the pack are with it all the time. Consequently, if every member of the family is out all day at work or school, it is useless thinking of a dog as a pet. How often have you known someone come home from work only to find chewed carpets in the sitting room and puddles in the hall and shout at the dog for doing these things? Yet it is the fault of the owner, not the dog, although dogs will do their utmost to fit in with your life style, they are not human.

Furthermore, it must be realised that dogs are not cheap to keep. As well as cans of food, there are the veterinary bills, the cost of kennels while you are on holiday, essential insurance premiums, dog grills in the car and the many other bits and pieces needed to keep a dog.

Having decided that a dog really is for you, the next stage is to think about whether to buy a pedigree dog or a mongrel. If the dog is to be a pet, pure and simple, I would suggest a mongrel every time as they tend to be more robust than a pedigree dog, they are not generally prone to all the inherited defects that bedevil many breeds these days and they are frequently of individual appearance. Another point in their favour is that nobody is going to steal a mongrel, whereas thefts of valuable pedigree dogs are by no means rare. If you do decide to choose a mongrel, a good place to look for it is the kennels of the local animal welfare organisation — you might well save the dog from a premature death. On the other hand, if you want a pedigree dog you can be pretty sure in advance what it is going to look like, how big it is going to grow and what its temperament will be like. Go to the library and find a good dog book which illustrates the different breeds. At first you will be bewildered by the variety but you can start by eliminating the dogs you do not want, because they need too much grooming, or are too big or too small, and then it is up to you to decide on a conventional or less conventional breed.

When every member of the family has agreed on the type of dog, think about whether to get a puppy or an older dog. If you decide on a puppy, you will have to make sure it has its injections — against canine distemper, canine viral hepatitis, leptospirosis, parvovirus, and rabies, if endemic. Most dogs join a household soon after weaning and there is much to be said in favour of this, but there are advantages to getting an older dog. It will have acquired a temperament and a personality and you will know that it is neither neurotic nor snappy, and it should already be house trained. Whatever type of dog you decide upon, do think carefully about holidays. You will have a responsibility to the dog and it really is not fair to leave it in kennels for a fortnight each summer. For the British reader, if you go on holiday in Britain every year there is no problem because you can make arrangements to take the dog with you, but if you feel that you have to migrate abroad annually, perhaps you should not keep a dog at all. Do not even contemplate taking it with you as it will have to spend six months in quarantine upon its return to Britain. Only in this way can the authorities try and prevent rabies from entering the country. Rabies is a dreadful disease that causes a painful and humiliating death. If it ever arrives in Britain it will affect the lives of everybody.

Food. Canned food is the commonest constituent of a dog's diet, but do look at the cans carefully. The majority of canned food available is not a complete diet — it is meant to be supplemented with biscuits or something similar. If that is the case it will say so on the label. Either choose a complete canned diet (which is expensive) or buy the necessary carboyhdrate filler to complement the canned meat. Do not feed your dog the bones from poultry or chops, as these can splinter when they are chewed and cause all sorts of problems. If you want to prepare all the food yourself this is perfectly possible, if somewhat tedious, and further information is contained in the chapter on feeding.

Finally, never feed your dog tidbits in the form of sweets or biscuits or alcohol. That is simply cruelty and you could kill your dog as a result of obesity or any one of a number of other ills.

Housing. Most dogs are kept in the home, so for a pet a cage is not required. Do not keep the dog in a kennel in the garden or on a running lead. Dogs are intelligent animals which need to be part of family life. If you are interested in keeping two or three bitches with a view to breeding from them you will almost certainly want to keep them outdoors in a breeding unit. You should be aware that you will then be required to have the unit licensed by the local authority who will come to inspect it, so read the chapter on legislation and familiarise yourself with the required standards before you start work or buy any expensive equipment.

Breeding. If your dog is a mongrel, take it your vet to be neutered. It is almost impossible to give away unwanted mongrel puppies, and if your dog gives birth to any they will probably have to be killed.

If your dog has a pedigree and you want to breed, make sure that the mate is registered with the Kennel Club as well, check that it has the characteristics that you want the puppies to have and arrange a time with the owner to mate the dogs. If your dog is a male the mating is the end of it and you will come to some agreement with the owner of the bitch with regard to the offspring. The owner of the mother has to think about the pregnancy, the birth and the puppies.

Ensure that the bitch is free of any internal or external parasites before mating, and then follow the information in the chapter on breeding and you ought to have no problems. When the puppies are born, check them to see that they are as they should be, and have enough strength of character to refuse to mutilate them by chopping off tails and ears and so on. Never mind what the show standards are; only by enough people standing against these barbaric practices will the standards be revised.

COMMON NAME:
Finch: Many species of finch, waxbill, weaver, bunting, whydah, nun and sparrow

SCIENTIFIC NAME:
Members of the families Fringillidae, Ploceidae, etc.

DISTRIBUTION:
Throughout Europe, Asia, Australia, Africa and Central and South America

HABITAT: Various but frequently grassland and parkland

ADULT SIZE: 6–30 cm (2½–12 in) including tail

General: These seedeaters do well in community aviaries, but beware, because some are incompatible or aggressive, while others might be perfectly peaceful but because one bird is quite a lot larger than another it might cause a panic when it flies. Some birds might be reasonably housed together, but if the aviary is overcrowded squabbling can result, and this in turn can completely ruin a breeding season.

Some of these birds, such as nuns, need to be watched carefully for overgrown claws. If they are allowed to get too long they can become caught up in the wire netting and the leg might break, or the bird can even die through hanging by a foot that it cannot disentangle. It is a good idea to get someone to show you how to clip a bird's claws the first time. After that it is no problem.

It is best to introduce newly imported birds into an aviary in the early summer so that they have plenty of time to become acclimatised before the cold weather — remember that they have come from climates that are much hotter than our native climates. Even so there must always be a cosy draught-free shelter that they can enter whenever they wish, and it is a good idea to heat it throughout the first winter. Do not worry if you see one of your precious birds bathing in a snow surrounded pond in the middle of February — it does not know that it is supposed to be delicate.

Food. The basic diet is seed, the seed mixture itself — various sorts of millet and canary seed — will vary according to which birds you intend to keep. To this should be added a small amount of Tonic Mixture — a wide variety of seeds — and some sprouted seeds should be given daily. Many of the birds in this section will take food eaten by softbills, such as chopped up insects, fat, fruit, livefood and other foods. As a general rule of thumb the shorter, more chunky the shape of the bill, the more likely it is that seed forms a great part of the diet, while if the bill is longer and sharper, other foodstuffs will probably be more important.

Like all seedeaters these birds need mineral grit to digest their food and a vitamin compound should be added periodically. Clean water is necessary for drinking; I like to provide this in a fountain clipped to the side of the cage/aviary and also in a wide shallow container for bathing.

Housing. Never keep these birds on their own — they are ultra gregarious. They are almost invariably sold in pairs and do better if they are kept in groups. Because of this an aviary is ideal, but they can be housed in cages. They are all very active so cages should be as long as possible. The perches should be as far apart as possible so that the birds can obtain a maximum of exercise, but make sure the birds' tails do not scrape on the walls! Natural perches should be used, not dowels, and these should be scrubbed clean regularly.

Breeding. Nowadays it is becoming rather easier to buy British or US-bred foreign finches and, if you can get hold of them, do not hesitate for they will be hardier than newly imported birds and should breed more readily. Wild populations are being depleted by pollution, destruction of habitat, hunting and trapping and it really is important that all foreign bird fanciers do their utmost to breed their stock these days.

To go about this put up plenty of nest boxes — quite a few more than you have pairs of birds. Some finches like pans to nest in but many like an enclosed nest box and you can buy these made from wicker. You can also use hollowed out coconuts with an entrance in one side and a few drainage holes at the bottom. These nests ought to be sited as near the top of the cage or aviary as possible and as far away from disturbances as you can.

It is important that the aviary is well-planted, for if a bird feels insecure it is not likely to breed, but in addition to this many species use bits of the plants in making their nests — weavers, for example, tear long strips from leaves such as those of pampas grass. Adequate nest material is essential so whenever you find some, as when you comb the dog, stuff it through the wire and someone will find it and use it; but do not use long horse or human hairs, these can get caught round toes and things.

COMMON NAME:
Frog and Toad

SCIENTIFIC NAME:
Various, but those belonging to the genera *Rana*, *Hyla* and *Bufo* are commonly kept

DISTRIBUTION: Worldwide

HABITAT: Moist areas with access to water for breeding

ADULT SIZE: 0.6-40 cm (¼-15 in)

General: People constantly confuse frogs and toads. Generally, toads are warty and frogs are smooth, and toads tend to walk while frogs hop. In addition, frogs are more dependent on water and for this reason their vivaria must be kept pretty humid which means that hygiene is really important. Tanks should not be kept in full sunlight and a fluorescent tube in the hood is a good idea. Unless you are a really experienced amphibian keeper you should not take spawn from the wild as was so commonly done a generation ago. Frogspawn is not the easiest of things to rear to maturity and most people lose it through lack of experience and care.

Many toads return to the same pond each year to breed and most toads breed in water but there are one or two odd ones, such as the Midwife Toad, where the male carries the strings of eggs around, wrapped about his back legs, until they hatch. On the other hand there are a few species of *Xenopus* that never leave the water. These should live in a tank full of water rather like fish, but it is virtually impossible to make their tanks look natural as plants are torn to pieces as the toads scrabble around.

Food. All amphibians are carnivorous and in the wild they will take any animal of suitable size. In captivity, therefore, they should be fed on livefood such as Bluebottles, mealworms, crickets, locusts, waxmoths, earthworms, small mice, chicks and fish such as Guppies or Goldfish. The chicks and mice should be supplied freshly killed. Multivitamin compound should be added. Tadpoles and small amphibians should be kept away from larger ones.

Housing. Trying to keep frogs and toads in an outdoor enclosure never works very well as the populations decline and disappear, and are preyed on by all sorts of animals. However, if you are lucky enough to have a large pond in your garden that is free of Goldfish, then you can enjoy a wild population of frogs. An acquaintance of mine is in this fortunate position and during the breeding season it takes a good fifteen minutes to walk the length of the garden carefully enough to avoid treading on the multitude of froglets that cover the grass.

A greenhouse is a great place for keeping all sorts of frogs from bullfrogs and Marine Toads to tree frogs and if it has suitable ponds and plants in it and can be maintained at a correct temperature, they will thrive. The temperature and humidity will depend on the species of amphibian and reference should be made to the conditions in which they live in the wild.

A large, well ventilated aquarium is also suitable. The floor should be covered in peat or loam with 25 per cent activated charcoal to keep it sweet. Pebbles beneath this layer helps drainage. The vivarium must be covered, for frogs can jump higher than you might think, and tree frogs can climb vertical glass with no trouble. The peat should be covered with growing moss to prevent it getting in eyes, food and water.

A variety of hiding places need to be constructed using slates, florists' bark and terracotta flower pots. Pot plants should be added for appearance and to provide further hidey holes and if you are keeping treefrogs they are vital for climbing about and sitting on. A large pond should be provided which needs cleaning at least twice a day. Frogs are very aquatic animals and mucky water can cause all sorts of problems as amphibians absorb water through their skin. Hygiene is absolutely vital and the whole tank must be carefully cleaned regularly and the plants taken away and hosed down and tidied up, but do make sure there are no animals sitting on the underside of leaves or snuggled down in the compost before you do this.

Breeding. The easiest species to breed are those from temperate zones; after a period of hibernation the frogs and toads enter the water in spring, and breed more readily than those from the tropics. Males and females are often difficult to tell apart though in some species the females are larger. During the breeding season, however, male frogs develop a large dark callous on their front feet and can be observed calling. After the eggs are laid they should be moved to a separate tank or the tadpoles might be eaten. Young tadpoles feed on algae but as they grow they become carnivorous. As they metamorphose into frogs, islands should be provided onto which they can climb.

211

COMMON NAME: Goat

SCIENTIFIC NAME: *Capra hircus*

DISTRIBUTION: Domestic goats are found worldwide, especially commonly in the tropics

HABITAT: In close association with humans, as they are kept to provide milk and meat

ADULT SIZE: 90 cm–1.60 m (3–5 ft) in length

General. Goat-keeping should not be undertaken lightly. Goats are difficult, suicidal, cantankerous animals that cannot put up with damp, so you will need plenty of room and time if you are absolutely set on keeping goats. A goat proof fence is the first essential. Goats will jump, climb, push and nibble, so you must supply such a fence, and a damp-proof shed.

Goats need to be part of a group so most people start by getting two female goatlings which are over a year old. They will be ready to mate the following autumn and thereafter you will have to mate them periodically if you are to have a regular supply of milk. They will usually produce two kids. If they are females you will be able to sell them. If they are billies they will be almost impossible to get rid of and most will have to be killed at birth.

Billies may occasionally be kept as pets but they are big, strong, hungry animals and, unless castrated, they smell extremely pungent.

There are several distinct breeds of goats and you should

choose one of these rather than 'scrub goats'. If you keep all the food for your charges somewhere in the same building in which they live, do ensure that the lids of the bins are absolutely goatproof, which is more difficult than you might imagine. They must also be ratproof or these rodents will soon be everywhere.

If you want milk from your goats there is no option to having them mated every so often which means the inevitable problem with kids. When you start to milk a goat, try and persuade a friend to show you how to do it before you try for the first time. The nanny will begin to get bored if you take too long and once she has lost interest she can make life pretty difficult for you. Before you decide which variety of goat to get for yourself, go to a few herds and sample the milk; it is surprisingly variable from downright rank to absolutely delicious and there is no point bringing home a milking goat if you have to throw away pints of the liquid each day.

Some people who take up goat keeping complain that they end up with too much milk, but even if you can't sell it, you can make cheese and yoghurt and ice cream.

Food. Hay and a mixture of concentrates or special goat nuts are a good basic diet which should be supplemented with root vegetables, hedge trimmings and wild plants, being careful to avoid anything poisonous like laurel, yew, rhododendron, spurge and foxglove. Goats are not sheep and should not be thought of as living mowing machines for the lawn. They browse far more than they graze and will strip any plants that they can reach through their fence.

Housing. Goats should be housed in a damp-proof building which can be divided into separate stalls for each goat. If you intend to milk the animals inside the shed, it is a good idea to make a separate milking stall with a raised platform so that the udders are raised to a convenient height, or you will end up with an aching back.

The walls between the stalls and the fence around the paddock should be nearly as tall as a man — goats can scale fences like a mountaineer.

Breeding. Nannies come into season every three weeks for two days during which time they make enough noise to drive you mad. Mate them in the spring and they will kid five months later in the autumn, or mate them in the autumn for a spring birth. Generally two kids are born.

COMMON NAME: Goldfish

SCIENTIFIC NAME: *Carassius auratus*

DISTRIBUTION: Originally China but nowadays domesticated worldwide

HABITAT: Large, still areas of water and slow-moving streams

ADULT SIZE: 20 cm (8 in)

General. The common Goldfish is familiar to everybody. It is bred in commercial quantities in the Far East and Italy whence it is exported. Sadly, in recent years it has become commonplace to see Goldfish being given as prizes at fairgrounds. This practice is perfectly legal but if you see it go and complain loudly to the stall-holder, and refuse to patronise his stall. It will only stop when there is no demand for prize Goldfish. Quite apart from the losses and cruelty involved in this trade, the chances of getting a healthy fish in a condition in which it will survive is fairly small. Instead, if you want to keep Goldfish, buy your stock from a reputable dealer. But do not keep it in a fish bowl, which is everything an animal home should not be. Goldfish live for around 25 years and you can either keep them in a large indoor aquarium or a garden pond.

The Goldfish Fancy has developed many varieties of the fish, some of which are scarcely recognisable as the common Goldfish. Some types are far too tender to live outdoors, while others may only do so during the summer months. Goldfish are not born gold, and indeed the original wild form is dull brown. Today they are found in all sorts of colours — red, blue, purple and black as well as various oranges and golds. Some varieties have long, flowing fins and tails and others possess grotesque ornamental head growths, while the Celestial resembles a bug-eyed monster.

Food. Goldfish are easy to feed and will take any of the commercial fish foods, though it should be noted that their diet should have a high level of carbohydrate. They feed at all levels of the tank.

Housing. Unlike freshwater tropical fish, Goldfish do not require heat, but they do need more space than tropicals. They are large fish so a generous tank is essential and it should be equipped with filters and aerators. Several fish may be kept together if the tank is large enough. An alternative to the indoor aquarium is the garden pond which ideally should be pretty large as the water in a small pond might be continually cloudy, due to the fish churning up the bottom. If you keep Goldfish in your pond, do not expect any amphibian tadpoles to survive as Goldfish will eat almost anything.

One point to watch if you do keep your fish outside is that they do not end up being eaten by a heron. These magnificent birds sometimes learn to haunt all the ponds in a particular area and the only effective way of deterring them is to cover the surface of the pond with netting. Unfortunately, this can never look anything but awful but with a bit of luck the marauding heron will get the message after a few weeks and go elsewhere.

Breeding. If you have a large pond containing plenty of plants and no major predators, you will almost certainly find a number of baby Goldfish thriving in the water a year or two after your adults have matured. Breeding Goldfish in an indoor tank is another matter altogether and really needs an experienced aquarist's attention to be successful.

COMMON NAME: Guinea Pig or Cavy

SCIENTIFIC NAME: *Cavia porcellus*

DISTRIBUTION: South America

HABITAT: Originally, the rocks on Andean and other hillsides, but Guinea Pigs have been domesticated for many centuries

ADULT SIZE: 25 cm (10 in)

General. These strange little rodents have been kept by South American Indians for centuries to use as food, and they are still treated as such. However in Europe, Britain and North America they are kept as pets and show animals. There are various types and colour varieties available, and the animals are gregarious so they should be kept together.

Guinea Pigs are highly strung animals so they must be approached and handled with care. They are also strange in that many of the common antibiotics prove fatal to them, which means that there may be considerable difficulty in treating them if they become ill. Never keep these animals in a garage as car fumes will kill them. They also suffer from heatstroke, so keep them out of the sun.

Food. Hay and a proprietary mixture of concentrates, or else suitable pellets, form a good basis for a Guinea Pig diet. But they cannot synthesise vitamin C, so have to have a daily supply of fresh fruit or vegetables which must not be wet or frosty.

Housing. Commercial Guinea Pig hutches are not adequate on their own, though they can be used in conjunction with an attached outside run which must have a weldmesh floor or the animals will burrow out. The whole thing can be moved periodically to a new part of the garden. A slab of concrete should be placed outside the hutch door, otherwise the claws will become overgrown.

Breeding. Females come into season once a fortnight, and if mated at that time they will give birth 60–74 days later to a litter of two or three babies. They can breed as early as four to five weeks so one needs to separate the sexes at this time. It is best not to mate animals earlier than about four months.

It is important to buy young animals as the life span is less than three years.

COMMON NAME: Horse (and Pony), Donkey
SCIENTIFIC NAME: *Equus caballus, Equus asinus*
DISTRIBUTION: Worldwide
HABITAT: Almost always in association with humans
ADULT SIZE: 75–180 cm (30–72 in) to the shoulder

General. A pony is of any size up to 14.2 hands. A hand is 10 cm (4 in) and the animal is measured from the ground to the withers, which is the point at which the neck meets the top of the shoulder.

Taking on a horse is a very expensive undertaking that demands considerable dedication and commitment and should not be undertaken lightly. You should contemplate whether you can provide suitable accommodation and the necessary time every day, throughout the year, to care for it.

Food. The feeding regime will vary according to what kind of housing you provide for your horse and what sort of work it has to perform, but grass, hay, water and daily feeds of grain or horse or pony nuts are the minimum requirements.

Housing. A paddock of considerable size and a sound stable are the only acceptable minimum requirements for keeping a horse. Preferably, the stable should incorporate a separate room to store hay, concentrates, tack and tools, and a running water supply.

Breeding. A mare is pregnant for eleven months and, while stud fees for a good stallion are high, it is just not worth economising, as a good foal will fetch much more than an indifferent one.

Donkeys

Donkeys are not small horses, but they are attractive, friendly characters that get on well with horses, and since horses are gregarious animals that live naturally in herds, a donkey will provide companionship without all the expense of a second horse.

Donkeys can range in size from tiny little beasts no taller than a poodle to the Spanish donkeys which are over 12 hands high. Talk to the Donkey Breed Society about quality stock before you buy a donkey or go to one of the donkey sanctuaries.

A donkey will eat far less food than a horse, and can survive on far poorer grazing.

COMMON NAME:
Lizard

SCIENTIFIC NAME:
Lacerta, Varanus, Tupinambis
and other genera

DISTRIBUTION: Worldwide
except for polar regions

HABITAT: Open parkland,
grassland, near rivers,
gardens and inside houses

**ADULT SIZE: 1.8 cm–1.8 m
(0.7 in–6 ft)**

General. Lizards are often feared, but none of them will ever attack humans, and there are only two venomous species in the world. Both come from the USA and Mexico — the Gila Monster and the closely related Beaded Lizard. Lizards are incredible little animals that come in all the colours of the spectrum. Some are silent and some call loudly like birds. There are lizards that swim, there are lizards that glide and every lizard can run very fast, some can even run on the water of creeks and streams, supported only by surface tension.

Lizards, however, are not for the inexperienced. They look tough they can be remarkably delicate and losses in consignments of imported lizards are very high indeed. Plenty of some species are now being bred in captivity and these are the ones to buy. You know how old they are, you know that they are healthy and you know that they are likely to do well in captivity. Even the best newly imported specimens are in a pretty poor state when they arrive.

It is not a good idea to handle lizards, and I am sure you know that most of them will shed their tails as a defence mechanism. A new tail grows in time but it is never as beautiful as the original. Lizards move very fast and you have to be very careful whenever you put your hand in their cage, otherwise they can shoot up your arm and leap for the curtain before you notice. Chameleons are the exception, but they are for the real expert.

Food. Most lizards are carnivores and will take any suitable sized animal food, such as crickets, but some of the large lizards will need rodents and day-old chicks. Beware, a large lizard may eat a

219

small lizard. Many otherwise carnivorous lizards will sometimes take a small quantity of chopped fruit and vegetables; iguanas, in particular, are almost vegetarian. Multivitamin powder, mineral grit and water also form part of their diet.

Housing. The best way to keep lizards is in a large glass tank with a close-fitting lid and a hood. It should be heated (for most species) to a temperature of between 26°C–32°C (80°F–90°F) by means of ceramic heater bulbs, soil warming cables or something similar. Light bulbs should only be used to provide light as there is evidence that constant light may be harmful. The heating should be at one end of the tank so that a lizard may move to a cooler place if it wishes. Good ventilation is imperative, as is a regular dose of ultraviolet light though too much will be detrimental. Heat sources must be inside weldmesh cages to prevent an animal from burning itself.

Choice of cage furniture will depend on the species of lizard, but typically the floor of the tank should be covered with a thick layer of unprinted newsprint, or gravel or peat. Several branches will be needed for arboreal or semi-arboreal species, and various rocks, hiding places and basking slabs should be provided. A large heavy water dish will be necessary. Plants (preferably in pots) may be used as long as they are big, tough ones. Little or fragile plants will soon die from being trampled constantly.

Breeding. Provide the right conditions, and these include temperature, humidity and length of daylight, and there is every likelihood that your lizards will breed, although some species, such as geckoes, are easier to breed than others. If you mist spray the tank to increase humidity, be careful of hot light bulbs which might explode, and electrical connections which might give you or your lizards a shock.

Some lizards give birth to live young, but most lay eggs. Some eggs are glued to the glass and some are laid on the floor and will need to be collected and cared for.

COMMON NAME:
Parrot, cockatoo, macaw, lovebird, parakeet, cockatiel, etc.

SCIENTIFIC NAME:
Psittacus, Cacatua, Ara, Agapornis, Psittacula, Nymphicus and other genera

DISTRIBUTION:
Throughout the tropics and sub-tropics. Introduced elsewhere

HABITAT: Forest, parkland, grassland

ADULT SIZE: 8–90 cm (5–36 in)

General. Parrots are not good pets. To start with they are gregarious, so they should not be kept on their own. A single parrot kept in the house is not a happy bird, and commercial parrot cages are completely inadequate and should not even be considered as suitable for one of these birds. A cockatoo or Amazon Parrot needs a minimum of several cubic metres (feet) of space. Chaining a parrot to a perch by one foot is equally undesirable. The bird becomes frustrated, painful lesions on the leg are common and a bird can break or dislocate a leg without much difficulty. The larger parrots are fairly intelligent animals and under these sorts of conditions they soon become bored, and a bored, frustrated parrot can inflict a very nasty wound. On top of all this they can make a horrendous din, so do not even think of keeping parrots unless you first build an aviary far enough away from any houses so that the noise will not disturb anyone.

Having said that, parrots are attractive, interesting birds so if you can fulfil all the necessary conditions they are fascinating to keep. All parrots are demolition experts, which means that aviaries have to be strongly constructed and any wooden parts have to be sheathed in metal or covered in weldmesh to protect them.

Captive-bred parrots are generally sold as youngsters but if you want the birds for breeding it is better to buy mature birds.

You might have become attracted to the idea of getting a parrot without thinking about prices. If that is the case you ought to be aware that parrots can cost several hundred pounds, and indeed many cost thousands.

221

Food. Most commonly kept parrots are fed on a seed mixture supplemented with considerable amounts of fruit and vegetables, nuts and insects. Some types require far more specialised feeding, since a large part of their diet consists of nectar.

Housing. Large, strong aviaries are essential with a separate flight for each pair of birds. Dividing walls between the flights should have weldmesh on each side of the framework, at least 2.5 cm (1 in) apart. A draughtproof shelter must be provided, with a weldmesh covered window in it to allow light to enter. This shelter may need to be heated, depending on the species of bird that you keep.

I prefer aviaries to be 2 m (6 ft) high — if they are appreciably higher than that catching birds can be difficult. The width of the flight will depend on your birds — obviously a little lovebird needs less width than a large macaw, but whichever you keep the flights should be as long as possible. Always feed your parrots in the shelter so that if you need to shut the birds indoors it is easy to do, since the only access between the flight and the shelter should be a 'pophole' which can be closed from outside the aviary.

Always lock aviaries when you leave them, not just because your birds are valuable, but because parrots will discover how to undo the most intricate of latches.

The aviary must be fitted with substantial perches made from non-poisonous wood, and these will need to be replaced periodically as they are destroyed. It is a waste of time planting the aviary as any shrubs will soon be converted into matchsticks, though grass and millet may be planted on the floor and the birds will enjoy wandering about on it.

The birds will need a large, indestructible water dish, and the food pots must not be plastic otherwise, when they are inevitably broken, the parrot might swallow sharp splinters of plastic.

Breeding. More species of parrot are being bred today than ever before, and if you give them the right conditions the chances are very good that your birds will breed. But do make sure you know someone who will take the babies, before you embark on the exercise.

Parrots of all sorts need to be supplied with large, very strong nest boxes and humidity is critical to ensure that the eggs hatch. A turfed area of the aviary floor is a good idea, as it can be sprayed regularly and the birds will pick up moisture to take back to the nest.

COMMON NAME:
Pigeon (Racing and Ornamental)

SCIENTIFIC NAME: *Columba livia*

DISTRIBUTION: Worldwide in association with humans

HABITAT: Throughout human settlements

ADULT SIZE: 30 cm (12 in)

General. All racing and ornamental pigeons are descended from the Rock Dove and have been associated with humans for a very long time. They are all easy to keep, but when first purchased they must be confined for a few weeks or they might return to their previous home. Pigeon racing is a well established sport and if you wish to become involved you will have to join a club. Racing pigeons live in a loft whereas ornamental varieties such as fantails are usually housed in a dovecote and kept at liberty. They reproduce prolifically and the size of the population could soon become an embarrassment. Whatever pigeons you decide to keep, you will be unpopular with your neighbours if they grow vegetables, since these birds can strip a crop faster than you would believe possible.

Food. Pigeons will eat almost any vegetable matter, but they are usually fed on a basic diet of either special pellets or mixed corn and, of course, they will need grit and fresh water.

223

Housing. Custom made pigeon lofts can be obtained from suppliers, but most start their lives as garden sheds. Dovecotes can be as ornamental as you like, but fancy pigeons will live in any suitable hole so a well made, weatherproof box divided internally into compartments and with entrance holes for the birds will suffice.

Breeding. These birds will breed without any help from you, unless you are specifically aiming to breed a winning or show specimen in which case the parents will have to be separated from the other birds. Pigeons lay two eggs and the chicks are fed a regurgitated, milk-like substance by the adults.

COMMON NAME:
Rabbit

SCIENTIFIC NAME: *Oryctolagus cuniculus*

DISTRIBUTION: Worldwide where introduced by humans

HABITAT: Downland in the wild state, otherwise in captivity

ADULT SIZE: 25-50 cm (10-20 in)

General. Originally from Mediterranean countries, the rabbit was introduced into Britain by the Romans twenty centuries ago, and thereafter it was taken and released in other parts of the world such as Australia where the populations have reached pest proportions. In captivity rabbits are easy to keep, but being gregarious they ought not to be kept on their own. However, unless you have a lot of room, keep only does as bucks will fight. Unfortunately, due to the fact that they will put up with a considerable amount of abuse, rabbits are frequently kept in a very poor state. They need proper care, housing and treatment.

There are several varieties of domestic rabbit, all varying in size and appearance. A rabbit will not remain tame unless it is frequently handled; but never pick one up by its ears.

Food. Rabbits cannot live by lettuce alone, they need a proper diet of hay, concentrates or pellets and a variety of fresh green vegetables.

Housing. Commercial rabbit hutches are far too small, though they are perfectly adequate if you fix an outside run to them so that your rabbits can move freely between the two. But, unless you can keep a more or less constant watch on the animals, make sure that the run has a weldmesh floor or the rabbits will burrow their way out faster than you might think. The whole structure can be moved from one part of the garden to another. There must be periodic access to a concrete floor, however, or the rabbit's claws will become overgrown.

Breeding. Do make sure you have found a home for any rabbits before you breed them. Gestation lasts about 31 days and the doe will have a litter of seven or eight blind, hairless kittens. They are weaned at six to eight weeks at which time they themselves can breed, so the sexes must be separated.

COMMON NAME:
Rodent — rat, mouse, gerbil
and hamster

SCIENTIFIC NAME: *Rattus norvegicus, Mus musculus, Meriones unguiculatus* and *Cricetus auratus*

DISTRIBUTION: The wild forms of rats and mice are found worldwide; the Mongolian Gerbil is from China and Mongolia; and the Golden Hamster originates in Syria. In captivity they are found everywhere

HABITAT: Savannah/grassland/steppes

ADULT SIZE: 15-25 cm (6-10 in)

General. All these animals are easy and pleasing to keep. Hamsters must be kept singly, since otherwise they will fight to the death. All the other species can, and indeed should, be kept together though it must be noted that unless you want to breed your animals you will have to keep only females, and that whilst rats are content to live together and welcome newcomers to their world, mice will not tolerate an introduction unless the newcomer is introduced carefully and slowly, and gerbils will only live harmoniously if the animals are introduced when they are very young.

If an animal is to remain tame it must be handled frequently or it may bite, and all rodents have long, sharp teeth. Never pick up a pregnant mouse by the tail or you may cause her considerable damage, nor should you lift a gerbil by the tail or you may end up holding the skin which breaks off, leaving the animal with a bald, rat-like tail.

Food. The best basis for rodent diets is a commercial seed and pellet mixture, supplemented with a variety of fruit and vegetables. It should also not be forgotten that most rodents are to an extent carnivorous, so they need livefood in the shape of crickets or mealworms.

Housing. Do not buy a metal rodent cage from your pet shop. At best they are far too small, badly designed and boring for the animals; at worst they are lethal (see the chapter on Housing).

By far the best home for a rodent is an aquarium fitted with a weldmesh top on a wooden frame. A small box should be supplied as sleeping quarters, and a quantity of old cardboard boxes, cardboard tubes and so on provide hiding places and interest for the occupants.

Breeding. If you keep both sexes of most common rodents together, they will breed, but if you wish to produce particular colour varieties you will need to do some homework on genetics. Remember that you can only mate hamsters with care or the male will be killed, and that pairs of gerbils must be kept together from the time they are weaned. Additional food will be required by pregnant females, and typical rodent behaviour when a mother is disturbed, or when a colony is overcrowded or otherwise under stress, is to eat the offspring. Therefore care must be taken to allow breeding to take place in peace and quiet.

Rodents are very prolific so one must be certain that the young animals can be disposed of before embarking on a breeding programme.

COMMON NAME:
Snake — Boas, Pythons and many others

SCIENTIFIC NAME:
Commonly kept snakes of the genera *Boa, Python, Natrix, Elaphe*, etc.

DISTRIBUTION: Worldwide except for the Arctic, Antarctic and one or two places such as Ireland

HABITAT: Forest, grassland, desert — pretty well everywhere

ADULT SIZE: 25 cm-8 m (10 in-26 ft)

227

General. The majority of snakes are to be found in the tropics, and the further you travel from the equator the less species will you find, as snakes need warmth to operate, which is why they hibernate during the winter in temperate parts of the world. Some species of snake live in trees, some live on the ground and some even spend their lives in the sea. Only about ten per cent of species of snake are venomous, and many of those are not lethal to humans. Many snakes are nocturnal.

Snakes are good animals to keep as pets, but keeping snakes should not be undertaken lightly. Like all animals there are aspects of their husbandry that can present problems and somebody taking on a snake must understand this, but the right snake is an even better pet, in my opinion, than the more commonly kept cats, dogs and ponies. Always remember that every single snake in the world is a born escapologist, which will somehow manage to squeeze through the tiniest space. If one does escape there is a pretty good chance that you will recover it if you think intelligently. First of all consider whether the snake is terrestrial or arboreal. If it is a tree-living specimen it will try to move upwards while something like a Python will get down to the floor as soon as it can. The next thing to look for is the nearest dark hole and after that, somewhere warm. Even if you do not find your snake immediately do not despair; it is amazing how many of them turn up weeks later.

When you are looking for a snake to buy, leave Grass Snakes alone. It is tempting to start with one because they are familiar, a reasonable size and fairly inexpensive, but believe me, they are not for beginners and if it is to be your first snake you will probably lose it fairly soon. The best first snake of all is a young Boa Constrictor or python. They are small, easy to handle, beautiful and a pleasure to look at, but if you like the idea of a Reticulate Python, think carefully. They can be snappy beasts, and although that will not matter now, a bite from a 3 m (10 ft) specimen is best avoided. Indian Pythons, Ball Pythons and African Pythons are better. If you are bitten by your snake the damage is usually minimal — no worse than the pricks and scratches you get when you are out collecting blackberries. I would rather handle a large, angry snake than a small, angry cat any day of the year.

Every so often your snake will slough, or change its skin. A few days before this happens the eyes will go cloudy and the snake will not feed and might strike at you because it cannot see too clearly. Then one day it will rub its nose on a conveniently rough surface to loosen the old skin, and over the next several minutes the snake will haul himself out from it, usually leaving a complete, inside out snakeskin, which you should remove. The snake will look particularly beautiful after a slough and will probably be ready for a drink and possibly a meal. The interval between sloughs varies enormously between a few weeks and several months.

Food. With one or two rare exceptions, wild snakes kill and eat animals of a suitable size. Some species will take almost anything, whereas other have highly specific tastes in food and these must be borne in mind with captive specimens.

A young snake will need feeding frequently, perhaps several times a week, but as it grows the interval between feeds will decrease (though often it is not constant), and sometimes a snake will fast for months. By law, all rodents, chicks and other similar food must be dead when it is offered to a snake.

Housing. Most captive snakes are kept in aquarium tanks, glass shop counters or something similar. They ought to be of adequate size — bigger than they often are. The cage furnishings will depend on the type of snake, but typically the floor should be covered with a thick layer of sheets of plain newsprint, or perhaps gravel or peat (but never sand) and a variety of perches, rocks and hiding places.

Some snakes need holes that are so small they can feel the sides when they are resting inside. A good heavy water dish that cannot be tipped over must be provided and the cage should be heated to between 26°-32°C (80-90°F), depending on the species of snake. It is not a good idea to provide the heating by means of a light bulb for more than a short while as there is evidence that this could be harmful. Ceramic heater bulbs, soil-warming cables or something of the sort should provide the heat, and a light used only as a light source. Whatever heat source you use, put it at one end of the cage so that the snake can move to a cooler place if it wishes. Do make sure that the snake cannot burn itself by making a wiremesh cage around light bulbs and heaters. Ultraviolet light in small doses is vital, but the constant use of UV is linked with skin tumours and eye problems.

Breeding. Just occasionally a snake is imported which gives birth after you have obtained her, but until recently hardly any captive breeding was being done. Fortunately, today more and more snakes are being produced in captivity, and about three years ago someone in Nottinghamshire was accepted on a government enterprise allowance scheme to breed snakes commercially. So, if you look after your snakes carefully and sensitively and keep proper records, there is a good chance that you might be able to breed from them.

COMMON NAME:
Softbill (denoting any birds
that are not seedeaters)

SCIENTIFIC NAME: Many;
typical families are Sturnidae
(Mynahs), Tanagridae
(Tanagers), Zosteropidae
(White eyes), Pycnonotidae
(Bulbuls)

DISTRIBUTION: Worldwide

HABITAT: Various

ADULT SIZE: From 7.5 cm
(3 in)

General. To my mind, some of
the foreign softbills are the most
pleasing of all birds to keep and
many of them will become delightfully tame. They are always
expensive but I do not consider it responsible to keep a single bird
— fanciers should try to breed as many species as possible. These
birds should preferably only be kept by experienced birdkeepers
because there is no doubt that they are not as easy as many other
types of birds. Keeping these, above all others, does need experience and understanding and because there are so many widely
differing types it is difficult to generalise, and much depends on an
individual's facilities. Many softbills, such as the tits, cannot be kept
together as they are far too aggressive.

Food. In the wild, softbills eat a wide variety of fruit, insects and
other small animals, vegetables and nectar. Many have highly
specific food requirements, and will not survive unless they are
absolutely right, so do not assume that what follows is correct for
a particular bird — read it up in some specialist books first.
Because many softbills are pretty demanding, many foreign bird
keepers start with common seedeaters and work their way up to
softbills after gaining experience with other, easier, birds.

As a general guide, begin with a good proprietory softbill
mixture which contains all sorts of things to keep your bird
healthy. It is made in different grades which are specified on the
packet, so you can buy a fine grade for a tiny zosterop and a
much coarser one for a big bird, such as a Javan Hill Mynah. You
will also need a pot of finely chopped fruit and perhaps vegetables
— but do go easy on banana which is not too good in quantity;

and, finally, provide some livefood. What kind will depend on the type of bird, but it could be *Drosophila* or maggots, mealworms, crickets, locusts, cockroaches, ants or bluebottles, and should be dusted with a vitamin supplement first. Fresh water should be available at all times.

Sponge cake soaked in a thin sugar and water or sugar and milk solution is appreciated by many birds, whilst things like humming birds and sunbirds need nectar. Many people who specialise in these types of birds have their own recipes but there are commercial nectars available and some of these are superb.

Housing. Some softbills, such as mynahs, are gregarious and quite happily live in community aviaries. Others are pugnacious and territorial and will not tolerate their kind apart from during a short breeding season, so if you are contemplating putting softbills into an aviary (where most do very well), do be careful. It is not as difficult as it may seem, just look at television programmes and in books, and watch similar types of bird around your home and see which are gregarious and which are not. Some of the more common softbills that can be kept in community aviaries, but not necessarily together because of size difference are:

White Eyes	Pied Mynahs
Pekin Robins	Pagoda Mynahs
Common Mynahs	Silver Eared Mesias
Bank Mynahs	Tanagers

Many of the softbills just cannot be left to winter without access to a well-heated birdroom, and if softbills are kept in cages particular attention must be paid to hygiene since by their very nature their food is wet and sticky and therefore so are their droppings. As large a box cage as possible should be used for softbills and the cage floor needs to be cleaned daily, while perches and walls need a good scrub frequently.

Breeding. All sorts of exotic softbills have been bred in captivity and the number is constantly rising. You will need to provide privacy, plenty of nest sites in a variety of types depending on the kind of bird, and as varied and nutritious a diet as possible.

Take care about the birds you keep in adjacent flights. All of them may be peaceable but if some are appreciably larger than others or simply frantically busy, their presence and activity may result in a general nervousness in an adjacent flight which inhibits breeding activity.

231

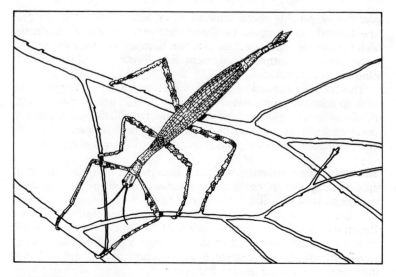

COMMON NAME: Stick Insect

SCIENTIFIC NAME: *Carausius morosus*

DISTRIBUTION: This species, the common one, came from India and other Asian countries, but there are several other species occurring throughout the tropics

HABITAT: Trees and shrubs in gardens, parklands and forests

ADULT SIZE: 10 cm (4 in)

General. The Indian Stick Insect is the best known species, frequently to be found in schools and homes, and it is by far the easiest to maintain in captivity. Males are rarely if ever encountered in this species though the females lay fertile eggs prolifically. Keep the animals at room temperature.

Some species of stick insect are winged and others are covered with thorns to complete the disguise. Leaf insects, which are closely related, also come in a variety of forms that are difficult to distinguish from surrounding vegetation. The length of a stick insect's life is nearly a year.

Do not handle stick insects as they are very fragile. Let them walk from one piece of foodplant to another rather than trying to move them.

Food. Privet is the easiest thing on which to feed common Indian Stick Insects. Some species feed on bramble, or rhododendron, or ivy, though they are reluctant to change from one to the other — check with the supplier as to what has been used. Wash the plant well to remove toxic residues before offering it to the animals, and never pick any foodplant if it might have been sprayed with gardening or agricultural chemicals.

The foodplant should be packed tightly in a jar of water in the tank to prevent the insects crawling down the stems and drowning. Newly emerged babies, and adults just before they die, need a drink of water: throughout the rest of their lives they obtain sufficient moisture from the leaves.

Housing. The best way of housing stick insects is to keep them in an aquarium with a nylon mesh top, and sheets of clean unused newsprint on the floor.

Breeding. Most stick insects reproduce freely, without any help from you. When the eggs are laid, separate them from any faeces to avoid confusion, and place them in a match box tray inside the tank. In due course they will hatch into tiny stick insects, but they do take a long time. No other care is necessary to stimulate breeding — you will soon find that you have an embarrassment of eggs.

COMMON NAME: Tortoise and Terrapin

SCIENTIFIC NAME: *Testudo, Pseudemmys* and other genera

DISTRIBUTION: Throughout the tropics, sub-tropics and temperate parts of the world

233

HABITAT: Grasslands, semi-arid deserts, edges of forests and along waterways

ADULT SIZE: 15 cm–1.8 m (6 in–6 ft)

General. Not long ago tortoises were cheap to buy from your local pet shop. Colossal numbers were imported in dreadful conditions that caused huge losses. It is now illegal to import many species, and those that are available are very expensive, and a licence from the Department of the Environment is necessary to sell them. As a result, nowadays, they are only kept by enthusiasts with specialist knowledge and experience who do their best to breed from their stock. Some pet shops now sell box tortoises from America, but if you are offered one and told that you keep it in the same way as a tortoise, take no notice, for although they are called box tortoises they are in fact terrapins which are altogether different. Tortoises live entirely on the land and are almost entirely vegetarian, whereas terrapins are pretty aquatic and are carnivorous.

Taking on a chelonian (tortoise or terrapin) is quite a commitment as they are long-lived animals. *The Guinness Book of Records* mentions one tortoise that lived over 116 years.

Never drill a hole through a tortoise's shell — it is the equivalent of drilling through one of your ribs. Neither should you ever buy the tiny terrapins that are offered for sale each year. They look lovely but they are far too small and will probably die. Some species of chelonian need to hibernate, and they should be allowed to do this somewhere completely frost-free, and when they wake in the spring they must be given a good drink and a soak in a shallow dish of tepid water before having their first feed. In a cold climate, tortoises only have a short season to recover from a long hibernation before they have to start building up a fat store for the next one.

Food. Tortoises should be fed a variety of chopped fruit and vegetables supplemented with a few mealworms, a little canned dog food plus a multivitamin liquid. Fresh water should always be available. Terrapins need meat, but do not put it in their water as it will pollute it. Young animals are best started on Tubifex and other aquatic livefood, but older animals will take anything of suitable size and some may take chopped raw meat or fish.

Housing. Tropical species need a large tank heated with a ceramic bulb heater to between 26–32°C (80–90°F). Light bulbs should only be used for lighting the tank as there is evidence that constant light may be harmful. Ultraviolet light (in small doses) is essential. For tortoises a suitable substrate could be peat but for terrapins gravel is better. They need a considerable pond in their tank and peat would soon pollute it. Heaters should be placed at one end of the tank so that an animal can move into a cooler spot. Mediterranean species can be kept in a secure well-planted garden but must be taken indoors well before the first frost.

Breeding. Tortoises will breed if given the right conditions, and every year captive-bred specimens are offered for sale. The eggs will need to be incubated. I am not aware of any captive breeding of terrapins.

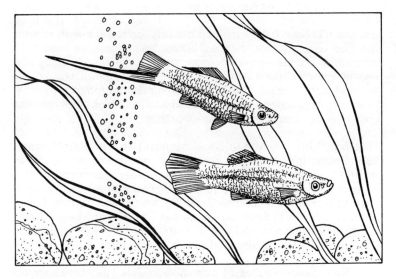

COMMON NAME: Tropical Fish. Many species, as for example Angel Fish, Neon Tetras and Congo Tetras

SCIENTIFIC NAME: Many, such as *Pterophyllum scalare*, *Paracheirodon innesi* and *Micralestes interruptus*

DISTRIBUTION: Originally tropical South America, African and South East Asia, but nowadays many are captive bred

HABITAT: Lakes and rivers

ADULT SIZE: 3–35 cm (1⅕–14 in)

General. Vast quantities of tropical freshwater fish that originally came from throughout the tropics are now produced by fish breeders in Singapore. Each week they send container-loads of fish to Japan, Europe, Britain and the United States. When the consignments arrive, the fish are very stressed and it takes some time before they have recovered and are ready for sale. If you can buy fish that have been native bred you will find they are of far superior quality. Never buy fish that do not appear in first-class condition, however beautiful they appear, as disease can infect a whole community tank.

Never put a newly purchased fish into an established community until you have quarantined it for some time in case of infectious disease.

Food. There are many varieties of fish food readily available. Some fish feed at the surface of the tank, some at the bottom, and others at different levels between these two extremes. The food you buy will have to be such that it meets the requirements of your fish and your aquarist shop will advise you if you are unsure. In addition to a commercial fish food, all your charges will enjoy and benefit from as much livefood as you can supply. If you collect livefood from a pond, take care that you do not introduce predators such as dragonfly larvae and hydra, which might well colonise your tank if you accidentally introduce them.

Housing. The only way to house tropical fish is in a large aquarium. Setting up a tank involves quite a bit of time and expense, and there is not much point buying one smaller than 90 cm (36 in) in length. The tank will have to be equipped with a hood, lighting, filter system, heater, thermostat, thermometer and aerator. When all these have been fitted, the tank must be landscaped with gravel, plenty of plants and rocks, and these and the water should be added some weeks before the fish can be introduced.

Breeding. Some species of tropical freshwater fish breed readily in captivity, others have never been bred. There are so many species of these animals that it is essential to read specialist books if you are interested in breeding. Many species lay eggs but some give birth to live young. When the babies (which are called 'fry') are born they are so tiny that they are almost impossible to see. Until they are fairly large they are regarded as edible by many adult fish, so often the best thing to do is remove the parent fish from a tank in which they have spawned in order to avert this cannibalism.

BREED SOCIETIES AND FANCY CLUBS

AUSTRALIA
African Lovebird Society of Australia, P.O. Box 19, Kenthurst, N.S.W.
Australian National Kennel Council, Royal Showgrounds, Ascot Vale, Victoria
Zebra Finch Society of Australia, 24 Ryvie Avenue, Cromer 2099, N.S.W.

AUSTRIA
Oevek, K.K.O., Spaunstrasse 40, A-4020 Linz

BELGIUM
Cat Club de Belgique (CCB), 33 Rue Duquesnoy, B-1000, Brussels
Federation International Feline (FIFe), 33 Rue Duquesnoy, B-1000, Brussels

CANADA
Canadian Cat Association (CCA), 14 Nelson Street West, Suite 5, Brampton,
    Ontario, L6S 1B7
Canadian Kennel Club, 2150 Bloor Street West, Toronto, Ontario, M6S 1M8
Golden Triangle Parrot and Parrakeet Club, Box 1574 Station C, Kitchener,
    Ontario, N2G 4PG

DENMARK
Landsforeningen Felis Danica, Tranehusene 44, DK-2620, Albertslund

FINLAND
Suomen Rotukisshayhdistysten, Keskuslittoo r.v. (SRK), Raappavuorenrinne 1 D
    59, SF-01620, Vantaa 62

FRANCE
Federation Feline Francaise (FFF), 12 Ave. Herbillon, F-94160, Saint Mande
Societe Centrale Canine, 215 Rue St. Denis, 75083 Paris, Cedex 02

GREAT BRITAIN
Anabantoid Association of Great Britain, 25 The Gowers, Chestnut Lane,
    Amersham, Bucks.
Arab Horse Society, Loughmoe, Shelley Close, Itchen Abbs, Winchester, Hants.

237

Association of British Riding Schools, The Moat House Bungalow, Alconbury Hill, Cambs.

Australian Finch Society, 478 New Hey Road, Wirral, Merseyside L49 9SB

Avicultural Society, Windsor Forest Stud, Mill Ride, Ascot, Berks. SL5 8LT

Bee Research Association International, Hill House, Gerrard's Cross, Bucks. SL9 0NR

British Beekeeping Association, 55 Chipstead Lang, Riverhead, Sevenoaks, Kent

British Bird Council, 1 King John's Road, Kingswood, Bristol BS15 1NN

British Border Fancy Canary Club, 139a Liverpool Road, Bickerstaffe, Ormskirk, Lancs.

British Chelonian Group, 105 Burnham Lane, Slough, Berks.

British Goat Society, Rougham, Bury St Edmunds, Suffolk

British Herpetological Society, c/o Zoological Society of London, Regent's Park, London NW1 4RY

British Horse Society, National Equestrian Centre, Kenilworth, Warwicks.

The British International Standard Rabbit Club, 24 Park Grove, Cardross, Dumbarton, Scotland

British Palomino Society, The Quinta, Bentley, Farnham, Surrey

British Rabbit Council, Pureso House, 7 Kirkgate, Sutton, Newark, Notts.

British Roller Canary Association, 21 Edge Avenue, Thornhill, Dewsbury, West Yorks. WF12 0EL

British Tarantula Society, 34 Phillimore Place, Radlett, Herts. WD7 8NL

British Veterinary Association, 7 Mansfield Street, London W1M 0AT

British Waterfowl Association, 6 Caldicott Close, Winsford, Cheshire CW7 1LW

Budgerigar Society, 49/53 Hazelwood Road, Northants. NN1 1LG

Canary Colour Breeders Association, 10 Castle Road, Studley, Warwicks. B80 7LS

Cat Association of Britain (CA), National Information Office, Lowfield Heath, Crawley, West Sussex RH11 0PY

'Clearwing Budgerigar Breeders Association, 16 Northgate Avenue, Reading, Berks. RG2 7HE

Crested Budgerigar Club, 68 Clarence Road, Fleet, Hants. GU13 9RY

Crested Canary Club, 19 Commerce Street, Alvaston, Derbyshire DE2 8TR

Domestic Fowl Trust, Honeybourne, Evesham, Hereford & Worcester

Donkey Breed Society, White Shutters, Exlade, Woodcote, Reading, Berks.

Donkey Foaling Bank, Hillside Farm, Adlestrop, Moreton-in-the-Marsh, Glos.

Foreign Bird Association, Langham, Dayseys Hill, Outwood, Redhill, Surrey RH1 5QX

Foreign Bird Federation, 48 Twickenham Road, Newton Abbot, Devon TQ12 4JF

Goldfish Society of Great Britain, 64 Ox Lane, Harpenden, Herts.

The Governing Council of the Cat Fancy (GCCF), Dovefields, Petworth Road, Whitley, Surrey GU8 5QU

International Bee Research Association, Hill House, Gerrard's Cross, Bucks. SL9 0NR

International Gloster Canary Breeders Association, 5 Halton Drive, Timperley, Altrincham, Cheshire

International Herpetological Society, 65 Broadstone Avenue, Walsall, West Midlands WS3 1JA

Irish Kennel Club, 23 Earlsfort Terrace, Dublin 2, Eire

Kennel Club, 1 Clarges Street, London W1

Kensington Kitten and Neuter Cat Club, Fairmont, 78 Highfield Avenue, Aldershot, Hants.

Lovebird Society, Long Acre, Highfield Road, Bubwith, Selby, North Yorks.

Lutino Albino Budgerigar Breeders Society, 22 Rectory Close, Long Stratton, Norfolk

The Marmoset & Tamarin Breeders' League, 40 Birchtree Avenue, Dogsthorpe, Peterborough, Cambs. PE1 4HW

National Bengalese Fanciers Association, 2 Bridge Street, Griffithstown, Gwent NP4 5JB

National British Bird & Mule Club, Milnsbridge, Bicron, Shrewsbury, Salop. SY3 8BT

National Cat Club, The Laurels, Chesham Lane, Wendover, Bucks.

National Cavy Club, 9 Parkdale Road, Sheldon, Birmingham B26 3UT

National Council for Aviculture, 87 Winn Road, Lee, London SE12 9EY

National Foaling Bank, Mereton Stud, Newport, Salop.

National Mongolian Gerbil Society, 4 Langdale Street, Elland, West Yorks. HX5 0JL

National Mouse Club, 6 Carlton Gardens, Stanwix, Carlisle, Cumbria

National Pony Society, Stoke Lodge, 85 Cliddesden Road, Basingstoke, Hants.

National Rat Club, 57 Myrtledene Road, Abbey Wood, London SE2

National Young Fanciers Society, 79 Boundary Road, Newark, Notts.

New Forest Breeding and Cattle Society, Beacon Corner, Burley, Ringwood, Hants.

Norwich Canary Plainhead Club, 21 Harrison Drive, Haydock, St Helens, Merseyside WA11 0EG

Old Varieties Canary Association, Pallinsburn & Ridley Ave., Blyth, Northumberland NE24 3BB

Parrot Society, 206 Raedwald Drive, Bury St Edmunds, Suffolk 1P32 7DW

Ponies of Britain Club, Brookside Farm, Ascot, Berks.

Pony Club, National Equestrian Centre, Kenilworth, Warwicks.

Red Canary Association, 18 Brierfield, Skelmersdale, Lancs. WN8 9JD

Royal Pigeon Racing Association, The Reddings, Cheltenham, Glos. GL51 6RN

Scottish Kennel Club, 66 Forres Street, Edinburgh, Scotland

Shetland Pony Society, 8 Whinfield Road, Montrose, Tayside, Scotland

Welsh Pony & Cob Society, 32 North Parade, Aberystwyth, Dyfed, Wales

Yorkshire Canary Club, Glebe Farm, Lower Dunsforth, Great Ouseburn, Yorks. YO5 9RZ

Zebra Finch Society, 87 Winn Road, Lee, London SE12

ITALY
Federation Feline Italienne (FFI), 20 Via Principi d'Acaja, 1-10138, Torino

NETHERLANDS
Felikat Mundikat, Rotterdamse Rijweg 94, NL-3042, A R Rotterdam

NORWAY
Norske Rasekattklubbers Riksforbund (NNR), Nordane, Valkyriegate 9, N-Oslo 3

SPAIN
Cat Club de Espana (CCE), 60 Olvido, Barcelona 26

SWEDEN
Sveriges Raskattklubbars Riksforbund 'SVERAK', PL 4094 a, S-524 00, Herrljunga

SWITZERLAND
Federation Feline Helvetique (FFH), Via Quiete 15, CH-6962, Viganello

UNITED STATES OF AMERICA
African Lovebird Society, Box 142, San Marcos, California 92069

American Cat Association (ACA), 10065 Foothill Boulevard, Lake View, Terrace, California 91342

American Cat Council (ACC), P.O. Box 662, Pasadena, California 91102

American Cat Fancier's Association (ACFA), P.O. Box 203, Point Lookout, Missouri 65726

American Federation of Aviculture, 2208 'A' Artesia Boulevard, Redondo Beach, California 90278

American Kennel Club, 51 Madison Avenue, New York, NY 10010

American Rabbit Breeders Association, 2411 East Oakland Avenue, Bloomington, Illinois 61701

Avicultural Society of America Inc., P.O. Box 157, Stanton, California 30680

Cat Fanciers' Association (CFA), 1309 Allaire Avenue, Ocean, New Jersey 07712

Cat Fanciers' Federation (CFF), 9509 Montgomery Road, Cincinnati, Ohio 45242

Crown Cat Fanciers' Federation (CCFF), P.O. Box 34, Nazareth, Kentucky 40048

Independent Cat Association, 211 East Oliver (Suite 201), Burbank, California 91502

International Cat Association (TICA), 211 East Oliver (Suite 208), Burbank, California 91502

National Parrot Association, 8 North Hoffman Lane, Hauppage, NY 11788

United Cat Federation (UCF), 6621 Thornwood Street, San Diego, California 92111

Zebra Finch Society of America, 8204 Woodland Avenue, Annadale, Virginia 22003

WEST GERMANY
Deutscher Edelkatzenzuchter — Verband (DEKZV), 48 Friedrichstrasse, D-6200, Viesbaden

Verband Fur das Deutsche Hundwesen, Postfach 1390, Dortmund

CONSERVATION AND WELFARE ORGANISATIONS

AUSTRALIA
Feline Association of South Australia, P.O. Box 104, Stirling, South Australia

CANADA
World Society for the Protection of Animals, Canada, 215 Lakeshore Blvde., Toronto, Ontario M5A 3WG

GREAT BRITAIN
Association of Responsible Animal Keepers, 13 Pound Place, Shalford, Guildford, Surrey GU4 8HH
Animal Aid, 7 Castle Street, Tonbridge, Kent TN9 1BH
Banham Zoo, The Grove, Banham, Norwich NR16 2HB
Battersea Park Children's Zoo, Albert Bridge Road, London SE14
Birdland, Riverside, Bourton-on-the-Water, Glos.
Brighton Aquarium, Marine Parade, 8 Madeira Drive, Brighton, East Sussex
Bristol Zoo, Clifton, Bristol BS8 3HA
British Butterfly Conservation Society, Tudor House, Quorn, Loughborough, Leics. LE12 8AD
British Hedgehog Preservation Society, Knowbury House, Knowbury, Ludlow, Shropshire
British Museum (Natural History), Cromwell Road, South Kensington, London SW3
British Trust for Conservation Volunteers, 36 St Mary's Street, Wallingford, Oxfordshire
British Trust for Ornithology, Beech Grove, Station Road, Tring, Herts. HP23 5NR
British Union for the Abolition of Vivisection, 16a Crane Grove, Islington, London N7
British Waterfowl Association, 25 Dale Street, Haltwhistle, Northumberland NE49 9QB
Cat Action Trust, The Crippets, Jordens, Beaconsfield, Bucks.
Cats Protection League, 20 North Street, Horsham, West Sussex
Cat Survival Trust, Marlind Centre, Codicote Road, Welwyn, Herts. AL6 9TU
Chessington Zoo, Leatherland Road, Chessington, Surrey KT9 2NE
Chester Zoo, Upton-by-Chester CH2 1LM
The Chipperfield Organisation, Heathersett, Chilworth Road, Southampton, Hants.
Compassion in World Farming, 20 Lavant Street, Petersfield, Hants. GU32 3EW
Connemara Pony Society, The Quinta, Bentley, Farnham, Surrey

Conservation Foundation, 11a West Halkin Street, London SW1X 8JL
Council for Environmental Conservation (CoEnCo), The London Ecology Centre, 45 Shelton Street, London WC2H 9HJ
Dale Pony Society, Hutton Gate, Guisborough, North Yorks.
Dartmoor Pony Society, Lower Hisley, Lustleigh, Newton Abbot, Devon
Department of the Environment (CITES Branch), Tollgate House, Houlton Street, Bristol BS2 9DJ
Donkey Sanctuary, Sidmouth, Devon EX10 0NO
Exmoor Pony Society, Capland Orchard, Hatch Beauchamp, Taunton, Somerset
Falconry Centre, Newent, Glos.
Farm and Food Society, 4 Willifield Way, London NW11 7XT
Farming & Wildlife Trust, The Lodge, Sandy, Beds. SG19 2DL
Fauna and Flora Preservation Society, c/o Regents Park, London NW1 4RY
Feline Advisory Bureau, 350 Upper Richmond Road, Putney, London SW15 6TL
Fell Pony Society, Packway, Windermere, Westmorland
Freshwater Biological Association, The Ferry House, Ambleside, Cumbria LA22 0LP
Friends of the Earth, 377 City Road, London EC1V 1NA
Greenpeace, 30-31 Islington Green, London N1 8XE
Hawk Trust, Freepost, Beckenham, Kent
Highland Pony Society, 51 High Street, Dunblane, Central Scotland
Humane Research Trust, Brook House, 25 Bramhall Lane, South Bramhall, Cheshire SK7 2DN
International Council for Bird Preservation, 219c Huntingdon Road, Cambridge CB3 0DL
Jersey Wildlife Preservation Trust, Les Augres Manor, Trinity, Jersey, Channel Islands
Kilverstone Latin American Zoo & Miniature Horse Stud, Kilverstone, Thetford, Norfolk
London Wildlife Trust, 1 Thorp Close, London W10 5XL
Marine Biological Association of the UK, The Laboratory, Cirader Hill, Plymouth, Devon
Marine Conservation Society, 4 Gloucester Road, Ross-on-Wye, Hereford & Worcester HR9 5BU
Ministry of Agriculture, Fisheries & Food, Animal Health Division, Hook Rise South, Tolworth, Surrey
National Anti-Vivisection Society, 51 Harley Street, London W1N 1DD
Nature Conservancy Council, Northminster House, Peterborough, Cambs. PE1 1UA
Nature Conservancy Council (Scotland), 12 Hope Terrace, Edinburgh EH9 2AS
National Federation of City Farms, The Old Vicarage, 66 Fraser Street, Bedminster, Bristol BS3 4LY
Otter Trust, Earsham, Bungay, Suffolk NR35 2AF
People's Dispensary for Sick Animals, PDSA House, South Street, Dorking, Surrey
Pet Health Council, 418-422 Strand, London, WC2R 0PL
Petwatch, P.O. Box 16, Brighouse, West Yorks. HD6 1DS
Royal Horticultural Society, Horticultural Hall, Vincent Square, London SW1P 2PE
Royal Society for Nature Conservation, The Green, Nettleham, Lincoln LN2 2NR
Royal Society for the Prevention of Cruelty to Animals, The Causeway, Horsham, West Sussex RH12 1HG
Royal Society for the Protection of Birds, The Lodge, Sandy, Beds. SG19 2DL
Scottish Society for the Prevention of Cruelty to Animals, 19 Melville Street, Edinburgh EH3 7PL
Scottish Wildlife Trust, 25 Johnston Terrace, Edinburgh EH3 7PL
Seal Rescue Service, 77 Gayton Road, Kings Lynn, Norfolk
WATCH, The Green, Nettleham, Lincoln LN2 2NR

Wild Birds Advisory Committee, Hut 6, Castle Grounds, Stormont, Belfast BT4 3SS, Northern Ireland

The Wildlife Rescue Service, The Old Chequers, Briston, Melton Constable, Norfolk

Wildfowl Trust, Gatehouse, Slimbridge, Glos. GL2 7BT

Wildlife Trade Monitoring Unit, 219c Huntingdon Road, Cambridge CB3 0DL

World Society for the Protection of Animals, 106 Jermyn Street, London SW1Y 6EE

World Wildlife Fund, Panda House, 11-13 Ockford Road, Godalming, Surrey GU7 1QU

Young People's Trust for Endangered Species, 19 Quarry Street, Guildford, Surrey GU1 3EH

Zoo Check, Cherry Tree Cottage, Coldharbour, Dorking, Surrey RH5 6HA

Zoological Society of London, Regent's Park, London NW1 4RY

NEW ZEALAND
New Zealand Cat Fancy Inc., P.O. Box 3167, Nelson

SPAIN
Loro Parque, Puerto de la Cruz, Tenerife, Canary Isles

SWITZERLAND
World Wildlife Fund, 1196 Gland

UNITED STATES OF AMERICA
American Association of Zoological Parks & Aquariums, Oglebay Park, Wheeling, WV 26003

American Humane Association, Box 1266, Denver, Co 80201

American Humane Society, 5351 S. Roslyn Street, Englewood, Co 80111

American Museum of Natural History, Central Park West at 79th, New York, NY 10024

American Ornithologists Union, c/o National Museum of Natural History, Smithsonian Institution, Washington, DC 20560

American Society of Mammalogists, Section of Mammals, Carnegie Museum of Natural History, 4400 Forbes Ave., Pittsburgh, PA 15213

American Society for the Prevention of Cruelty to Animals, 441 East 92nd Street, New York, NY 10028

Animal Protection Institute, P.O. Box 22505, Sacramento, CA 95822

Animal Welfare Institute, P.O. Box 3650, Washington, DC 20007

Bat Conservation International, c/o Dr Merlin D. Tuttle, Milwaukee Public Museum, Milwaukee, WI 53233

Cousteau Society Inc., 777 3rd Ave., New York, NY 10017

Desert Tortoise Council, 407 W Line Street, Bishop, CA 93514

Humane Society of the United States, 2100 L St., N.W., Washington, DC 20037

International Primate Protection League, P.O. Drawer X, Summerville, SC 29483

National Audobon Society, 950 Third Avenue, New York, NY 1002

New York Zoological Society, Bronx, NY 10460

The Sierra Club, National Wildlife Federation, 1412 16th St., Washington, DC 20036

World Society for the Protection of Animals, U.S.A., P.O. Box 190, 29 Perkins Street, Boston, MA 02130

World Wildlife Fund, U.S.A., 1601 Connecticut Ave., N.W. Washington DC 20009

VIRGIN ISLANDS
Caribbean Conservation Organisation, P.O. Box 4187, St. Thomas

BIBLIOGRAPHY

Publications marked ** are journals.

Advances in Animal Welfare Science, M.W. Fox & L.D. Mickly (eds.) (MTP Press Ltd., 1985)

**All Cats*, Pacific Palisade, California

All the World's Animals, Primates, Graham Bateman (ed.) (Torstar Books, Croydon, 1987)

Amateur Naturalist, The Gerald & Lee Durrell (Hamish Hamilton, London, 1982)

**American Cage Bird Magazine Inc. The*, 1 Glamore Court, Smithtown, NY 11787

Amphibians of Europe, D. Ballasina (David & Charles, Newton Abbot, 1984)

Animals in Education, The Use of Animals in High School Biology Classes & Science Fairs, Heather McGriffin & Nancie Brownley (eds.) (Institute for the Study of Animal Problems, 1980)

Animals in the Home & Classroom, Terry Jennings (Pergammon Press, 1971)

**Aquarist & Pondkeeper, The* Buckley Press Ltd., 58 Fleet Street, London EC4Y 1JU

**Aquarium, The* Pet Books Inc., Maywood, NJ

Audobon Society Field Guide to North American Reptiles & Amphibians, The John L. Behler (Alfred A. Knofp, Random House, New York, 1979)

Australian Finches, I.C. Immelman (Angus & Robertson, 1982)

Australian Parrots in Field & Aviary, A. Lendon (Angus & Robertson, 1973)

**Beecraft*, 21 West Way, Copthorne Bank, Crawley, West Sussex RH10 3QS

Best In Show, Breeding & Exhibiting Budgerigars, Gerald S. Binks (Ebury Press/Pelham Books, 1976)

Bird Business, The Greta Nilsson (Animal Welfare Institute, Washington, DC, 1981)

Bird Diseases, L. Arnall & I.F. Keymer (Ballière Tindall, 1983)

Breeding Endangered Species in Captivity, R.D. Martin (ed.) (Academic Press, New York, NY, 1975)

**British Bee Journal*, 46 Queen Street, Geddington, Kettering, Northamptonshire NN14 1AZ

**Cage & Aviary Birds*, Prospect Magazines, Prospect House, 9-13 Ewell Road, Cheam, Sutton, Surrey SM1 4QQ

Care and Management of Wild Mammals in Captivity, The Lee S. Crandall (Chicago University Press, 1964)

Cat Fanciers Association Yearbook, 1309 Allaire Avenue, Ocean, NJ 07712

**Cats*, 5 Leigh Street, Manchester

Cats Annual (5 Leigh Street, Manchester)

**Cats Magazine*, P.O. Box 37, Port Orange, Florida

Catwatching, Desmond Morris (Jonathan Cape, 1986)

**Cat World*, Scan House, Southwick Street, Southwick, Brighton

**Cat World International*, P.O. Box 35635, Phoenix, Arizona

Coldwater Aquariums & Simple Outdoor Pools, Neil Wainwright (Frederick Warne, London)

Conservation Review, The, Conservation Foundation, 11a West Halkin Street, London SW1X 8JL

Dictionary of Birds in Colour, The, Bruce Campbell (Peerage Books, London, 1974)

Encyclopedia of Cage & Aviary Birds, C.H. Rogers (Pelham Books, London)

Endangered Birds: Management Techniques for the Preservation of Threatened Species, Stanley A. Temple (ed.) (University of Wisconsin Press, 1977)

Endangered Ones, The, James A. Cox (Crown Publishing Co. London, 1975)

Endangered Parrots, Rosemary Low (Blandford Press, Poole, 1984)

Endangered Species Handbook, The Greta Nilsson (Animal Welfare Institute, Washington, DC, 1983)

**Exchange & Mart*, Link House, 25 West Street, Poole, Dorset BH15 1LL

**Fancy Fowl*, Crondall Cottage, Highclere, Newbury, Bucks.

Finches & Softbilled Birds, H. Bates & H. Busenbark (TFH Publications, New Jersey, 1965)

First Aid & Care of Wild Birds, J.E. Cooper & J.T. Eley (eds.) (David & Charles, Newton Abbot, 1979)

**Fur & Feather*, Idle, Bradford, West Yorks. BD10 8NL

Goldfish, Marshall Ostow (Barron's Educational Series Inc., New York, NY, 1985)

Good Pets Guide, The Alison Prince (Armada, London, 1981)

Handbook of Foreign Birds, The (Vols 1 & 2), A. Rutgers (Blandford Books Ltd., Poole, 1977)

**Horse & Hound*, Kings Reach Tower, Stamford Street, London SE1 9LS

International Cat Association Year Book, 221 East Olive, Suite 208, Burbank, California

**Journal of the British Tarantula Society*, 36 Phillimore Place, Radlett, Herts.

Keeping Bees, Peter Beckley (Pelham Books, London, 1977)

Man Meets Dog, Konrad Lorenz (Methuen and Co., London, 1954)

Manual of the Care and Treatment of Children's & Exotic Pets, A (British Small Animals Veterinary Association, London)

**Our Cats*, 4 Carlton Mansions, Clapham Road, London SW9

**Parrot Breeder*, Carterton Breeding Aviaries, Brize Norton Road, Carterton, Oxon

Parrots & Related Birds, H.J. Bates & R.L. Busenbark (TFH Publications, New Jersey, 1967)

Parrots of the World, J.M. Forshaw (Landsdowne Press, London, 1973)

Parrots – Their Care & Breeding, R. Low (Blandford Press, Poole, 1980)

**Pedigree Digest*, Pedigree Petfoods, Melton Mowbray, Leics.

Pet Animals & Society, R.S. Anderson (ed.) (Balliére Tindall, London, 1975)

Pet Keeper's Guide to Reptiles & Amphibians, A, David Alderton (Salamander Books Ltd., London, 1986)

Pets & Human Development, Boris Levinson (Charles C. Thomas, Springfield, Illinois, 1972)

Pets & Their People, Bruce Fogle (Collins, London, 1983)

**Pony*, D.J. Murphy Ltd., 104 Ash Road, Sutton, Surrey SM3 9LD

Private Life of the Rabbit, The, R.M. Lockley (André Deutsch, London, 1965)

Rabbit Keeping, Gay Nightingale (John Bartholomew & Son Ltd. London, 1979)

**Riding*, IPC Magazines, Kings Reach Tower, Stamford Street, London SE1 9LS

RSPCA Official Pet Guides (Collins)

Seawater Aquaria, L.A.J. Jackman (David & Charles, Newton Abbot)

**Snake Keeper*, Michael Connolly, 159 Stanley Hill, Amersham, Bucks. HP7 9EY

Starting with Tropical Fish, Jose & John Thorne (The Aquarium Press, London)

Studying Insects, R.L.E. Ford (Frederick Warne, London, 1973)

Tackle Riding This Way, C.E.G. Hope (Stanley Paul, London, 1970)

Tarantula Classification & Identification Guide, Andrew Smith (Fitzgerald Publishing, London, 1987)

Teach Yourself Riding, C.E.G. Hope (Brockhampton Press, London 1972)

** *Today's Aquarium*, Aquadocumenta, London, 70 Wood Vale, London N10 3DN

Tortoises & How to Keep Them, M. Knight (Brockhampton Press)

** *Tropical Fish Hobbyist*, TFH Publications, Jersey City, NJ

Turtles, Extinction or Survival, S.R. Riedman & R. Witham (Abelard-Schuman, New York, NY, 1974)

Understanding Your Dog, Michael Fox (Blond & Briggs Ltd., London, 1974)

University Federation for Animal Welfare Handbook on the Care & Management of Laboratory Animals (Livingstone, London)

Usborne First Book of Pets & Petcare, The, Rose Hill (Usborne Publishing Ltd., London, 1982)

World Directory of Environmental Organisations Conservation Directory (The Sierra Club, Washington, DC)

World's Disappearing Wildlife, The, Maurice & Robert Burton (Marshall Cavendish, London, 1978)

Writer's & Artist's Yearbook (A & C Black, London, annual)

You and Your Aquarium, Dick Mills (Dorling Kindersley, London, 1986)

You and Your Cat, David Taylor (Dorling Kindersley, London, 1986)

You and Your Dog, David Taylor (Dorling Kindersley, London, 1986)

SUPPLIERS

This is only a representative list of the thousands of firms that supply animals and goods to the pet keeper.

GREAT BRITAIN

Abbot Bros., Thuxton, Norfolk	Waterfowl and poultry
Biopet, 4 Windmill Road, Sunbury-on-Thames, Surrey	Reptiles, amphibians and equipment
Bioserv, 38-42 Station Road, Worthing, Sussex	Reptiles, amphibians and equipment
Birdquest International, 20 Lancaster Avenue, Besses o' the Barn, Whitfield, Manchester M25 6DE	Birds
Bob Partridge, Marlow Bird Farm, 32 Marlow Road, Leicester	Pigeons
Broadway Pet Stores, 612 Romford Road, Manor Park, London E12	Animals of all sorts
Cobwebs, The Tropical Butterfly Garden, The Boating Lake, Cleethorpes, South Humberside	Invertebrates
County Kennels, P.O. Box 34, Aberystwyth	Dogs
Eric Higginbottom, Laboratory Livefoods, High Bradfield, Sheffield S6 6LJ	Livefood
Entomological Livestock Supplies, Unit 3, Beaver Park, Hayseech Road, Halesowen, West Midlands B63 3PD	Invertebrates
G. & M. Cages, 26 Gypsey Road, Bridlington, East Yorkshire	Cages
Geoff A. Smith, Pet Farm, Attlebridge, Norwich, Norfolk NR9 5SU	Birds
Gerrard & Co., Gerrard House, Worthing Road, East Preston, Sussex	Biological material
I.D.M. Pets, 206 Alexandra Avenue, South Harrow, Middlesex	Animals and equipment
Ipswich Pet Cemetery, I.J. Chittock, Cemetery Lodge, Tuddenham Road, Ipswich, Suffolk	Pet cemetery
J.G. Animals, 19 Streatham Vale, London SW16	Reptiles
John E. Haith, Park Street, Cleethorpes, South Humberside, DN35 7NF	Bird seed
K.P. & S. Nets, Castle Street, Axminster, Devon	Ferrets
Leonard F. Jollye Ltd, The Granaries, Crews Hill, Enfield, Middlesex EN2 9BB	Bird seed
Martins Pet Supplies, 48 Queens Road, Nuneaton	Birds
Monkfield Aquatica, Monkfield, Bourn, Cambridgeshire CB3 7TD	Livefood
Mr Fish, 90-92 Bromham Road, Bedford MK40 2QH	Fish
Newman Cages, Lynchwynd, Cove Road, Fleet, Aldershot, Hampshire GU13 8RT	Cages
N. Cousins, 4 The Chase, Ely, Cambridgeshire CB6 3BH	Invertebrates
Oval Pet Centre, 17 The Oval, Sidcup, Kent	Dogs
Palmers Pet Stores, Parkway, Camden Town, London NW1	Animals and equipment

Parrot House, High Wycombe, Buckinghamshire	Parrots
Paul Sullivan, 34 Willow Avenue, Torquay, Devon	Reptiles
Porters, 81 Plashet Grove, East Ham, London E6 1AF	Equipment for bird-keepers
Reflections Aquatic Centre, 232 North Lane, Aldershot, Hampshire	Fish and equipment
Register of Accredited Breeders & Recognised Suppliers, M.R.C. Laboratory Animal Centre, Woodmansterne Road, Carshalton, Surrey	Rodents
Shotgate Koi, 240 Southend Road, Wickford, Essex	Koi carp
Stapeley Water Gardens, Stapeley, Nantwich, Cheshire	Fish and equipment
The Butterfly Farm, Bilsington, Ashford, Kent TN25 7JN	Butterflies
The Vivarium, 55 Boundary Road, Walthamstow, London E17	Reptiles and amphibians
Tom Carnihan, 27 Willow Lane, Great Houghton, Northamptonshire	Falconry furniture
Toplands Hatchery, Slaughterford, Chippenham, Wiltshire	Chicks
Valley Aquatics, Plantation House, Flip Road, Haslingden, Lancashire BB4 5EJ	Fish and equipment
Watkins & Doncaster, Four Throws, Hawkhurst, Kent	Biological material and equipment
Waveney Wildfowl, Bungay, Suffolk	Waterfowl
Winforton Rabbits, Byton, Presteigne, Powys	Rabbits
Winkfield Equestrian Centre, Crouch Lane, Winkfield, Berkshire	Horses
Worldwide Butterflies, Compton House, Over Compton, Sherborne, Dorset DT9 4QN	Butterflies and equipment
Xenopus Ltd, Holmesdale Nursery, Mid Street, South Nuffield, Redhill, Surrey RH1 4JY	Amphibians and livefood
Xotic Pets Ltd, Unit D2, Salcombe Road, Meadow Lane Industrial Estate, Alfreton, Derbyshire DE5 7RG	Livefood

USA

Al's Tarantula Ranch, P.O. Box 822, Kenore, WA 98028	Tarantulas
Animal City, 8500 Alvarado Road, P.O. Box 1076, La Mesa, CA 92041-0318	Animals
Better Pets, Waterbury Plaza, 194 Chase Avenue, Waterbury, CT 06704	Animals
Blue Ribbon Pet Farm, 23400 SW 217th Avenue, Homestead, FLA 33031	Animals
Custom Parrot Network, 7800-Bt River Road, Bergen, NJ 07407	Parrots
Hoagy's Bird Ranch, 8755 Galena, Riverside, CA 92504	Birds
Indian River Exotics, 3425 Pawnee Drive, Mims, FLA 32754	Animals
N.W. Pet Supply, P.O. Box 305, Boring, Oregon 97009	Animals
Night Flight Farm, P.O. Box 142, Nesbit, MS 38651	Animals
Parrots of the World, 239a Sunrise Highway, Rockville Centre, New York, NY 11570	Parrots
Petfarms Inc., 5400 North West 84th Avenie, Miami, FLA 53166	Animals
Pet Ranch, 3015 Pioneer Way, P.O. Box 744, Jamul, CA 92035	Animals
Pick a Bird, 22122½ Ventura Boulevard, Woodland Hills, California	Birds
Scarlet Oak Aviaries, 27935 Pergi Road, Glenwillow, Ohio 44139	Birds

INDEX

weldmesh 26
white lettuce 58
white millet 58
white worms 89
Wild Rat 10
World Wildlife Fund 141
wormery 41

yellow millet 58
Young Ornithologists' Club 141
yuhina 60

Zebra Finch 57, 58, 96, 129
zoos 171, 172
zosterops 60